Atomic Tragedy

ATOMIC TRAGEDY

HENRY L. STIMSON AND
THE DECISION TO USE THE
BOMB AGAINST JAPAN

SEAN L. MALLOY

CORNELL UNIVERSITY PRESS ITHACA AND NEW YORK

First published 2008 by Cornell University Press

Printed in the United States of America

Library of Congress Cataloging-in-Publication Data

Malloy, Sean L. (Sean Langdon), 1972–
    Atomic tragedy : Henry L. Stimson and the decision to use the bomb against Japan / Sean L. Malloy.
        p.   cm.
    Includes bibliographical references and index.
    ISBN 978-0-8014-4654-2 (cloth : alk. paper)
  1. Hiroshima-shi (Japan)—History—Bombardment, 1945.
2. Nagasaki-shi (Japan)—History—Bombardment, 1945.
3. Stimson, Henry Lewis, 1867–1950.   4. Atomic bomb—Moral and ethical aspects—United States.   5. World War, 1939–1945—United States.   6. World War, 1939–1945—Japan.   7. United States—Military policy—Decision making.   I. Title.

    D767.25.H6M26 2008
    940.54'2521954—dc22   2007048069

Cornell University Press strives to use environmentally responsible suppliers and materials to the fullest extent possible in the publishing of its books. Such materials include vegetable-based, low-VOC inks and acid-free papers that are recycled, totally chlorine-free, or partly composed of nonwood fibers. For further information, visit our website at www.cornellpress.cornell.edu.

Cloth printing   10 9 8 7 6 5 4 3 2 1

To my parents, Judy, Jim, and Treacy,
and to my wife, Patricia

For history is a way of learning,

of getting closer to the truth. It is only by

abandoning the clichés that we can even define

the tragedy. When we have done that, we will no

longer be merely acquiescing in the deadly inertia

of the past. We will have taken the first and

vital step in making history.

—WILLIAM APPLEMAN WILLIAMS,

THE TRAGEDY OF AMERICAN DIPLOMACY

Contents

Acknowledgments

THIS BOOK HAS BEEN A LONG TIME IN THE MAKING. IN THE PROCESS, I have incurred the kinds of debts that are impossible to repay with a sentence or two of acknowledgment. But however inadequate, I want to start by thanking some of the many people who made this journey possible. Needless to say, many of those named in these acknowledgments may differ with my conclusions in one way or another. Any errors are mine alone.

Barton J. Bernstein served not only as my thesis adviser and mentor but also as a continuing model of scholarly inquiry and generosity. I am thankful to him for many probing conversations that have shaped the way I think about war, morality, history, and the atomic bomb. Bart has also been unfailingly generous in sharing documents and unpublished research on a wide range of subjects related to nuclear history. David M. Kennedy has provided both valuable feedback on various drafts of this book and invaluable advice on the craft of writing history. To the extent that I have been able to render a complex and nuanced story in an engaging fashion, David deserves much of the credit.

As I have discovered, to write on nuclear history is to step into a rich, exciting, and often contentious scholarly debate. Though I have tried to scrupulously indicate in my footnotes where I draw upon the works of others, I should also acknowledge some larger conceptual debts at the outset. In addition to Bart Bernstein, pioneering works by Martin J. Sherwin and Tsuyoshi Hasegawa have greatly shaped my thinking about the issues associated with the atomic bomb. Sherwin, along with Lloyd Gardner and one other anonymous reader, provided helpful comments and suggestions on my initial manuscript. Robert S. Norris has not only contributed to the scholarly debate over the development and use of the atomic bomb but also been tremendously generous in sharing his vast knowledge and rich collection of documents on this subject.

I also wish to acknowledge the following scholars who have contributed in various ways to the development of this book: Stephen Andrews, Brian H. Balogh, Kai Bird, Elizabeth Borgwardt, Chuck Carlson, Lynn Eden, Elizabeth Eraker, Jan Goggans, Michael Gordin, Gregg Herken, Jim Hershberg, David Holloway, Chad Martin, and Timothy Naftali. Finally, though I have never met or corresponded with Gar Alperovitz or Richard B. Frank—two scholars with very different views on the atomic bomb and the end of World War II—my own understanding of these issues has been greatly enriched by wrestling with their work.

The University of California, Merced, has provided a rich and stimulating environment in which to complete this book. The experience of helping launch a new university has been tremendously exciting, and I want to extend my thanks to the faculty, staff, and students at UCM for their energy and inspiration. My colleagues in the World Cultures and History program at Merced have made me a better teacher and scholar. I particularly want to thank Jan, Gregg, Ruth Mostern, Cristian Ricci, and Bradford Johnston for their help and support in good times and bad.

Obviously, this book would not have been possible without the efforts of a number of people at Cornell University Press. My editor, Alison A. Kalett, deserves special acknowledgment. Alison did far more than listen patiently when I first pitched her this book. She took the time to read all the chapters in draft as I produced them over the ensuing years, offering advice along the way that made this a far better book. I greatly appreciate Alison's skill, dedication, and good humor in working to bring this project to fruition. Thanks also to

Candace Akins, Cameron Cooper, Jamie Fuller, Scott E. Levine, Peter J. Potter, Susan Specter, and everyone else at Cornell University Press who guided this manuscript from submission to publication with ease and professionalism. Thanks to the *Journal of Strategic Studies* for allowing me to include parts of an earlier article.

All works of history are built on the quiet, tireless work of librarians and archivists. While I cannot thank each by name, I would like to particularly acknowledge the assistance of Carol Leadenham, Ronald Bulatoff, and the rest of the fantastic staff at the Hoover Institution Archives, Diane Kaplan of Yale University's Manuscripts and Archives, Roger Meade of the Los Alamos National Laboratory, Daniel J. Linke of the Seeley G. Mudd Manuscript Library at Princeton, Peter Nelson of Amherst College Archives and Special Collections, Jacque Roethler of Special Collections at the University of Iowa, Leslie Morris of the Houghton Library at Harvard University, and the staffs of the Herbert Hoover Presidential Library, the National Archives II facility at College Park and the manuscripts department at the Library of Congress. The great libraries at UC Berkeley and Stanford were a source not only of books, articles, and microfilm but also of inspiration.

On the long road to completing this project, I received generous funding from a number of sources, including the history department of Stanford University, the MacArthur Fellows program at Stanford's Center for International Security and Cooperation, and the Miller Fellows program at the Miller Center of Public Affairs at the University of Virginia. The David and Lucile Packard Foundation generously provided me with a grant to conduct research at the Herbert Hoover Presidential Library. More recently, I received grants from the University of California's Graduate and Research Council and UC Merced's Humanities Funds Committee that helped me to complete this book.

The greatest debts I incurred in the course of this project were to my family: to my parents, for helping me get here, and to my wife, Patricia, for her constant love, understanding, and support.

Sean L. Malloy

Richmond, California

Atomic Tragedy

Introduction

"Its Use Must Weigh Heavily on Our Minds and on Our Hearts"

AT 5:00 A.M. ON AUGUST 8, 1945, HENRY L. STIMSON AWOKE TO WHAT he laconically described as "a rather sharp little attack." Stimson had likely suffered a mild heart attack, the prelude to a major coronary occlusion that would nearly kill him two months later. For the previous five years, Stimson as secretary of war had helped guide the American military effort in World War II, culminating in the use of a nuclear weapon against the Japanese city of Hiroshima on August 6. The dawn of the atomic age coincided with his own physical collapse, the result of age and accumulated stress. His doctors insisted that he leave Washington immediately for a "complete rest," but the secretary of war still had a duty to perform.[1] He left for work at the Pentagon as usual that morning before journeying across the Potomac for a meeting with President Harry S. Truman.

At the White House, Stimson presented the president with damage reports and photographs dramatically illustrating the effect of the atomic bomb dropped on Hiroshima. According to one of the reports, the "most conservative estimate" placed the death toll at "at least 100,000" people.[2] Upon viewing the reports and photos, Truman made a point of stressing "the terrible

Figure 1. President Harry S. Truman and Secretary of War Henry L. Stimson inspect damage reports and photographs from Hiroshima on August 8, 1945, two days after the use of the atomic bomb on that city. Despite suffering a mild heart attack, Stimson remained on the job in order to brief the president on the aftermath of the Hiroshima bombing. Upon receiving Stimson's report, Truman reflected on "the terrible responsibility that such destruction placed upon us here and himself." (Corbis)

responsibility that such destruction placed upon us here and himself."[3] Stimson clearly felt the weight of that responsibility. In a statement to the press the next day, the secretary of war confessed that the effects of the new weapon were "so terrific that the responsibility of its possession and its use must weigh heavily on our minds and on our hearts."[4]

Behind the scenes, Stimson worked frantically in the aftermath of Hiroshima and Nagasaki (bombed August 9 with some forty thousand dead) to control the atomic fire that he had helped to unleash. When the Japanese offered to surrender on August 10 with the sole condition that they be allowed to retain their emperor after the war, Stimson urged Truman to accept the offer. He also pleaded that the "humane thing" would be for the United States to unilaterally cease all conventional and nuclear attacks on Japanese cities while negotiations were ongoing. In calling for an immediate end to the bombing, Stimson specifically cited (according to Secretary of the Navy James V. Forrestal) "the growing feeling of apprehension and misgiving as to the effect of the atomic bomb even in our own country."[5]

Figure 2. A picture by an unknown photographer showing the immediate aftermath of the Hiroshima bombing. This photograph was among ten images discovered after the war by an American soldier (Robert L. Capp) assigned to the occupation forces. The photos were among rolls of undeveloped film hidden in a cave on the outskirts of Hiroshima. We have no information as to the identity of the photographer. Mr. Capp donated these photos to the Hoover Institution Archives in 1998 with the provision they not be reproduced until 2008. Mr. Capp has since passed away, and I am grateful to his wife and family for allowing me to reproduce these photographs in time for their inclusion here. (Robert L. Capp Papers, Hoover Institution Archives, Stanford, Calif.)

Truman did order a halt to the atomic bombing of Japan after the attack on Nagasaki.[6] The war, however, dragged on while Secretary of State James F. Byrnes dispatched a note that attempted to finesse the surrender issue, reassuring the Japanese about the postwar status of the emperor without explicitly abandoning the unconditional surrender formula. Truman rebuffed Stimson's plea to cease the conventional bombing of Japanese cities on August 10. Concerned that further indiscriminate attacks on Japanese cities and civilians might compromise surrender negotiations, the commander of the American strategic air forces in the Pacific, General Carl A. Spaatz, ceased such bombing on his own initiative the next day. But on August 14, acting on Truman's order to "go ahead with everything we've got," over seven hundred American heavy bombers flew raids against Japan, including extensive incendiary bombing of two Japanese cities.[7] American planes were still returning to their bases following those missions when the president announced that Japan had accepted the Byrnes note.

Stimson was not in Washington to receive the news of the Japanese surrender. Only partially successful in his attempts to sway Truman to do the "humane thing," the battered and exhausted secretary of war had finally left Washington on August 12 in order to recuperate at the exclusive Ausable Club in upstate New York. There, in the shade of the Adirondacks and the quiet of the forest, the old statesman thought a great deal about the terrible new weapon he had helped unleash upon the world. He returned in early September, determined to confront the menace posed by the bomb before it could be used again in anger. On September 21, his seventy-eighth birthday and last day in office as secretary of war, Stimson stood before Truman and his cabinet to present a dramatic plan aimed at "saving civilization not for five or for twenty years, but forever."[8]

Who Was Henry L. Stimson?

The press labeled him "the human icicle." Close friends eulogized him as "a Puritan" and a "New England conscience on legs." In person, they respectfully addressed him as "the Colonel," a rank he had won as a fifty-year-old volunteer during World War I.[9] A rigorous guardian of morality in both public and private affairs, he supposedly did not welcome divorced persons into the Stimson household.[10] A self-described "conscientious dry," he abstained from drinking liquor until the age of seventy-eight, when his doctor prescribed it following a heart attack. He was an unapologetic opponent of women's suffrage and an unabashed elitist who believed public policy should be guided by the "richer and more intelligent citizens of the country."[11] He consistently maintained that Anglo-Saxons were superior to the "lesser breeds" and once asked to have one of his government aides reassigned to other duties on "the slight possibility he might be a Hebrew."[12]

Though his most famous contribution to world history was as a reluctant midwife to the atomic age, the values that defined Stimson's character were those of the Victorian era. His rigid bearing and his deeply ingrained prejudices render him a distant and forbidding figure to modern eyes. Yet the Victorian values that appear merely narrow and petty when applied to Stimson's personal life were also responsible for shaping his many notable contributions to public life. His devotion to duty and commitment to morality in the conduct of national and international affairs inspired intense respect and loyalty from those who served under him during a career in public service that spanned five decades and six American presidents. A distinguished roster of men that included future Supreme Court justice Felix Frankfurter as well as pillars of the post-World War II American establishment such as John J. McCloy, Robert Lovett, George Harrison, and Harvey and McGeorge Bundy looked to Stimson as the embodiment of "wisdom and integrity and selflessness" as well as "a terrific human being" with a "gentle but penetrating wit and humor."[13]

War was a specter that haunted Stimson's long career. His most active involvement in public life came during a time of increasingly destructive global conflict. A superficial examination of his resume might suggest that he was a man not uncomfortable with warfare. He served as secretary of war twice, enlisted in the army in World War I, and was a vocal advocate of U.S. intervention in World War II before helping lead the American war effort, culminating with the use of the atomic bomb against Japan. This history—and his close association with Theodore Roosevelt—has led many observers to conclude that Stimson was, in the words of journalist Evan Thomas, one of a "group of militant nationalists" who were "especially avid about fighting wars."[14] Stimson biographer David F. Schmitz expressed a similar conclusion, asserting that "[l]ike Theodore Roosevelt, Stimson believed in the virtue of struggle and war and the positive influence of expansion."[15] Legendary American historian Charles Beard was blunter, privately blasting him as an "Old Republican hand of the imperialist school—war for glory and trade and to divert attention from domestic troubles."[16]

Stimson was undeniably an "old Republican," though he made a point of serving under presidents of both parties. His dedication to public service was marked by an intense loyalty to the presidents whom he served—whatever he believed to be their personal or political failings. At times in his career Stimson was also an imperialist. And "the Colonel" unabashedly embraced the pageantry and camaraderie he forever associated with his own time in uniform. But though never a pacifist, in the early years of the twentieth century Stimson learned to fear war as a mortal threat to the existence of world civilization.

"There is nothing more confusing about Henry Lewis Stimson," journalist Drew Pearson observed in 1931, "than the fact that despite his naïve and tenacious worship of the folderol of militarism, he is a devoted disciple of peace."[17]

As a conservative, Stimson had an attachment to law, order, and morality that led him to question the notion that war was a legitimate or useful tool of state policy. His lament that "the glory of war departed when they abolished the horse" reflected more than simply a romantic attachment to the cavalryman's life.[18] As the industrial revolution spread to the battlefield during World War I, he concluded that "war, perhaps the next war, would drag down and utterly destroy our civilization."[19] The better part of Stimson's long public career was devoted to preventing that next war or, at the very least, moderating its effects on civilians.

Previous studies of Stimson have largely neglected his sincere commitment to containing, if not eliminating, the violence of war.[20] Long before the advent of nuclear weapons, he was intimately concerned with the danger posed by technological terrors such as the submarine. As secretary of state under Herbert Hoover, Stimson passionately campaigned for arms control and international cooperation based on mutual trust, embracing an idealistic diplomatic agreement (the 1928 Kellogg-Briand Pact) that called for outlawing war among nations. Though he welcomed the fight against a lawless Nazi regime as just and necessary even before taking office as secretary of war in June 1940, Stimson brought with him into office a well-developed set of ideas about the conduct of that war. Throughout World War II, he opposed the indiscriminate use of force against civilians for both moral and practical reasons. "The reputation of the United States for fair play and humanitarianism," he insisted to Truman in 1945, "is the world's biggest asset for peace in the coming decades." Privately, Stimson lamented that "I, the man who had charge of the Department which did the killing in the war, should be the only one who seemed to have any mercy for the other side."[21]

The atomic bomb obviously posed a tremendous challenge to someone of Stimson's sensibilities. How was a rigidly moral man of the Victorian era to respond to what he dubbed a "terrible" new weapon in the midst of a horribly bloody war?[22] As secretary of war, Stimson had a responsibility to end the war as soon as possible with a minimum loss of American lives. He could not afford to shun the development and use of a weapon that might hold out that possibility. But neither did he throw out his moral and ethical standards as civilian head of the Manhattan Project. A man of demonstrated competence and un-questioned probity, arguably the most intelligent and conscientious public ser-vant of his generation, he found himself at the sunset of his career and life struggling with a project of immense moral and geopolitical complexity.

The Atomic Bomb and the Context of Use

This book uses the lens of biography to offer a new perspective on the over-lapping diplomatic, military, political, and scientific developments that culmi-nated in the first use of nuclear weapons in August 1945. In the pages that follow, I strive to recapture one man's complicated relationship to the bomb and in the process open up new avenues of inquiry into one of the most im-portant events in world history. Stimson's struggle never focused on a simple binary choice between using the bomb or launching a bloody invasion of the Japanese home islands. Rather, the A-bomb decision—or, more accurately, decisions—encompassed a complex and often overlapping set of calculations. What I refer to as the "context of use" included a host of diplomatic, military, political, and moral questions the answers to which combined to determine the way in which the bomb was eventually used.

One set of questions concerned America's enemies, the Axis powers. If the bomb was available to the United States before the end of the war, should it im-mediately be used against the Axis or held in reserve as a deterrent? If it were to be used, should Germany or Japan be the first target? What types of targets within those two countries were appropriate for such a weapon? Did the special properties of fission weapons, most notably radioactivity, raise ethical concerns that complicated their potential use? Should an explicit warning or other diplo-matic effort precede first use against the Axis? What role should the bomb play in the larger calculations over how to secure Japanese capitulation?

Another set of questions concerned relations with the other Allied powers, particularly Great Britain and the USSR. To what extent should the United States cooperate with the British in developing and perhaps using atomic weapons during the war? Should it attempt to maintain a nuclear monopoly after the war? Or would it be better to share the secret with the Soviets in hopes of gaining Stalin's cooperation in the postwar international control of atomic energy? If the United States did share the secret of the bomb, what price, if any, should American leaders insist upon in exchange for entrance into the atomic partnership? Should a deal on international control be struck before or after combat use of the bomb? In addressing these overlapping questions, U.S. leaders had to consider the impact of the bomb project on both wartime alliances and the postwar world. Looming over all these questions was the prospect of a nuclear arms race and the fear that the bomb might become "a Frankenstein which would eat us up."[23]

The atomic destruction of two Japanese cities punctuated the closing days of the bloodiest conflict in human history while simultaneously ushering in a new era of fear, terror, and insecurity that still haunts the world today. Truman's use of nuclear weapons has been scrutinized, defended, and criticized in numbing detail since the end of the war, resulting in a veritable cottage industry of popular and scholarly writings on the bomb.[24] While interesting new evidence is still emerging from Japanese and Soviet archives on the end of the Pacific War, on the American side scholars are increasingly left to parse minutiae, often in support of well-worn positions.[25] Some of the most intense scholarly exchanges on this issue in recent years have involved American casualty estimates for an invasion of Japan that never took place—and likely would not have even if the bomb had never been used.[26] Approaching the use of the bomb not as the result of a single decision but rather as the compound product of a series of choices that went back to the start of the American nuclear program offers a more sophisticated way of treating this complicated issue. By breaking down the decision into components, it also allows us much more flexibility in judging the impact of individuals in determining how the bomb was used.

No single person was in a position to shape every one of the choices that factored into the eventual use of the bomb. Though Franklin D. Roosevelt presided over the Manhattan Project from its inception, he died while several important decisions still hung in the balance. FDR also delegated a number of questions to his advisers, particularly with respect to how the bomb might be used in combat against the Axis. When Harry S. Truman stepped into the presidency in April 1945, he inherited important assumptions about the bomb. Although he must bear final responsibility for his decision to use nuclear weapons, Truman's choices were limited if not foreclosed by earlier decisions over which he had no control (and no knowledge) prior to taking office. Indeed, one of the weaknesses of much of the literature on the bomb is a narrow focus on Truman and the last months of the war.[27]

Some historians have highlighted Truman Secretary of State James F. Byrnes as the key player in the decision to use the bomb.[28] Byrnes was undoubtedly the most influential member of Truman's inner circle in the months prior to the use of the bomb. But he, too, was a relative newcomer to the Manhattan Project who inherited many of the choices and assumptions formulated in the early years of the program. And while General Leslie R. Groves may have been the Manhattan Project's "indispensable man" (in the estimation of biographer Robert S. Norris), his powers had limits.[29] Specifically, Groves had little say over the various high-level diplomatic issues involving Britain, the USSR, and Japan that played a crucial role in determining the context of use. Though in practice Groves was usually left to run the technical side of the bomb project as he saw fit, higher-level decision makers could and did intervene to overrule him at times.[30]

Henry Stimson was in a unique position to shape many of the decisions about the use of the bomb. He was briefed on the possibility of a fission bomb in November 1941. By the time the Japanese attacked Pearl Harbor, the secretary of war was among a select few charged with overseeing the American nuclear weapons program. To the end of the war he remained an important nuclear adviser, serving as a conduit between the president and the military and scientific personnel working under Groves at Los Alamos and elsewhere. In that context, Stimson's role was similar to that played by presidential science advisers James B. Conant and Vannevar Bush.[31] Unlike Bush and Conant, however, Stimson had decades of foreign policy experience, including a stint as secretary of state, upon which to call as he weighed the diplomatic ramifications of the bomb. With his bipartisan credentials as a servant to Democratic and Republican administrations, his extensive record of national and international service, and his close ties to the army's military leadership (most notably the army chief of staff, General George C. Marshall), Stimson was a powerful voice in the diplomatic and military debates over the atomic bomb.[32]

I do not want to overstate Stimson's role in the various atomic bomb decisions. At a number of crucial moments, Roosevelt and Truman chose to take matters into their own hands. When it came to the delicate diplomatic issues surrounding the American nuclear program, FDR at times concealed the details of his decisions from his own closest advisers, including the secretary of war. At the Potsdam Conference in July 1945, Stimson found himself painfully isolated from Truman and Byrnes as they weighed many of the important diplomatic decisions with respect to the bomb. Moreover, Stimson willingly deferred and delegated a number of important questions related to the bomb, particularly in the area of nuclear targeting. In doing so, he unknowingly contributed to narrowing the range of options open to American policymakers in summer 1945. Nevertheless, in evaluating the series of decisions that culminated in the atomic destruction of Hiroshima and Nagasaki, it is vital to understand the role played by Henry L. Stimson, a deeply moral man faced with terrible and difficult choices.

An Atomic Tragedy

The title of this book is inspired by a letter that Stimson wrote in 1946, a year after his retirement as secretary of war and four years before his death at age eighty-three. Writing to an old friend about the use of the bomb, he confided his fear that "the full enumeration of the steps in the tragedy" might taint his reputation as a moral statesman devoted to the cause of peace.[33] That Stimson should look back on the destruction of Hiroshima and Nagasaki as tragic is not surprising given the role he played in the affair. At several key junctures during World War II, his actions (or in some cases, inaction) contributed to the use of the bomb in such a way as to violate his own standards of war, morality, and international relations. It is not my intention to paint Stimson as a hypocrite or liar. Rather, in the pages that follow I trace how the pressures of war, the temptations posed by nuclear weapons, and Stimson's deference to authority and waning energies led a wise and thoughtful man, often inadvertently, to compromise his most cherished values.

In addition to reflecting Stimson's ambivalence about the atomic bomb and its implications for the world, the title *Atomic Tragedy* emphasizes the contingent nature of the events of August 1945. Perhaps the most unfortunate consequence of the narrative advanced by postwar defenders of the bomb has been to encourage a widespread belief that its use against Japanese cities and civilians was unavoidable and that no other outcome was realistically possible.[34]

Approaching the use of the bomb as a compound product of many decisions—technical, diplomatic, political, military, and moral—over a prolonged period of time greatly expands the range of possible outcomes. It is possible (but not certain) that a more creative use of diplomatic threats and

promises on the part of the United States might have secured a Japanese surrender at an earlier date, perhaps even prior to the use of the bomb.[35] But failing
that, it is also possible that the United States might have used the bomb
against Japan without deliberately targeting civilians for mass killing. Moreover, independent of decisions about use against Japan, it is possible that the
United States could have handled the diplomatic aspects of the bomb in such
a way as to increase the chances of postwar international control and diminish
the threat of a nuclear arms race.[36]

Even in the midst of a bloody and perilous world conflict, there were those
in the United States government, Stimson perhaps foremost among them, who
retained a deep concern with limiting the effects of war on civilians and fostering trust between nations as the foundation of the peace that followed. In light
of those convictions, many of Stimson's actions with respect to the bomb are
tragic and lamentable. His failures were understandable given the pressures
faced by the aging secretary of war. They were not, however, inevitable. This
book is about how an experienced, principled man faltered when confronted
by the tremendous challenge posed by the intersection of war, diplomacy, and
technology. It also contains relevant lessons for present and future generations
who must grapple with the ongoing legacy of this atomic tragedy.

Chapter 1

The Education of Henry L. Stimson

AMID WHAT NEWSPAPER REPORTS DESCRIBE AS "AN AIR OF TENSITY,"
Henry L. Stimson rose to address the representatives of the world's great
powers in a drawing room of St. James's Palace in London.[1] Moved by the
horrors unleashed in a global conflict that was still fresh of the minds of all
present, Stimson lamented that the war had produced a terrible new weapon,
the use of which had "revolted the conscience of the world." This technological terror was "particularly susceptible to abuse . . . in a way that violates
alike the laws of war and the dictates of humanity." In any future conflict, he
warned, warring nations would "be under strong temptation, perhaps irresistible temptation," to use this instrument "in the way that is most effective
for immediate purposes, regardless of consequences." Stimson closed with a
sharp question for the assembled diplomats: "whether in this day and age, and
after the experiences of the last war, the nations of this conference are justified
in continuing to build these instruments of warfare, thereby assuming responsibility for the risk of repeating in any possible future wars the inhumane
activities which have been condemned by the verdict of history."[2]

Figure 3. Secretary of State Stimson delivering an address calling for the abolition of the submarine as a weapon of war at the London Naval Conference, February 11, 1930. In the course of his address, Stimson warned that the submarine was "particularly susceptible to abuse . . . in a way that violates alike the laws of war and the dictates of humanity." (Corbis)

The occasion for Stimson's dramatic address was the London Naval Conference of February 1930. The weapon in question was the submarine, "the abuses of which were directly responsible for calling the western world into the greatest European war of history." In response, Stimson, who was representing the United States as secretary of state under President Herbert Hoover, publicly declared that "technical arguments should be set aside in order that the submarine may henceforth be abolished."[3]

Not all the powers at the conference were ready to follow Stimson's dramatic lead. In the face of French and Japanese opposition to abolition, Hoover's secretary of state had to be content with a vague agreement to "humanize" submarine warfare in order to limit its effects on noncombatants.[4] Undeterred by this setback, the secretary of state returned to Washington dedicated to meeting the challenge to peace posed by high-technology weapons combined with rising militarism and nationalism around the world. Stimson is best remembered today as secretary of war during World II, where he presided over the creation and use of atomic weapons against Hiroshima and Nagasaki. But his response to the challenges posed by nuclear fission was shaped by a set of values that were ingrained early in his life and evolved over time in response to a rich variety of experiences at home and abroad. Understanding that background is crucial to illuminating his dilemma as civilian overseer of the Manhattan Project.

Stimson's Trinity: Parkhurst, Root, and Roosevelt

Henry Lewis Stimson was born on September 21, 1867, in an America still recovering from the wounds of the Civil War. His father, Lewis Atterbury Stimson, was a member of a moderately wealthy New York family with American roots dating back to the mid-seventeenth century. In 1865, Lewis Stimson met, and became enchanted with, a young woman named Candace Wheeler. After pursuing Candace all the way to Venice, Italy, the two were married at the American embassy in Paris in November 1866. A son, Henry, followed ten months later.[5]

Henry and his younger sister (named Candace after their mother) had a colorful if not always happy childhood. They spent their early years living in New York City before embarking on an extended family sojourn in Europe as their father, a successful Wall Street broker, began a second career training as a physician in Paris, Berlin, and Zurich. Following their mother's untimely death in 1875 (likely as a result of diabetes), the two children returned to New York City, where they spent much of their time under the care of their grandfather, Henry Clark Stimson.

At the age of thirteen, young Henry was shipped off to Phillips Academy in Andover, Massachusetts. The "little New York City boy with his narrow shoulders and slender build" flourished in the rustic setting, and it was there that he developed a love of the outdoors that lasted the rest of his life. Technology and commerce also played an important part in his extracurricular education. While a student at Andover, he designed and built an electric telegraph and telephone system for sending messages between dorms and then charged his fellow students for the privilege of using it.[6]

Stimson went on to study at Yale (his father's alma mater), where he enjoyed academic and personal success. "Stimmy," as his classmates called him, graduated in 1888, having won several academic prizes as well as the attention of a young woman, Mabel Wellington White, who would eventually (after a lengthy and secretive engagement) become his wife and lifelong companion. He was also tapped to become a member of Skull and Bones, the illustrious secret society that provided a continuing web of social connections for a privileged few among Yale's student body. As a young man on the rise, Stimson was influenced by religion, the law, and three New Yorkers, all of which combined to shape his world in the tumultuous decade of the 1890s.

Religion had long played an important role in the Stimson family. His uncle, Henry A. Stimson, was a Presbyterian minister, and Stimson's education at Andover included regular attendance at prayer meetings. While at Yale, he served as a student missionary in one of New Haven's rougher neighborhoods. As he pondered his future after graduation, young Henry seriously considered a career in the ministry. Though he was uncertain whether he was truly cut out for the cloth, he earnestly wanted, as he explained to his aunt, "to do good in some way."[7] Pressured by his father, Stimson eventually chose law school over the church. Religion, however, continued to play an important role in his life. After completing his training in the law at Harvard, he returned to New York City, where he regularly attended services at the Madison Square Presbyterian Church. It was there that he first encountered a charismatic minister on a mission to redeem the spiritual and civic life of a wicked city.

Dr. Charles Parkhurst, a strict New England Presbyterian, was appalled by the vice that he saw in the streets and back alleys of New York City. Upon investigation (which included undercover visits to some of the city's most notorious dens of sin), an outraged Parkhurst discovered that the police and the Tammany Hall Democratic political machine were taking bribes in return for providing protection to prostitutes, madams, saloon owners, and other moral reprobates. Stimson was sitting in the pews at the Madison Square church in February 1892 when Parkhurst gave the first in a series of sermons that sent shock waves through the city and beyond. From his pulpit, Parkhurst unleashed a torrent of fire and brimstone on the "polluted harpies" and the "lying, perjured, rum-soaked, and libidinous lot" who governed New York City.[8] These sermons were the first shots in a lengthy war that pitted Parkhurst and his Society for the Prevention of Crime against Tammany Hall and its allies. With support from other religious and civic reformers (including Stimson's uncle as well as police commissioner Theodore Roosevelt), Parkhurst wedded his strict Presbyterianism to an earthly campaign of municipal reform.[9]

The most immediate result of Stimson's experience with Parkhurst's good-government crusade was to lead him away from the Tammany-dominated Democrats and toward the reform-minded wing of the Republican Party.[10] This political shift proved to be permanent—despite his record of bipartisan national service, Stimson remained a steadfast Republican until his death in 1950. More generally, his experience with Parkhurst's crusade helped leverage his private faith into participation in the growing national movement for political and economic reform. Though Stimson's values remained conservative to the core, his was not the moss-backed conservatism of the status quo. When he began his ascent into public life at the start of the twentieth century, it was as a reformer steeped in righteous morality and guided by the stirrings of the Social Gospel to change the world for the better.

Faith provided a call to action, but it did not necessarily offer a blueprint for solving the complex problems that beset a rapidly urbanizing and industrializing America at the end of the nineteenth century. Looking back near the end of his life, Stimson explained his relationship to God by saying that though he believed strongly in organized religion, "I don't intellectually believe in dogma."[11] While Presbyterianism provided the moral core of Stimson's worldview, it was not religious dogma but rather the law from which he drew both his livelihood and the intellectual framework that guided his approach to national and international affairs.

Heeding his father's advice, Stimson had passed on the ministry to attend Harvard Law School in 1888. After an initial struggle that found him in a "state of rebellion against life, law, and Harvard in general," he rallied and found stimulating intellectual companionship with a group of fellow students that included such notables as Ezra Thayer (future dean of Harvard Law).[12] While at Harvard, Stimson was also exposed to a broader set of ideas about the world than could be found in dusty casebooks or contentious mock trials.

Unsatisfied with confining himself to a narrow education in the law, Stimson found in the work of Harvard philosophers George H. Palmer, Josiah Royce, and John Fiske an ideal fusion of purpose, order, and morality. Drawing from the work of these men, particularly Royce and Fiske, Stimson developed a belief in what he later referred to as "a law of moral progress."[13] Biological evolution through natural selection (which Stimson readily accepted as compatible with his religious convictions) had taken mankind as far as it could. Future developments would hinge not on the blind interaction of natural forces but rather on the ability of men to use their minds and moral sensibility to perfect human civilization. In the short term, this belief allowed Stimson to

Figure 4. Stimson upon his graduation from Yale in 1888 (left) and later as a successful New York City attorney at the prestigious firm of Root and Clarke in the 1890s. (Henry L. Stimson Papers, Manuscripts and Archives, Yale University, New Haven, Conn.)

tolerate the more tedious aspects of his legal education and embrace the law as a tool for the gradual evolution of human society toward a more perfect moral order. In the long term, his belief in a "law of moral progress" informed Stimson's work on the national and international stage.

Before he could change the world, Stimson had to make his place in it. Earning his law degree in 1890 at the age of twenty-two, he made use of his network of Yale connections to land a job as a clerk at a prestigious New York City corporate law firm headed by Elihu Root. While he would eventually come to see Root as a "second father," in the early years of their association the benefits that Stimson accrued from the relationship were of a more material nature.[14] Starting as a clerk at the salary of $750 a year, he was elevated to the status of full partner on January 1, 1893. Having managed a place in a good firm and passed his bar examinations, Stimson was finally able to make good on his long-delayed engagement to Mabel White, and the two were married in July of that year. Secure in his personal and professional life, Stimson slowly began to grapple with how to put his talents into the service of a good greater than himself. In this task, Elihu Root played a crucial role.

Root was the quintessential American conservative: a man who devoted his considerable intellect to the preservation of order and the protection of capital. The most respected corporate lawyer in late-nineteenth-century New York, he had a client list that was a virtual *Who's Who* of the city's corporate titans. Root's legal and political philosophy was built on the rock of precedent. Change at the local, national, and international level should be based on gradual legal evolution; he had no patience for well-meaning but untested schemes for rearranging human affairs. This emphasis on precedent would become central to Stimson's approach to law, society, and policy. The other pillar of Root's thought was an abiding belief in the power of capitalism to solve the problems of the United States and the world. His passionate rhetorical defense of the free market and his close association with many of the era's corporate giants won Root the informal title of "the attorney for capitalism."[15] These beliefs also resonated with Stimson, who for the rest of his life embraced law and commerce as dual engines of peaceful change in national and international affairs.

In 1899 Root turned over his lucrative private practice to Stimson and the other younger partners in order to accept the position of secretary of war under President William McKinley. Root's initial charge was to use his administrative talents to organize the insular empire that the United States had wrested from Spain following the war of 1898. Controversy dogged Root's service as secretary of war. He was a frequent target of anti-imperialists, who accused him of condoning torture and other atrocities committed by American troops against Filipino insurgents fighting for their independence.[16] Root's experience as a defense counsel and his political attachment to his Republican patrons led him to mount a zealous if narrow defense of the army's actions in the Philippines, but his inclinations eventually led him to pursue a very different course for the United States in world affairs.

As a conservative, Root abhorred the chaos and dislocation caused by war. War fostered instability and bred radicalism. After a brief return to private practice, Root agreed to serve as secretary of state under Theodore Roosevelt. In his new office, he promoted law as a substitute for international conflict. War, he believed, should be labeled "criminal conduct" rather than regarded as a legitimate tool of state policy. Acknowledging that such a shift in human behavior would take "generations and centuries in the life of nations," Root rejected calls for the creation of a world government as dangerously idealistic.[17] Rather, as secretary of state from 1905 to 1909, he applied his passion for order and precedent to the growing movement for international judicial arbitration. He advocated the creation of a permanent international court as well as the gradual extension of international law in order to expand the realm of questions open to judicial settlement.

Root's efforts on behalf of a legal and judicial solution to the problem of war were recognized with the 1912 Nobel Peace Prize. Aghast at the chaos unleashed by the outbreak of World War I, he redoubled his effort to codify alternatives and impediments to war in a formal, institutional form. "Conciliation, good-will, love of peace, [and] human sympathy, are ineffective," he asserted in 1915, "without institutions through which they can act."[18] For the rest of his life, Root worked toward building those institutions, most notably helping to draft the charter for the World Court in the aftermath of the war. He was increasingly handicapped, however, by his advancing age (Root was seventy-three at the end of the First World War) and by the surge tide of provincial American nationalism that crested in the wake of World War I. It would fall to Root's young protégé to carry on the legacy of "practical idealism" in pursuit of a solution to the growing menace of war in the industrial age.[19]

From his position in Washington, Root began to groom Stimson for service on the national and international stage. In a stroke of good fortune, Stimson found that he had not only a powerful mentor but also a strong personal connection to the brash, young chief executive under whom Root served. Stimson had first met Theodore Roosevelt in 1894 as a fellow member of the Boone and Crockett Club, an organization of sportsmen and conservationists founded by the future president in 1887. They shared a background of privilege. Both men had been born to wealthy New York families and received Ivy League educations. They also shared an interest in reform dating back to Parkhurst's campaign to clean up New York City. Both men gloried in proving their manhood through outdoors adventures in the West. In the 1880s, Roosevelt had famously traveled to the Dakota badlands, where the Harvard College and Columbia Law School graduate embraced ranching as a relief from the pressures of city life. In that same decade, Stimson began his excursions to the American West while still an undergraduate at Yale. He witnessed an uprising by the Ute tribe in Colorado in 1887, climbed mountains in the Rockies, had a peak named after him in what is now Glacier National Park in Montana, and shot innumerable game animals. Stimson later claimed to "have killed nearly all varieties of North American big game, including moose, elk, caribou, two kinds of deer, three kinds of bears (eleven in all), Rocky Mountain sheep, Rocky Mountain goat and antelope, as well as various kinds of small game."[20]

When unable to travel West, Stimson did his best to re-create the rustic life at Highhold, the Long Island estate he purchased in 1903. On Highhold's hundred acres in the farming land of West Hills, Stimson constructed horse stalls, a hay barn, a coachman's cottage, and a windmill; planted corn and oats; purchased "the fastest hound in Rappahannock"; and, with the exception of his numerous letters of complaint to the Long Island Railroad, seems to have enjoyed a quiet retreat from the pressures of his daily work in the city. Shortly after moving into his new home, Stimson inaugurated the "Annual Highhold Games," at which he played the role of the country gentleman providing sport, entertainment, and refreshments for hundreds of neighbors, including Roosevelt, who owned an estate in nearby Sagamore Hill.[21]

Though their shared exaltation in the "strenuous life" helped cement the bond between the two men, it was Root who first suggested to the president in 1905 that Stimson's talents might be put to good use on the national scene. When he was summoned to lunch with Roosevelt on December 8, 1905, Stimson expected a pleasant chat about bear hunting. Instead, the president, on Root's advice, asked him to consider taking the position of United States Attorney for the Southern District of New York.[22] Upon accepting the president's offer and receiving his appointment in 1906, Stimson vaulted into the national ranks of the Progressive movement. Though he had little interest in foreign affairs at the time, Stimson's career as a Progressive reformer greatly influenced his later approach to problems of war and peace in the nuclear age.

Like Root, Stimson embraced precedent, order, and capitalism as bedrocks of American life. To a greater degree than his mentor, however, Stimson understood that unchecked industrial capitalism was itself a radical threat to the stability of American society. Picking up on a thesis most famously advanced by historian Frederick Jackson Turner, he concluded that with the closing of the frontier also came the closing of "the great safety valve against discontent" that had long preserved social and economic peace in the United States. Stimson got a firsthand taste of this discontent in 1900 when his National

Guard unit was called upon to help put down a strike by Italian and Italian–American workers at the Cornell Dam in upstate New York.[23]

Stimson understood that industrial capitalism could not be indefinitely propped up by force. "The bitterness with which certain business men confront the necessary reforms of the future," he warned, was "pathetic and dangerous."[24] And though he had "not the slightest sympathy with or faith in the tenets of Socialism," he strongly objected when the New York State Assembly attempted to deny seats to Socialists who had won election in the midst of the 1920 Red Scare. Failing to seat the Socialists would be "a blow at the very foundations of democracy." It would also increase the danger of revolution by excluding legitimate dissent from the political arena.[25]

Throughout his career, Stimson insisted that reform, not repression, was the best response to radicalism. Moved by his personal experience with the growing unrest among the working class and informed by Dr. Parkhurst and the Social Gospel, Stimson championed the activist use of government power to curb the excesses of unregulated industrial capitalism. As a United State attorney, he gained a reputation as a trustbuster. Aided by a brilliant group of hand-selected young attorneys (including future Supreme Court justice Felix Frankfurter), he conducted a lengthy and ultimately successful fraud prosecution of the New York sugar trust, his biggest triumph.

Stimson's laudable commitment to public service was tinged with a paternalism and elitism that was characteristic of the Progressive movement as a whole. He insisted that political and economic reform be directed by an educated, male elite, preferably Republicans who shared his own class and social background. "[T]he Republican Party, which contains, generally speaking, the richer and more intelligent citizens of the country," he insisted, "should take the lead in reform and not drift into a reactionary position." He opposed giving women the vote on the grounds that "like other dilution of the suffrage, [it] would tend towards more ineffective and worse government."[26]

In domestic policy, Stimson consistently extolled the virtues of strong executive authority from the state house to the White House. Privately he insisted that the American people were as "ignorant as babies about their foreign relations" and that it was the responsibility of men like himself to take the lead in crafting foreign policy and shaping public opinion on matters of international importance.[27] On an international level, this translated into a diplomacy rooted in quiet, often informal negotiations between cosmopolitan elites. Stimson's elitism and distrust of democracy when it came to deciding matters of foreign policy was perhaps the least appealing aspect of his legacy. It was also an attitude that helped facilitate his career as a Washington insider serving a bipartisan series of presidents at a time of growing executive power in the realm of foreign policy.

Disdain for the American masses whom they sought to uplift and reform was not uncommon among the Progressives. But unlike more successful Progressive politicians, Stimson lacked the charisma and oratorical skills necessary to actually win elections in an age of mass suffrage. Stimson learned this lesson the hard way. In 1910, he made his first and only bid for elected office, running as Theodore Roosevelt's hand-picked candidate for governor of New York. For the Long Island squire it was a humbling experience in the messy world of retail politics. Unable to extricate himself from TR's considerable shadow (a cartoon in the *New York Times* depicted Stimson as a small girl grabbing at the coattails of the elder Roosevelt) and ill prepared for the populist give-and-take of the campaign trail, Stimson was decisively defeated by his Democratic opponent in the same election that catapulted Woodrow Wilson into the governorship of neighboring New Jersey and onto the fast track for the presidency.[28]

Electoral defeat in 1910 did not significantly dim Stimson's career in government. Though he never again stood for elective office, his political connections to the Roosevelt wing of the Republican Party and his growing reputation for quiet, loyal service behind the scenes made him a valuable commodity in Washington. In 1911, President William Howard Taft tapped him to head the War Department. It was the first of several positions that forced Stimson to directly grapple with one of the defining issues of the twentieth century.

War and Empire at the Dawn of the Century

The origins of Stimson's aversion to war are not hard to trace. As much as he admired Theodore Roosevelt, temperamentally and intellectually he remained the disciple of Elihu Root. While Roosevelt's love of the strenuous life translated easily into a bellicose patriotism that often glorified war, the same association did not hold true for Stimson.[29] This crucial distinction was clear as early as 1898 in their divergent responses to the Spanish-American War. America's "splendid little war" was high season for upper-class patriotic vigor. Several influential men in Stimson's circle took advantage of the conflict to dramatize their masculinity in the service of American nationalism.[30] Roosevelt and his fellow "Rough Riders" were the most notable example, but Stimson's law partner and close friend Bronson Winthrop also served, embarking to the Philippines as a quartermaster. Stimson, in contrast, found the war to be an inconvenience to his professional and social life and its imperial aftermath distasteful to his republican sensibilities.

Though at thirty he was nine years younger than Roosevelt and four years younger than his partner Winthrop, Stimson lacked his comrade's boyish enthusiasm for the war.[31] Stimson remarked on Winthrop's departure for the Philippines by lamenting that "his patriotism has sadly interfered with my possibility of bear-hunting this fall." When he was not decrying the impact of the war on his hunting expeditions and "the even tenor of our ways in New York City," he was concerned with the effect that military service might have on his law career.[32] Though he felt duty-bound to answer the call should the need arise, he was not anxious to spend a prolonged period away from his lucrative private practice. As a compromise, Stimson briefly considered service in the navy, which he believed "would be much more convenient for a man in my position, as the emergency need for the Navy will probably not last so long as the garrison need for the Army and I could probably get back to my work much quicker."[33] He eventually solved this dilemma by enlisting in a New York National Guard unit that allowed him to serve on a part-time basis without the inconvenience of an overseas posting.

Seemingly uninterested in the war itself, Stimson quietly opposed the exercise of imperial power that followed in its wake. He later admitted to being "greatly scandalized" by McKinley's decision to annex the Philippine Islands.[34] Though his mentor and close friend Elihu Root accepted the task of organizing America's newly won insular empire, Stimson's position on the Philippines at the turn of the twentieth century was closer to that of the Reverend Parkhurst. From his pulpit, Parkhurst repeatedly blasted the American conquest and subjugation of the Philippines as immoral and unjust. "[T]o promote civilization by the use of swords and artillery," he insisted in 1899, "is false to the word, example, and life of Jesus Christ and of all his apostles and alien to the entire genus of Christianity." In response to the torture scandal in the Philippines that took place under Root's watch, Parkhurst declared that the abuses were the inevitable fruit of an immoral war.[35]

Though more restrained in his language than Parkhurst, Stimson left no doubt in his private correspondence as to where his sentiments lay on the subject. Writing to a close friend in the aftermath of the war, Stimson decried "a loose tendency on the part of the press . . . to talk of 'imperialism' in a glib way which indicates that a good many people think we can permanently bring such places as the Philippines under the United States Government and still maintain that Government in the form of a single Republic." He dismissed this suggestion out of hand, noting sharply, "I cannot see how we can permanently govern any piece of territory, no matter how remote or how inferior its population, by any other system of government than a representative one."[36] He saw no grounds for a permanent relationship without admitting the Philippines into the union, a development that he strongly opposed on the grounds that Filipinos, whom he believed to be racially inferior, would taint the American body politic.

Though his motives were far from altruistic as far as the Filipinos were concerned, Stimson's convictions put him quietly but firmly in the anti-imperialist camp. Tellingly, however, he never spoke publicly on the issue of the Philippines during the heated debate over annexation and its immediate aftermath. Perhaps he saw the whole thing, like the war itself, as a distraction from his personal and professional pursuits. It seems likely, however, that he was also motivated by a desire to avoid antagonizing or embarrassing Root and Roosevelt, who were prominently identified with the pro-imperialist position. Linked to his belief in the need for benevolent rule by educated elites was a deep loyalty to his own political patrons and bosses. Though he never shied from offering dissenting opinions in private discussions with those whom he served, Stimson was always careful to keep such disagreements out of the public eye. Admirable in some ways, Stimson's reputation for loyalty enhanced his status as the ultimate political insider. But this same tendency often led him to muzzle his own moral and political views in public in deference to the interests of those in power.

A decade after the great debate over empire, Stimson was forced to reconsider the issue thanks to his new position under President Taft. As secretary of war from 1911 to 1913, Stimson was tasked with presiding over the imperial spoils of 1898, including the Philippines and Puerto Rico, as well as the still-under-construction Panama Canal. Whatever his personal opinions on the subject, his new job required him to manage and defend the American empire in Asia and the Caribbean. In short order, however, he went from a tepid official endorsement of U.S. policy to a vocal apologist for the "white man's burden."

The catalyst for Stimson's imperial transformation was a visit to Panama, Cuba, and the Dominican Republic in July 1911. In this course of his Caribbean voyage, Stimson's views on race quickly trumped his more abstract concerns about the deleterious effects of empire. Throughout his life, Stimson expressed a belief in the superiority of the white (and particularly Anglo-Saxon) race over what he once referred to as the "lesser breeds."[37] The secretary of war's exposure to the native peoples of Santo Domingo led him to conclude that "a little benevolent despotism" was called for in administering that country.[38] After visiting "that spot of darkness" and its "fat bullock of a president," he confided to his father, "I have rarely been more impressed with the 'white man's burden' than when I saw what that little force of revenue men were standing against . . . in the most damnable hole of loneliness and misrule that I have yet run up against."[39]

Stimson's newfound enthusiasm for imperialism also extended to the Philippines. As secretary of war, he reversed course and strongly advocated retaining the islands under American control. When Parkhurst penned a 1913 editorial excoriating the United States for its brutal subjugation of the Filipino independence movement, Stimson responded with a peeved letter to the crusading reverend. "As against this comparatively small percentage of life lost in the work of restoring law and order," he admonished, "you should consider the far greater amount of life that has been actually saved by the measures of civilization which have been made possible by this law and order."[40] Whereas he had previously rejected imperialism as a distraction from the vital work of reform at home, as secretary of war under Taft he embraced it as part of a greater struggle to impose order on a chaotic world.

By the end of the 1920s, Stimson would revise his attitude toward imperialism yet again. Serving as a special emissary to war-torn Nicaragua in 1927 and then as governor general of the Philippines in 1928–29, Stimson slowly began to appreciate the limits of U.S. power in the developing world.[41] In both cases he attempted to achieve his desired ends through personal diplomacy with indigenous elites. Convinced in the aftermath of World War I that "[w]e have passed the era of caveman methods in regard to international alliances," Stimson asserted in 1929 that the loyalty of developing nations could be won only by cultivating their trust.[42] By the time he took office as secretary of state under Herbert Hoover, Stimson had come full circle in his views on empire. Disillusioned with the "white man's burden" and the often heavy-handed use of American marines that went along with it, he worked with Hoover to scale back the exercise of U.S. power in Latin America.[43]

Stimson's imperial struggles highlighted two fundamental and sometimes clashing aspects of his approach to international relations. On the one hand, he clearly believed in the supremacy of the white race and of Euro-American civilization in particular, a conviction that led him at several points in his career to support so-called benevolent imperialism in the developing world. On the other hand, like his mentor Elihu Root, Stimson harbored a growing distaste of war as a tool of state policy. The fierce resistance to the exercise of naked American power in places such as Nicaragua eventually led him to question whether it was possible to impose his vision of civilization without the kind of destructive conflicts that he so deeply wished to avoid.

"Praying Earnestly for Peace"

It was the mundane task of bureaucratic reform, not the agonies of empire, that occupied most of Stimson's tenure as secretary of war under Taft. The force he oversaw in those years was a shadow of the armies he would later help raise during World War II. By law the army was limited to no more than one hundred thousand men, with an actual strength closer to seventy-five thousand. The army's Aeronautical Division (buried within the Signal Corps) consisted of a grand total of one airplane and one pilot at the time Stimson took office in 1911.[44] The greatest enemies confronting the small, all-volunteer army were boredom, inefficiency, and disease. All too often, the army found itself on the losing end of these battles. The newly installed secretary of war quickly discovered an epidemic of venereal disease "far in excess of that obtaining among other nations and which causes more disability than all other diseases combined."[45]

Though his new position lacked glamour, Stimson relished both the sleepy atmosphere of peacetime Washington and the opportunity to bring Progressive reform and "scientific management" to the hidebound military bureaucracy.[46] Each day he walked to his office in the War-and-Navy Building followed by his devoted dog, an Airedale named Punch, who would sleep beneath the secretary's desk until it was time for the afternoon walk back home for lunch. Punch would sometimes follow his master into White House meetings with Taft, much to the annoyance of the president. Aside from the president's "lack of interest in dogs," Stimson enjoyed good relations with Taft, whom he later hailed as "a very pleasant and jolly man to serve under."[47] The only major crisis Stimson faced in his personal relations with the president arose from the challenge of hosting Taft at a dinner party. Deeming the furniture at his residence inadequate to support the president's three-hundred-pound frame, Stimson commissioned a special chair for the occasion. Recounting the story years later, Stimson's longtime friend George Wharton Pepper recalled that, "to make sure of its strength I sat in it, the Secretary of War sat on my lap and the wife of the Secretary sat on his. The chair stood this triple test and was deemed safe for the Chief Executive."[48]

In the waning days of the Taft administration, Stimson confronted a much more serious crisis, one that tested his distaste for war as a tool of policy. In February 1913, the administration was confronted with the possibility that the Mexican government under Francisco Madero might collapse into civil war. Stimson was not averse to using force if necessary to protect U.S. citizens, and he deployed troops on the Mexican border in case it should be necessary to dispatch such a "relief expedition." Unlike president-elect Woodrow Wilson, however, Taft was not eager to become involved in the turbulent Mexican political situation. Stimson was also cautious, confiding to his father on February 13 that there was "no ground [for] intervention yet and I hope there won't be."[49]

Taft and Stimson left office without committing U.S. troops to Mexico. When the crisis flared up again in 1914, Stimson, then a private citizen, castigated Wilson's handling of the Mexican situation, which he believed had resulted in the United States "inevitably drifting into a war."[50] Though he felt duty-bound to serve should a full-scale war break out, he expressed great surprise when it appeared his offer of military service might actually be accepted. He privately admitted that he was "praying earnestly for peace." When the crisis cooled off again in June 1914, Stimson declared, "I confess to being unwarlike enough to be much relieved personally."[51] His sense of relief, however, was short-lived. Within months, events in Europe thrust him into a public debate on war and peace in the industrial age.

Colonel Stimson and the War to End All Wars

World War I was the defining moment in Stimson's evolution from a minor figure in American domestic politics to a crusader for international peace.

Prior to that conflict, his distaste for war had primarily been a matter of temperament. The devastation unleashed by industrialized warfare from 1914 to 1918 led him to see the prevention of future conflicts as nothing less than a matter of life and death for human civilization. Just as domestic reforms had been necessary to prevent industrial conflicts from tearing the United States apart, international reforms guided by the steady application of humane legal principles would be necessary to protect the world's industrialized nations from the ravages of war.

Predictably, Stimson's attitude toward the conflict in Europe was shaped at the intersection of law, commerce, and morality. In the early days of the war, he was content to stump for military preparedness without advocating American intervention. But when a German submarine torpedoed and sank the passenger liner *Lusitania* on May 7, 1915, Stimson decided that the issues of the war transcended narrow questions of national interest. In attacking civilians on the high seas, the Germans were not only threatening American lives and commerce but also undermining the legal and moral foundations of international progress. Neutrality rights, he insisted, were the first step on the path toward the abolition of war. While admitting that the world was still a long way from "abolishing war in the name of its inhumanity and in substituting for it a rule of peace and reason," Stimson insisted that "by far the greatest advance which has been thus slowly made in putting brakes upon the savagery of war has been in the development of the rights of the neutral." The United States, he exhorted a Carnegie Hall audience in June 1915, must be ready to defend these hard-won rights in order that "out of this doctrine of neutrality may ultimately be realized our dreams of peace which will be universal and permanent."[52]

By 1917 Stimson had concluded that American intervention was a necessary and just response to the threat to peace posed by the Central Powers, and particularly by Germany under the kaiser. When President Wilson asked for a declaration of war in April 1917, Stimson rushed into uniform to serve with a fervor that surprised his close friends. His law partner Bronson Winthrop (whose service in the Spanish-American conflict Stimson had lamented some twenty year earlier) tried to convince him that active military service at his age was foolish and that he "ought to be headed for a sanitarium rather then the War Department."[53] Stimson, however, would not be dissuaded. He had come to share Wilson's belief that "the world must be made a safe place for

Figure 5. Stimson in uniform during World War I. Upon U.S. entry into the conflict, Stimson volunteered for service at the age of forty-nine. He did so despite the advice of friends who warned that he "ought to be headed for a sanitarium rather then the War Department." While serving as an artillery officer, Stimson spent a brief period with the American Expeditionary Force (AEF) in France before returning stateside with a promotion to colonel. (Henry L. Stimson Papers, Manuscripts and Archives, Yale University, New Haven, Conn.)

democracy," and he was determined to play his own part in the grand endeavor.[54] On May 31, 1917, only months short of his fiftieth birthday, Stimson secured a commission as a major in the United States Army. A little more than a year later, he was placed in command of battalion of artillery in a quiet section of the western front near Lorraine.

Promoted to the rank of colonel and shipped back stateside after only three weeks on the front lines in France, Stimson had a brief and relatively uneventful military career. He gloried in the camaraderie of fellow soldiers, and his overseas service filled him with admiration for both the American fighting man and his British and French counterparts.[55] But as much as he enjoyed the pageantry of the military, Stimson's service left him with no romantic notions about the nature of modern warfare. The chaotic aftermath of the war (including the triumphs of the Bolsheviks in Russia) only reinforced his conviction that such conflicts could no longer be tolerated in the future.

Both personality and experience had led Stimson to cherish the values of order and stability. By 1918 it was clear that those values were no longer compatible with the conduct of modern warfare. The days of Rough Riders and splendid little wars were over. As he put it many years later, "To us oldsters the glory of war departed when they abolished the horse."[56] Not only was modern war highly costly in human life, but it also threatened to disrupt the economic and political fabric of the industrial capitalist West and unleash revolutionary forces far beyond the battlefield. Upon his return to civilian life, Stimson quickly announced his support for "trying almost anything which may offer any chance to diminish the likelihood of another such catastrophe to civilization as this war."[57]

Crafting an Alternative to War

For twenty years after the end of World War I, Stimson worked both publicly and privately to promote alternatives to war in hopes of avoiding "another such catastrophe." The apogee of his involvement in the international peace movement came during his service as secretary of state under Herbert Hoover. The tribulations of worldwide economic depression and militant nationalism only strengthened his belief that the United States, western Europe, and Japan were inextricably connected as part of "a complex industrial civilization which could not withstand modern war."[58] His approach to preventing war was rooted in a combination of international law, arms control, a capitalist Open Door policy for world trade, and the fostering of mutual trust among world leaders. While Stimson and his cosmopolitan allies in other capitals ultimately failed in their task of preventing another world war, these years were crucial in forming the lens with which he viewed the atomic bomb and during World War II.

Stimson's quest for peace in the aftermath of World War I was built on the foundation of international law. It was this attachment to law and precedent that led both Root and Stimson to distrust the Covenant of the League of Nations that Woodrow Wilson brought back from Paris in 1919. While pleased that the league would create "regular institutions which will work toward peace," Stimson followed his mentor Root in fearing that it was not sufficiently grounded in the existing canon of international law.[59] He also had specific reservations about Article X, which committed league members to collectively guarantee the political and territorial integrity of all the signatory nations. While he approved of the idea of collective security, Stimson worried that in the absence of widely accepted judicial alternatives to war as a means of resolving international disputes, Article X would "artificially freeze the status quo and commit the United States to defend it by force." Attempting to outlaw war without substituting other means of effecting international change amounted to putting a "strait-jacket on progress" and would result in more conflict rather than less.[60]

Instead of relying on Wilson's well-meaning but untested covenant, Stimson hoped to build on the existing body of international law, gradually extending its reach by treaty and mutual agreements among like-minded nations. The "safe course of procedure," he insisted, was "to go conservatively, creating institutions which would develop public opinion along the lines of rapprochement and then leave it to time and experience to do the rest."[61] Here Stimson was following not only Root but also Harvard philosopher John Fiske, who had similarly argued for the gradual development of moral self-control as the best means of perfecting human civilization. Initially Stimson believed that it might take centuries to craft the necessary institutions and shape public opinion to the point where it would be possible finally to outlaw war. He was, however, greatly encouraged by the progress on this issue during the 1920s. The successful naval disarmament conference at Washington in 1920–21, coupled with the creation of the World Court and a series of agreements on boundaries and debts reached by European nations, seemed to indicate a growing international consensus on the futility of war. These trends appeared to reach their logical conclusion in 1928 with the promulgation of the Kellogg-Briand Pact.

Crafted in Paris in 1928, the Kellogg-Briand Pact outlawed war as a tool of state policy. The signatories, which included most of the nations in existence at the time, promised that they would "condemn recourse to war for the solution of international controversies, and renounce it as an instrument of national policy in their relations with one another."[62] It is easy in hindsight to be dismissive of the idealism enshrined in the pact. Significantly, it lacked any enforcement provisions for dealing with violators. Stimson, however, believed that it was those who accepted war as a tool of state who were dangerously naïve. Preventing the outbreak of war was the only way to preserve the complex, interdependent relationships that sustained modern industrial societies around the world.

Consequently, he believed that that the Kellogg Pact was a sound, conservative document that represented the culmination of centuries of international law. By the early 1930s, Stimson was convinced that "the time had arrived when that dream [of outlawing war] had a reasonable chance of becoming a reality."[63]

Stimson, never a pacifist, acknowledged that it would not be possible to totally banish human conflict from the face of the earth. He insisted, however, that "we can abolish war as a regular instrument of national policy."[64] In making this argument, he explicitly drew on the precedents of Anglo-American domestic law, noting that "we have reason to hold that faith because the same evolution has taken place in the domestic affairs of nations." To illustrate the power of public opinion to resolve disputes short of force, he often cited the example of the U.S. Supreme Court. "For one hundred years," he observed, "our Supreme Court has existed without any sanction behind it in respect to disputes between states and yet its decisions have always been respected."[65] As an international equivalent, Stimson pointed to the World Court, which Elihu Root had played a role in creating. In order for the Kellogg-Briand pact to be effective, it was vital that the World Court develop "judicial means instead of war to settle the inevitable controversies between nations . . . and clarify the standards and rules of international conduct by which such controversies can be prevented or minimized."[66]

As secretary of state from 1929 to 1933, Stimson followed in Root's footsteps as he worked with President Herbert Hoover to translate the promises of Kellogg-Briand into a practical American foreign policy. The secretary and his new boss differed sharply in personality and temperament. Hoover was careful, calculating, and driven to work at a rate that Stimson found appalling. Stimson's preference for the more leisurely pace of the country gentleman, on the other hand, struck his new boss as a symptom of "slackness."[67] Hoover reportedly remarked that his secretary of state was "a pathological case, that he thought clearly for a couple of hours and then crashed mentally because not enough blood went to his brain."[68] When Stimson did act, however, he preferred to do so decisively. In securing approval for the administration's policies, he was constantly urging Hoover to "march toward the guns" and impose his will on the Congress. Hoover, more attuned to the nuances of domestic politics, preferred to act with a restraint that Stimson found galling. He was particularly agitated by the president's reluctance to push the Senate to ratify the World Court treaty.[69]

Though he often chafed under Hoover, Stimson remained the good soldier for the duration of his tenure, loyally serving the president despite mounting personal and policy disputes. But it was not simply his famed loyalty that kept Stimson from abandoning his unpopular boss. For all their differences, the colonel and the Quaker shared a powerful set of assumptions about war, law, and morality. Both men had been deeply affected by World War I and shared revulsion at the chaos and destruction sown by modern industrialized warfare. They also shared a commitment to arms control as a logical and necessary response to the problem of war.

For Stimson, the international arms race that had preceded World War I illustrated the danger of relying too heavily on military means to deter war. Though he supported modest military preparedness, Stimson lectured officers at the Army War College in January 1931 on the dangers inherent in taking such an approach too far. "There is a natural limit to the possibility of military preparedness," he asserted, "arising out of the fact that if a nation adopts a military defense which is perfect for itself and seems to its own citizens no more than is appropriate to itself, it is dead sure that that same defense seems to other nations so excessive as to be pointed at them."[70] This was an observation that proved just as true in the nuclear age as it was in the age of the dreadnought, and it later informed Stimson's post-World War II plea for nuclear arms control.

Stimson's first overseas trip as secretary of state was as the head of the American delegation to the London Naval Conference, where he made his dramatic plea for the abolition of submarines. Arms control and the abolition of weapons that posed special dangers to civilians seemed a logical starting point on the path toward a permanent peace. But Stimson's hopes for disarmament quickly ran into a thicket of problems. The leaders of the other major powers at London responded skeptically to his assertion that "the enactment of the Kellogg Pact created a new starting point for international negotiations for the preservation of peace."[71] Meanwhile, to Stimson's great frustration, Hoover refused to allow U.S. participation in the kinds of diplomatic alliances that most European leaders believed a necessary prerequisite for further disarmament. As a result, talks at London faltered, and Stimson eventually brought home a modest treaty with Japan and Britain that actually sanctioned an increase in naval tonnage without any substantial progress on the issue of outlawing submarine warfare.[72]

Hoping to avoid the tensions that had scuttled agreement on limiting naval armaments, the secretary of state sought to build ties of trade among nations and trust among leaders. He strongly believed that free trade was a vital pre-condition for the spread of both peace and democracy. The globalization of commerce and ideas, Stimson observed, not only increased wealth but also created "a better mutual understanding" among industrialized nations.[73] He objected to increased tariffs and other manifestations of economic nationalism as harmful to the world economic system in which the United States was inex-tricably enmeshed. "The outstanding lesson of the present world situation," he insisted during the first year of the Depression, "is that the prosperity of each is dependent on the prosperity of all and that in the long run no nation can develop its own national well-being at the expense of its neighbors."[74] This linkage of trade, democracy, and peace remained a constant in Stimson's ap-proach to international relations and helped shape Stimson's approach to the atomic secret during World War II.

When all else failed, Stimson relied on personal contacts with like-minded leaders in other countries to overcome the inflamed nationalist passions of the masses. This attitude flowed naturally out of his Victorian elitism and was re-inforced by his experiences in Nicaragua and the Philippines during the 1920s. Stimson sincerely believed that he had succeeding in taming national-ism and anti-Americanism in those countries by dealing frankly and openly with the indigenous leaders he met there. He repeated this lesson to the end of his life, remarking to Truman in September 1945 with respect to the future of atomic energy, "The chief lesson I have learned in a long life is that the only way you can make a man trustworthy is to trust him; and the surest way to make him untrustworthy is to distrust him and show your distrust."[75] Build-ing on this maxim, Stimson made several personal visits to the capitals of Europe while serving as secretary of state, hoping to overcome the rising tide of militarism and nationalism through personal contacts with leaders ranging from British socialist Ramsay MacDonald (with whom he became good friends in spite of their political differences) to Italian fascist Benito Mus-solini (who took Henry and Mabel Stimson on a wild speedboat tour around the Gulf of Anzio).[76]

Hoover and his secretary of state also worked to cultivate trust in Latin America, striving to undo the legacy of decades of heavy-handed U.S. inter-vention in that region. Stimson, who had only recently acted as agent of that policy, was particularly frustrated by the failure of U.S. military intervention to produce a lasting peace settlement in Nicaragua. By the time he took office as secretary of state, he had come to believe that efforts to spread democracy and capitalism at the barrel of gun were doomed to failure.[77] Hoover agreed, bluntly declaring, "[W]e have no desire to be represented abroad by marines."[78] In the midst of a period of intense economic and political turmoil in Latin America, the Hoover administration not only avoided new military commitments in the region but also managed to end the twenty-year U.S. occupation of Nicaragua and pave the way for a similar development in Haiti. In response to a military conflict between Peru and Columbia, Stimson took the unprecedented step of allowing the League of Nations to take the lead role in seeking a peaceful resolution.[79] The decision to allow the league to inject itself into Latin American affairs, a direct blow to both the spirit and the letter of the Monroe Doctrine, underscored Hoover and Stimson's genuine commitment to multilateral political and legal solutions to the problem of war.

Stimson illustrated the depths of his commitment to fostering trust in international relations by closing down the secret State Department code-breaking operation known as the "Black Chamber." Since 1921, American code breakers had been intercepting and reading diplomatic cables between foreign capitals and their embassies in Washington. Stimson did not approve. It was, he remarked in his diary, an "unethical thing for this Government to do to be reading the messages coming to our ambassadorial guests from other countries." Any information gained as part of such an operation was offset by the "impairment of relations of the only class of officers who are supposed to deal internationally on a gentleman's basis." And gentlemen, Stimson believed, "do not read each other's mail." To do so not only was immoral but also undercut the diplomatic trust necessary to avoid future wars.[80]

Ultimately, Stimson's gestures of trust and his personal contacts with world leaders were insufficient to overcome the lingering resentments of World War I, quell the ardor of fascist ideologues, or trump the popular appeal of militant nationalism. The dramatic failure of capitalism at home and abroad dashed his hope that trade would foster democracy and peace around the world. Meanwhile, popular opinion in the United States was increasingly isolationist. At the Geneva Conference in 1932, he lamented to German Chancellor Heinrich Bruning that "the situation in the world seemed to me like the unfolding of a great Greek tragedy, where we could see the march of events and know what ought to be done, but to be powerless to prevent its marching to its grim conclusion."[81] Nowhere was this more dramatically demonstrated than in the

Manchurian crisis, an event that paved the road to the war in the Pacific that ended fourteen years later with the use of the atomic bomb.

Stimson had long looked to Japan as a friendly, Westernized power that would help the United States maintain an open door for trade in China while collaborating on broader measures to end the threat of war to the industrialized world. Meeting with Japanese leaders on his way to the Philippines in 1928, he made a point of informing them that he did not belong to "the aggressive jingo school" but rather, like Root, sought a long-term accommodation between the two Pacific powers.[82] It was thus doubly troubling to Stimson when Japan invaded the Chinese province of Manchuria in September 1931. Not only did this action violate the Kellogg-Briand Pact (of which both China and Japan were signatories) and threaten the open door to American commerce in China, but it also belied the notion that Japanese leaders shared his commitment to the principle of peaceful change in international affairs.

Torn between his desire to avoid provoking a Japanese nationalist backlash and his conviction that no nation should be allowed to "run amok and play havoc with its peace treaties," Stimson responded cautiously in the initial month of the crisis.[83] By mid-November, however, escalating Japanese attacks, including the bombing of Chinese civilians in the city of Jinzhou (Chinchow), shocked him into action. Lamenting that the situation in Manchuria constituted "a deadly threat to the authority of the great peace treaties which after the World War had been conceived by the nations of the world in a supreme effort to prevent a recurrence of such a disaster," Stimson pressed Hoover to take a firm stand against Japanese aggression.[84]

In attempting to formulate a response following the bombing of Jinzhou, Secretary of State Stimson confronted a problem that has long bedeviled advocates of international peace. Under what circumstances is it legitimate to employ force to bring about a restoration of international law? Put another way, when is war acceptable to advance the cause of peace? In the response to German aggression on the high seas in World War I, Stimson had believed the case to be clear-cut: there could be no peace in the face of such a blatant challenge to the very foundations of international law. In the case of Manchuria, however, he was not so sure. Unwilling to even privately contemplate war against Japan at this point, the secretary of state advocated economic sanctions, perhaps coupled with an indirect threat of force, to compel the Japanese militarists to back down. Though he lamented that "the only police force I have got to depend upon today is the American Navy," Stimson strongly believed that there was no need to actually wield that power in anger. He assured Hoover that the mere threat of force would be enough and that the odds that such pressure would lead to a war with Japan were "a thousand to one."[85]

The secretary of state's deliberations on how to balance force and law were ultimately short-circuited by Hoover. The president was staunchly opposed to involving the United States in foreign quarrels and made it clear he would not approve any policy that carried the slightest hint of provocation. The strongest American response came in the form of the so-called Stimson Doctrine, a rhetorical defense of the Kellogg-Briand Pact and the Open Door policy. In notes dispatched to China and Japan on January 7, 1932, Stimson declared that the United States did "not intend to recognize any situation, treaty, or agreement which may be brought about by means contrary to the covenants and obligations of the Pact of Paris of August 27, 1928." Stimson hoped that the nonrecognition doctrine that bore his name might form the basis for coordinated economic and diplomatic action against Japan, perhaps including a trade embargo. But in the face of Hoover's continuing opposition to any kind of intervention, the secretary once again played the good solider, publicly muting his concerns over the inability of words alone to halt Japanese militarism in Manchuria.[86]

Privately, both the president and his secretary of state were frustrated and angry. In January 1933, Undersecretary of State William R. Castle recorded in his diary, "Poor Hoover feels that Stimson comes very close to disloyalty and poor Stimson feels that his loyalty is a terrible strain on his conscience." Each man, Castle lamented, "will leave Washington on March 4th hoping that he may never see the other again and that is a tragedy."[87] With Hoover's defeat at the hands of Franklin D. Roosevelt in 1932, Stimson's public career appeared to be headed for an inglorious end. But while he was destined to spend the rest of the 1930s watching the escalating world crisis from the sidelines, the Democratic Roosevelt would ultimately entrust Stimson with the most dramatic and difficult assignment of his life.

Chapter 2

The Road to Pearl Harbor

GIVEN THE FRUSTRATIONS THAT MARKED HIS FINAL YEARS AS SECRE-
tary of state, it was hardly surprising that in the waning months of the Hoover
administration Stimson found himself "looking forward to the fourth of March
[1933] with intense relief."[1] After attending Franklin D. Roosevelt's inaugura-
tion, Stimson was the guest of honor at an intimate farewell dinner with close
members of his staff. While there was some talk of the banking crisis gripping
the nation, the overall mood was one of profound release as Stimson and his
companions "gathered around the piano and had singing until midnight." It
was, Stimson noted in his diary, "the best time we have had in Washington."[2]

Removed from the daily pressures of the State Department, Stimson soon
discovered it "very difficult to reconcile myself to going back to the routine
practice of law in New York; the combination of subways and skyscrapers seem
more unattractive than ever."[3] Even in the bitter spring of 1933, with the
Hoover administration cast out of office, the Japanese unyielding in their conquest of Manchuria, and Adolf Hitler in power in Germany, Stimson remained
strongly committed to the peaceful ideals embodied in the doomed Kellogg-

Briand Pact. The pact, he continued to assert, was part of "a system of positive law among the nations, which should guide their course toward peace."[4] Stung by failure of joint action in response to the Manchurian crisis, as a private citizen in the 1930s he tirelessly promoted new forms of international organization and cooperation to meet the dangers of modern industrialized warfare.

"Organized Self-Control"

Pondering the events that had buffeted his term as secretary of state, Stimson concluded that the greatest danger facing the world was that the same technological advances that had helped to create "complex industrial civilization" had also given birth to a generation of weapons (such as the submarine and the bomber aircraft) that rendered war infinitely more destructive. While mankind's power over the material world had grown astronomically in recent decades, "[h]is moral and social power did not increase so rapidly." "Man's technique," Stimson asserted in 1934, "has temporarily outstripped his power of organization and distribution."[5] This was a lesson learned the hard way in World War I and one that the great powers of the world needed to heed as they struggled with the legacies of that conflict.

Foreshadowing the approach that he would eventually take toward the nuclear challenge, Stimson in 1934 suggested that the time had come for what he dubbed "organized self-control" at the international level.[6] Just as the power unleashed by the industrial revolution had required the growth of governmental organization at the national level to guard against its abuse, international cooperation and organization were needed to perform a similar function on a global scale. Drawing again on Fiske and Root, Stimson insisted that as part of the "price of liberty" in an interdependent world, all industrialized nations would have to learn to accept impositions on their international freedom of action.[7] For the United States, "organized self-control" translated into a program that was "the very opposite of isolationism, namely . . . affirmative cooperation with other nations" and with larger international organizations such as the League of Nations and the World Court.[8] This cooperation would ideally include both collective security agreements to deal with threats to peace and economic agreements to end tariffs and other barriers to trade. Looking overseas, in 1934 he advocated the creation of a United States of Europe in which political impediments to trade across European borders would be entirely eliminated.

The alternative to this admittedly ambitious internationalist program, Stimson argued, was "suicide by war." Though his commitment to collective security implied a willingness to use force against aggressors, for much of the decade Stimson remained optimistic that international cooperation could prevent war before it occurred. "[W]hen mankind realizes that he is now living in a world which is likely to be torn down by attacks on its underpinnings," Stimson reasoned, "he is, speaking generally, intelligent enough to devise means of warding off those attacks; in other words, having a better control of war in such a civilization than could be evolved when war was a pleasant pastime."[9]

Stimson's hopes for organized self-control at the international level were in tatters by the latter half of the 1930s. The Italian invasion of Ethiopia in 1935, German and Italian intervention in the Spanish civil war, and the Japanese invasion of China in 1937 combined to undercut his hopes for collective security and international self-restraint. Each of these incidents was troubling individually, but in combination they were evidence of an organized assault on the very foundations of international law. In Stimson's analysis, the race hatred that manifested itself with particular virulence in Nazi Germany and the general restrictions on personal freedom that characterized the governments of Italy and Japan were rooted in a rejection of the "sovereignty of reason rather than force."[10] These same characteristics, Stimson believed, explained the behavior of the Axis nations at the international level. "[B]y an inexorable consequence," Stimson declared, "these violations of the principles of independence and freedom in the outside world have been made by governments which had previously destroyed the principles of freedom and individual rights within their own borders."[11]

The weak response of the Western democracies to the fascist challenge mocked Stimson's hopes for collective action to contain aggression. Bitterly disappointed by appeasement in Europe and surging isolationism in the United States, he watched with dismay as another war appeared increasingly inevitable. In a letter to the *New York Times* in March 1939, Stimson invoked Abraham Lincoln in an implicit acknowledgment that conflict with the fascist nations had become virtually inevitable. "[I]n our modern interdependent world," he declared, "Lincoln's saying holds true, that a house so divided against itself cannot permanently stand."[12] Having reluctantly concluded that the interwar efforts at replacing force with law had failed, he become a vocal advocate of coordinated action to check the Axis nations in order to bolster the longer-term prospects for peace.

Following the outbreak of war in Europe in September 1939, Stimson advocated American military aid to Britain and France. With the fall of France in spring 1940, he concluded that the United States would have to take more dramatic steps in order to quash the Nazi menace to world peace. In a national radio address on June 18, 1940, Stimson placed the European war in the context of the ongoing "struggle for a lawful world." Should the fascist powers prevail, he warned, it would mean "the termination of freedom throughout the world not only in international affairs but in the individual freedom of the citizens of each country." In addition to a full and final repeal of American neutrality laws, he urged that the United States send its own warships to escort convoys carrying arms to Britain, a policy that virtually guaranteed a clash with German U-boats in the Atlantic.[13] Just as in World War I, force would be necessary to restore the rule of law.

Stimson's status as one of the most visible public supporters of American intervention in Europe helped convince Franklin D. Roosevelt to select him as secretary of war. It was Stimson protégé and Roosevelt confidant Felix Frankfurter who first suggested him for the post.[14] Stimson's status as an eminent Republican statesman would add a powerful public voice for intervention, give a bipartisan stamp to FDR's foreign policy, and help further divide the already fractious Republican Party in the months before the 1940 election. Despite doubts about Stimson's age (he was seventy-two), Roosevelt telephoned him on June 19, 1940, and offered him the post of secretary of war.

Between War and Peace, 1940–41

Though he had spent much of the previous twenty years working for international peace, Stimson arrived in Washington in 1940 as one of the most prominent public advocates of American military intervention in Europe. From his perspective, there was no contradiction between these two positions. The Axis nations, and Nazi Germany in particular, represented such a powerful threat to "the existence of this kind of world which we have been trying to create and the methods of freedom and self-government," that peace was a practical impossibility.[15] In "a broken world," Stimson asserted that the only hope for the resumption of the progressive trends in international law and

Figure 6. President Franklin D. Roosevelt congratulates Stimson following Senate approval of his nomination as secretary of war, July 10, 1940. Though sometimes frustrated by FDR's tendency to vacillate when making tough decisions (he once compared the task of pinning down the president on such matters to "chasing a vagrant beam of sunshine around a vacant room"), Stimson developed a tremendous respect for a man whom he came to value as "a real personal friend." (Corbis)

world peace that he had championed since 1919 was to fight and defeat Nazi Germany in a military conflict.[16]

After surviving a bruising confirmation hearing that mirrored the intense public debate over American intervention in Europe, Stimson took charge of the War Department for the second time on July 10, 1940. By design, much of the daily work of the department was left in the hands of his civilian and military assistants, particularly Army Chief of Staff George C. Marshall and Undersecretary of War Robert P. Patterson. Stimson also plucked three crucial aides from the private sector in the months following his appointment. John J. McCloy (Amherst, Harvard Law, Wall Street lawyer), Robert A. Lovett (Yale, Skull and Bones, Wall Street banker), and Harvey H. Bundy (Yale, Skull and Bones, Harvard Law, and State Street lawyer) formed the indispensable core of the secretary's staff.[17]

Stimson enjoyed an intimate rapport with his handpicked War Department aides. There was, Lovett recalled, "a peculiar family relationship, with the Colonel in the role of pater familias."[18] Judging from the accounts of those who worked under him, Stimson's approach to personnel management relied heavily on shouting, mild obscenities, and angry gesticulating. McCloy, Lovett, and Bundy shared Stimson's politics (all three were Republicans) as well as his devotion to quiet, loyal service removed from the public eye. They tolerated his outbursts of temper with good humor and could often be found at the Stimson estate after hours engaging in a vigorous game of "deck tennis" with the secretary of war. "He might give you hell for disagreeing with him," Harvey Bundy recalled, "and then the next day he'd call you up on the telephone and apologize."[19] This level of personal comfort, combined with his staff's first-rate administrative skills, allowed Stimson to focus his energies on pressing political-military matters without worrying about the daily functioning of his department.

While his staff managed the details of military mobilization, Stimson concentrated much of his energy in 1940–41 on matters of high-level policy. Though he had publicly assured his anti-interventionist critics that as secretary of war he would have "nothing to do with policy," once in office he often intruded into territory generally reserved for the secretary of state.[20] Distressed by "the efforts of the little group of isolationists to play politics with the matter," Stimson quietly worked with pro-interventionist journalists and private citizens to influence the debate over going to war. Meanwhile, he sought to influence the one man who he believed could and should openly lead the United States into the battle against Nazi Germany: Franklin D. Roosevelt.[21]

Stimson found working with "Franklin" to be rewarding and frustrating in equal measures. In 1932, Stimson had dismissed Roosevelt as an "untried rather flippant young man who is trying to make his place."[22] As secretary of war, however, Stimson gained new respect for the Democratic Roosevelt. He almost invariably agreed with Roosevelt on fundamental questions of national security and appreciated the president's efforts to prepare the country for war, even if they did not always see eye-to-eye on tactics. Roosevelt's administrative habits often drove Stimson into bouts of frustration. After visiting Roosevelt's Hyde Park home during the 1932 interregnum, Stimson commented that the jumbled surroundings "gave the impression of confusion . . . it did not give the impression of calm and simplicity."[23] On this judgment, which he soon learned applied to more than the president-elect's taste in furnishings, Stimson's opinion was not to waver. "I doubt," he ruefully remarked of Roosevelt in 1940, "whether we shall be able to hold him to any very systematic relations because that is rather entirely antithetic to his nature and temperament."[24]

On the basic necessity of American action in Europe to save Britain, Stimson and Roosevelt were in total agreement. They differed, however, on the question of how actively—and publicly—to pursue this policy. The secretary of war privately fumed at the president's "rather disingenuous attitude" with respect to intervention.[25] Reacting to Roosevelt's decision to conduct a secret naval war in the Atlantic, he warned that the "American people should not be asked to make the momentous decision of opposing forcefully the actions of the evil of the leaders of the other half of the world possibly because by some accident or mistake American ships or men have been fired upon by soldiers of the other camp."[26] Stimson did not oppose Roosevelt's war; he simply wanted the president to be more forthright in acknowledging it publicly. FDR, fearful of the domestic political repercussions, continued to inch toward war with Germany while refusing to publicly divulge the depth of American involvement or ask Congress for a declaration of war. Stimson, as he had throughout his long career as a Washington insider, swallowed his objections and continued to work behind the scenes to ready the United States for a wider war.

The Limits of Deterrence: B-17s, Japan, and Pearl Harbor

In an ironic twist, it was developments in the Pacific, where Stimson hoped that war could be avoided, that finally brought the United States into World War II. Though he had long advocated a tough line with Japan, at the time he took office in 1940 Stimson did not believe war in the Pacific was either necessary or desirable. Japanese leaders would bluff to the limit but never actually risk war with the more powerful United States. As he explained to Roosevelt in October 1940, "when the United States indicates by clear language and bold actions that she intends to carry out a clear and affirmative policy in the Far East, Japan will yield to that policy even though it conflicts with her own Asiatic policy and conceived interests."[27] In November 1940, after Roosevelt had agreed to a total prohibition on scrap metal exports to Japan, Stimson was confidently predicting that "our little friends in Japan will gradually be brought to a realization that their pipedream of Asiatic conquest is coming to an end."[28] But as evidence mounted in 1941 that American economic pressure was, in fact, inciting the Japanese to expand their campaign of conquest in Asia, the secretary of war grew increasingly concerned. In desperation, he latched onto the promise of the newest high-technology weapon in the army's arsenal in order to achieve America's diplomatic goals in the Pacific without the need for war.

Since World War I, Stimson had lamented the tendency of technological innovation to produce terrifying new weapons that threatened the existence of modern civilization. In practice, however, he was not immune to the temptation of employing high-technology weapons (or at least the threat of such weapons) to overcome vexing diplomatic or military problems. Even as he orchestrated the withdrawal of U.S. troops from Nicaragua in 1931, then secretary of state Stimson had suggested sending Marine aircraft to help pacify the countryside from the air. "We have a superiority in mechanics," Stimson noted in reference to U.S. airpower, "and we ought to use it."[29] As secretary of war nine years later, he was highly receptive to the role of science and technology in the race to rearm America, a position that often put him at odds with hidebound army officers and the even more conservative leaders of the U.S. Navy.[30]

Stimson's role as an advocate of science within the War Department was in part shaped by an unusual family connection. His cousin and close confidant Alfred L. Loomis had leveraged a spectacular run on Wall Street into a second career as a gifted amateur physicist and powerful scientific patron.[31] During the 1920s and 1930s, Loomis's lavishly funded private laboratory in Tuxedo Park, New York, attracted some of the world's best scientists. During these years, Loomis tutored his older cousin in matters of science while Stimson passed on his wisdom in foreign affairs. With the outbreak of World War II, Loomis devoted himself to the war effort, working closely with Vannevar Bush, director of the federal government's Office of Scientific Research and Development (OSRD), and MIT president Karl T. Compton on a number of projects, most notably the development of radar and airborne navigation aids.

The high-tech weapon that Stimson seized on in fall 1941 as the solution to the problem posed by Japan was not one in which Loomis was directly involved. It was, however, a fine example of American industrial and scientific prowess. The B-17 "Flying Fortress" strategic bomber was the culmination of a doctrinal and technological revolution promoted by a handful of influential officers in the Army Air Corps during the 1920s and 1930s. It was designed to fly great distances at high altitudes and deliver its bombs with pinpoint precision on the "key nodes" of the enemy's industrial infrastructure, crippling their ability to make war with a minimal loss of life on either side. Though the B-17 and its associated technologies (most notably the Norden bombsight) had been in development since the early 1930s, it was not until 1941 that planes began rolling off American assembly lines in large quantities.[32] In the midst of the ongoing standoff with Japan, the B-17 suddenly appeared to have tremendous value as a diplomatic tool.

In April 1941, Marshall suggested to the secretary of war that the deployment of B-17s to American forward bases in the Pacific would ensure that "the Japs wouldn't dare attack Hawaii, particularly such a long distance from home."[33] Stimson quickly seized on the potential deterrent power of the B-17, asserting in September that "the American bomber which at present holds the top notch in the world's race by virtue of its control over the narrow seas—has completely changed the strategy of the Pacific."[34] American technology and know-how had provided him with a weapon that would prevent an unwanted war in the Pacific without the need for a diplomatic compromise. Japanese leaders, confronted with the threat of the B-17, would have no choice but to back down. Marshall played along by working to leak word of the deployment of the B-17 to the Japanese through the American press corps.[35] As late as October 28, Stimson confided to Secretary of State Cordell Hull that the deterrent power of American strategic bombers not only would prevent war in the Pacific but also might "shake the Japanese out of the Axis."[36]

The violent denouement of Japanese-American negotiations in December 1941 provided Stimson with a brutal lesson in the limits of deterrence. Ironically, it was the ungentlemanly work of American code breakers that finally convinced him that the deployment of American strategic bombers had failed as a diplomatic tool. Decoded messages indicating menacing fleet movements and a November 25 deadline for negotiations with the United States finally shattered his long-held confidence that Japanese leaders could be bullied or deterred into abandoning their dreams of an Asian empire. Unwilling to advocate a retreat that might embolden the Axis powers, he set about preparing for the forthcoming Japanese blow. "The question," Stimson remarked after meeting with Roosevelt and Secretary of State Hull on November 25, "was how we should maneuver them into the position of firing the first shot without allowing too much danger to ourselves."[37]

In a final miscalculation, Stimson and his aides assumed that the "first shot" would be aimed at the Philippines. To his surprise, Japanese planes struck Hawaii and the Philippines nearly simultaneously on December 7. While the cream of the American Pacific Fleet lay devastated at Pearl Harbor, the B-17s that he had counted on to deter the Japanese burned on the runaways at Clark Field and Hickam Field. Harvey Bundy later recalled that the secretary of war was "terribly distressed" to find that the vaunted planes on which he had pinned his hopes "went up like powder in a keg when the war started."[38]

Despite the military and diplomatic failures that had led to the disaster on December 7, Stimson found a silver lining in the smoke that hung over Pearl Harbor. He privately professed "relief that the indecision was over and that a crisis had come in a way which would unite all our people."[39] Although he would have preferred a more direct path to confronting Nazi Germany, the Japanese attack and ensuing German declaration of war finally brought about the conflict that Stimson had believed inevitable since 1939.

Stimson's relationship to the conflict, which began in December 1941 with the attack on Pearl Harbor, has often been misunderstood. Accounts of his service as secretary of war inevitably focus on his role in bringing the nation into World War II and guiding the army's role in securing a military victory in Europe and the Pacific. It is true that Stimson embraced war with the Axis powers as a just and necessary conflict. It is also true that once the battle was joined, he was guided by a strong desire to "end the war in victory with the least possible cost in the lives of the men in the armies which I had helped to raise."[40] But the pursuit of military victory never fixed the limits of Stimson's wartime vision. His ultimate goal remained that which he had pursued since the end of World War I: building the foundations of lasting world peace. In June 1942, Stimson reminded Hull and Secretary of the Navy Frank Knox that the ultimate goal in winning the war was "to lay the foundation of the step forward in international democracy which we are all hoping for."[41]

With his eyes fixed on shaping a lasting postwar peace, the secretary of war faced a difficult balancing act in overseeing the conduct of the war effort. While he sought a speedy victory, the indiscriminate use of force might embitter allies and enemies alike, sowing the seeds of future wars. And though he understood that cooperation with the Soviet Union and Great Britain was vital to defeating the Axis powers, he worried that agreements made during the pressure of war might prejudice postwar efforts to create an open, prosperous, democratic, and peaceful world order. It was with this complicated calculus of war and peace in mind that Stimson wrestled with the challenge and opportunity posed by nuclear fission during World War II.

Chapter 3

"A Most Terrible Thing"

ON NOVEMBER 6, 1941, DR. VANNEVAR BUSH ARRIVED AT STIMSON'S War Department office with "an extremely secret statement." Bush, director of the Office of Scientific Research and Development (OSRD), had in hand a report by the National Academy of Sciences that concluded it would be possible to develop "a fission bomb of superlatively destructive power" within three to four years. Though Albert Einstein (at the urging of fellow émigré physicist Leo Szilard) had first alerted President Franklin D. Roosevelt to the possibility of such a bomb in August 1939, the fledgling American nuclear effort lacked high-level leadership and had received only paltry funding through fall 1941. That was about to change. Bush and his colleague Dr. James B. Conant, head of the National Defense Research Committee (NDRC), planned to use the academy's report to jolt the administration into a full-scale effort to pursue a bomb. Stimson's diary entry for November 6 contained his first recorded comment on the atomic bomb. It was, he confided, "a most terrible thing."[1]

From the outset of the serious American nuclear effort, all the key decision makers understood that the bomb was a special and unique weapon.[2] While he had only a limited grasp of the scientific principles behind nuclear fission, the secretary of war never treated the bomb as simply another powerful explosive. From late 1941 onward, he and a handful of others within the Roosevelt administration wrestled with its implications for both the course of the war and the shape of the postwar world. With Roosevelt's blessing, Bush and Conant assembled a Top Policy Group, which included Stimson, Vice President Henry Wallace, and Army Chief of Staff George C. Marshall, to take charge of an accelerated research effort. At a meeting of the new committee on December 16, 1941, Bush was already looking ahead to "full-scale construction" of the massive engineering and production facilities required to produce a bomb. Once that point was reached, he suggested, the program should be turned over to control of the army and hence to Stimson as head of the War Department.[3]

The secretary of war expressed no objection to taking charge of the bomb project. Lobbying by Bush, Conant, and Stimson's cousin, gifted amateur physicist Alfred L. Loomis, had convinced him that the atomic secret could hold the key to victory or defeat in the struggle against the Axis powers. His sense of dread, however, had not lessened. Following the December 16 meeting, he privately characterized the bomb as "diabolical."[4] While he welcomed the scientists' aid in winning the war, Stimson's Victorian values and his horror at the excesses of industrialized warfare left him acutely sensitive to the perils of unleashing nuclear fire upon the world.

After the war, Stimson joined other American A-bomb insiders in implying that the use of the bomb against heavily populated Japanese cities was inevitably embedded in the decision to develop such a weapon in the first place.[5] In the decades since the destruction of Hiroshima and Nagasaki, a number of historians have supplemented this explanation by highlighting the gradual slide toward the targeting of civilians that took place throughout World War II. The so-called moral threshold argument holds that the use of nuclear weapons against Japanese civilians in August 1945 was the logical extension of the destructive precedent set by both Axis and Allied conventional bombing, including the firebombing of Tokyo in March 1945 that killed as many as a hundred thousand Japanese in a single night. In the words of historian Robert P. Newman, "Who would dare call the use of this superbomb illegitimate when all agreed that it was quite legitimate to mass 210 B-29s to drop an equivalent explosive force?"[6]

A close examination of the contemporary evidence casts doubts on post-war claims about the inevitability of use and dispels the myth that American leaders were so inured to the brutality of total war that they were untroubled by the nuclear incineration of Japanese civilians. Thinking about use of nuclear weapons remained conditional at upper levels through at least 1944. Roosevelt and Stimson energetically pushed the development of the bomb while deferring considerations about what to do with a finished weapon. And even as he supported research and development on nuclear weapons, Stimson remained opposed to the targeting of civilians for both ethical and practical reasons.

In choosing to defer serious consideration of the difficult moral questions posed by the bomb, Stimson and other high-level policymakers in Washington effectively delegated many of the practical decisions about use to the scientists and military officers working at the top-secret Los Alamos laboratory. Though some of the atomic scientists shared Stimson's concerns over the immorality of waging warfare against civilians, wartime work at Los Alamos under director J. Robert Oppenheimer was dominated by technical concerns and resulted in a weapon optimized for the destruction of cities and the killing of civilians. This disconnect between high-level policymakers in Washington and the scientists and engineers who produced the weapon contributed greatly to the atomic tragedy of August 1945.

"Unsuitable as a Weapon": Early Thinking about Use, 1940–42

Ethical questions about the use of the bomb and the mass killing of civilians predated the start of the serious American nuclear program. In March 1940, two German émigré physicists working in Great Britain, Rudolf Peierls and Otto Frisch, were already grappling with the ethical issues raised by the atomic bomb. Prohibited from joining the British war effort because of their nominal status as enemy aliens, Frisch and Peierls studied the problem of atomic fission independently at Birmingham University. Their findings indicated that perhaps as little as one kilogram of uranium 235 (U235) would be required to produce an explosive chain reaction. Writing to the British government in March 1940, they predicted that such a "super-bomb" would be "practically irresistible" and that there was "no material or structure that could be expected to resist the force of the explosion."[7]

Even as they provided the impetus for a crash program to build the bomb, the two émigré physicists expressed reservations about the use of such a weapon. Nuclear fission weapons would produce intensely radioactive byproducts. "Owing to the spread of radioactive substances with the wind," they warned, "the bomb could probably not be used without killing large numbers of civilians." The likelihood of massive civilian deaths, they suggested, "may make it unsuitable as a weapon for use by this country [Great Britain]." As an alternative, they suggested use "as a depth charge near a naval base," though they acknowledged that even then it would be difficult to entirely avoid civilian casualties caused by radioactive fallout.[8]

Frisch and Peierls achieved mixed results in their attempt to alert the British leadership to the dilemmas posed by nuclear fission. They were successful in jolting the government into a serious examination of the military implications of atomic weapons. While the American research effort languished, by July 1941 a British group code-named the MAUD Committee had confirmed the two émigrés' predictions about the feasibility of a wartime bomb.[9] Its final report accurately predicted that the "gun" method of bringing two masses of U235 together at high speeds would result in nuclear fission and the liberation of a tremendous amount of explosive energy. The MAUD Committee concluded that the weight of the finished weapon would be "well within the capacity of a modern bomber" and that it should be dropped from high altitude so that it would produce a "large radius of damage." Such a weapon was "likely to lead to decisive results in the war."[10]

The two German émigrés were considerably less successful in initiating high-level discussion of the ethical dilemmas posed by atomic weapons. Setting a precedent that would continue on both sides of the Atlantic, the MAUD Committee ducked this issue even as its own findings raised troubling questions about the bomb's effects. On the issue of radiation, the final report acknowledged that "the area devastated by the explosion would be dangerous to life for a considerable period of time." It also concluded that if the carrying plane was to survive the blast, the bomb would have to be dropped from such as height as to render its delivery highly inaccurate.[11] Taken together, these two propositions strongly implied that the effects of an atomic bomb would be both lingering and indiscriminate, akin to those produced by chemical or biological weapons. The MAUD Committee's report, however, avoided any discussion of the ethical implications of these conclusions. Noting this omission, British scientist Dr. Charles Darwin pointedly asked after reading it whether "our own prime minister and the American president . . . are willing to sanction the total destruction of Berlin and the country round."[12]

Across the Atlantic, a handful of American scientists were also interested in the lethal effects of nuclear radiation. Unlike Frisch and Peierls, however, they expressed no ethical qualms about its potential for the mass killing of civilians. A special committee of the National Academy of Sciences chaired by University of Chicago physicist Karl T. Compton suggested in May 1941 that "violently radioactive materials . . . destructive to life" might be "carried by airplanes to be scattered as bombs over enemy territory."[13] No mention was made of potential targets for Allied radiological warfare, though the suggested method of delivery would have inevitably entailed spreading the poisons across a relatively wide area. The objections to this scheme among American scientists appear to have centered on the technical challenge of delivering radiological agents rather than on moral concerns over potential civilian casualties. In response to a 1943 proposal to use radioactive poisons against the enemy's food supply, physicist J. Robert Oppenheimer coolly replied that "we should not attempt a plan unless we can poison food sufficient to kill a half a million men."[14]

The American scientists' flirtation with radiological warfare, combined with Frisch and Peierls' earlier warnings, conclusively demonstrate that they were aware of the lethal (and potentially militarily useful) properties of the bomb's byproducts, even if they sometimes underestimated the degree of danger. But Stimson and other top-level American policymakers appear to have been insulated from these discussions of radiation and the mass killing of civilians. Bush and Conant acted as the gateway between the scientists on both sides of the Atlantic and the civilian and military decision makers within the Roosevelt administration. The two American scientist-administrators had read the MAUD Committee's reports as well as those produced by the National Academy of Sciences and were well aware of the dangers posed by radiation. But none of their reports to Roosevelt, Stimson, and the Top Policy Group in 1941–43 addressed the possible mass poisoning and killing of civilians. Though there is no evidence that Bush and Conant deliberately misled their superiors, they almost certainly understood that dwelling on the lingering and indiscriminate effects of the bomb might raise troubling concerns in the minds of the government officials who oversaw the American nuclear effort.

Stimson, for one, was acutely sensitive to the dangers of indiscriminate force in the pursuit of victory and consistently objected to the intentional killing of civilians. In October 1939, he supported liberal newspaper columnist Dorothy Thompson when she called upon the Allies to refrain from bombing German cities "because they are the cities of Western civilization."[15] "The problem," Stimson asserted, "is, if possible, not to destroy any nation of Europe or elsewhere but to bring them back into European civilization if they have departed from it—as the present German government has departed."[16] In casting about for a solution to this problem, Stimson as Secretary of War eagerly embraced technological solutions that promised to bring victory without compromising his cherished moral values.

One such potential solution was the "precision bombing" doctrine developed during the 1930s at the U.S. Army's Air Corps Tactical School (ACTS). The plans drafted by the Army Air Forces (AAF), instead of contemplating indiscriminate attacks on enemy cities and civilians, called for daylight strikes against carefully selected military-industrial targets using high-tech weapons such as the B-17 bomber equipped with the Norden bombsight. The architects of the precision bombing doctrine claimed that it combined the virtues of morality and efficacy by promising a speedy end to the war without having to directly target civilians. As AAF Major General Laurence S. Kuter bluntly declared in August 1944, "[I]t is contrary to our national ideals to wage war against civilians."[17] Stimson agreed. The secretary of war personally approved the AAF's strategy following a meeting on September 11, 1941, and remained an enthusiastic supporter of precision bombing throughout the war.[18]

In practice, American bombs often strayed from their targets and killed civilians in both Axis and Axis-occupied countries. Stimson's aides and AAF leaders sought to obscure this ugly reality by selectively presenting the secretary of war with photographic evidence of the "miraculous" and "marvelous" accuracy of American bombers.[19] His relative inattention to the less-than-precise results of American bombing and willingness to accept the assurances of his aides on this matter foreshadowed Stimson's later blindness on the issue of nuclear targeting and the mass killing of Japanese civilians.

Given his opposition to the mass killing of civilians, it is not surprising that Bush and Conant downplayed the effects of radiation as they sought Stimson's aid in jump-starting the A-bomb project. Even without this information, he was still clearly troubled by the bomb, referring to it in his diary at various points as "the terrible," "the dire, "the awful," and "the diabolical."[20] As secretary of war, he had a clear responsibility to pursue the development of any weapon that promised "military superiority" to the nation that developed it first.[21] But it does not follow that Stimson was automatically committed to first use of such a weapon once it was developed, particularly if such use involved the mass killing of civilians. Stimson backed full-scale development of the bomb while deferring difficult practical and ethical questions about use until the project was closer to fruition. In a similar vein, he simultaneously presided over what he called the "dirty business" of developing chemical and biological weapons, neither of which were ultimately used by the United States during World War II.[22]

Roosevelt's approach to the potential use of the bomb was similar to that of his secretary of war. The president readily assented to Bush and Conant's pleas for an expanded American nuclear program. In March 1942, he approved transferring the program to Stimson and the War Department and added his own admonition that "the whole thing should be pushed not only in regard to development, but also with due regard to time."[23] On the question of use against the Axis, however, FDR remained noncommittal. The August 1943 Quebec Agreement signed by Roosevelt and British Prime Minister Winston Churchill explicitly deferred this question. Reflecting the unique status of the bomb within the Allied arsenal, they agreed that "we will not use it against third parties without each other's consent."[24] The president's refusal to explicitly commit to using the bomb against the Axis does not imply that he shared the moral concerns voiced by Frisch and Peierls or even the vague sense of dread expressed by Stimson. It does indicate, however, that he preferred to keep his options open when it came to the potential combat use of nuclear weapons.

Roosevelt's handling of the A-bomb from the inception of the project until his death in 1945 was marked by a pattern of silence and delay punctuated by sometimes contradictory policy directives. This was very much in character for FDR, who liked to hedge his bets when deciding questions of any magnitude. Stimson repeatedly complained that trying to pin down Roosevelt on matters of any importance was like "chasing a vagrant beam of sunshine around a vacant room."[25] In the case of the bomb, this tendency created both immediate challenges for those responsible for managing the Manhattan Project and longer-term puzzles for historians seeking to divine Roosevelt's intent. Yet for all his complaints about the president's management style, on the issue of the bomb, the secretary of war shared a commitment to full-scale development while preferring to defer to a later date questions related to its potential use.

The Military Policy Committee and Nuclear Targeting, 1942–43

While Roosevelt and Stimson put off considering the question of use, officers and administrators attached to the Manhattan Project quietly began laying the groundwork for the military application of nuclear weapons. In September 1942, Bush suggested that the time had come to establish "a small group of officers to consider strategic uses and tactics" with respect to the bomb. Marshall was skeptical on the grounds that such a group was "premature" and posed the danger of leaks.[26] Nevertheless, Stimson agreed to establish a Military Policy Committee (MPC) that included Bush, Conant, and representatives from the army and navy "to consider and plan military policy relating to the project."[27] General Leslie R. Groves was tapped as the military head of the American nuclear effort and agent of the MPC.

One of the most important questions considered by the committee was whether Germany or Japan should be the focus of planning for potential use. Germany was the seemingly obvious choice. The specter of a Nazi A-bomb had been the driving force in the American atomic project from the outset. Einstein later remarked that he "would never have lifted a finger" had he known that the Nazis were not going to produce a bomb during the course of the war.[28] Even after the American nuclear program began in earnest, some Manhattan Project insiders worried that the Allies might have to "stand the first punishing blows" of Nazi A-bombs before they could respond in kind.[29] As physicist Leo Szilard lamented in May 1942, "Nobody can tell that whether we shall be ready before German bombs wipe out American cities."[30] It was not until November 1944 that a special Anglo-American intelligence unit operating in Europe discovered that the Germans had abandoned any attempt to build nuclear weapons during World War II only weeks after Szilard's 1942 warning.[31]

Stimson, who strongly favored an overall Allied strategy that gave priority to the defeat of Nazi Germany, shared the scientists' focus on the atomic bomb as a counterweight to the Nazi efforts in this area. Assistant Secretary of War John J. McCloy later recalled that he had "many conversations with him in regard to the menace of a possible German development of an atomic weapon," usually after hours at Stimson's Washington estate.[32] British and American officials pursued an array of covert operations aimed at disrupting the German nuclear program, including commando raids, conventional bombing, and a proposed plot to kidnap or assassinate German physicist Werner Heisenberg.[33] Anticipating a strategy later considered during the cold war, Bush in January 1943 even suggested using Allied nuclear weapons against suspected research sites inside Germany in order to preemptively destroy the Nazi bomb program.[34]

Given the persistent focus on Germany, the Military Policy Committee's deliberations produced a seemingly surprising result. On May 5, 1943, in the committee's first and only formal discussion of the targeting issue, Japan was selected for the first use of the bomb. Ironically, it was fear of the German nuclear program that was the deciding factor in reaching this conclusion. Bush, Conant, and the military members of the committee were swayed by concerns that the Germans could use knowledge gained from an American bomb to further their own efforts. They were particularly worried about what would happen should a nuclear "dud" land in German hands. Japan, on the other hand, was not believed to have an active nuclear weapons program. Thus, the "Japanese were selected as they would not be so apt to secure knowledge from it as would the Germans."[35]

Having settled on Japan as a focal point for future planning, the MPC also considered what specific targets would be best suited for the first use of the bomb. From the beginning, Anglo-American scientists had considered two possible scenarios for combat use. One envisioned use against land targets, exploding the bomb either on contact with the ground or in the air above the target. The other contemplated use was as an underwater explosive for destroying ships and harbors, a possibility raised by Frisch and Peierls in 1940 as a way of possibly reducing civilian casualties. Initial American research encompassed both land and sea uses of the bomb. In May 1942, Conant mentioned "underwater use" as well an airburst weapon intended for targeting "industrial plants . . . [and the] destruction of dwelling houses over a radius of two to three miles."[36]

The targeting issue was discussed at the same May 5, 1943, Military Policy Committee meeting that selected Japan over Germany for first use. Though some consideration was given to targeting the city of Tokyo, "the general view appeared to be that its best point of use would be on a Japanese fleet concentration in the Harbor of Truk." The stated reason was that if the bomb failed to explode, "it would land in water of sufficient depth to prevent easy salvage."[37] There is no indication that moral concerns over radiation or civilian casualties played any part in this recommendation—which was tentative in any case, given that the bomb would not be available for at least a year. Nevertheless, the committee's deliberations offer an important insight into the military's initial attitude toward nuclear weapons, which emphasized an isolated naval base rather than a city as a target.

Stimson, Roosevelt, and the Top Policy Group were not involved in this initial discussion of nuclear targeting. In June 1943, Bush unsuccessfully attempted to engage Roosevelt in a discussion of "possible use against Japan, or the Japanese fleet," pointing out that "the program would shift if we had in mind use against Japan as compared with use against Germany."[38] The president, however, had no apparent interest in the details of nuclear targeting at this point. As for Stimson, there is no record that he ever saw or responded to the Military Policy Committee's recommendations in 1943. This is unsurprising given that the secretary of war showed seemingly no interest at all in targeting questions until spring 1945, only months before the bomb was used in combat.

The apparent high-level indifference to the targeting question in 1941–44 cannot be attributed to a failure to comprehend the revolutionary potential of atomic weapons. As indicated by the intensive discussions of the bomb's diplomatic implications during this same period (outlined in chapter 4), both Roosevelt and Stimson clearly recognized the significance of nuclear fission from the beginning of the serious American effort. Why, then, did they not pay more attention to the issue of nuclear targeting in the early years of the Manhattan Project?

Practical reasons likely account for a large part of the failure of American leaders to closely engage with the targeting question prior to 1945. Preoccupied with the tremendous task of mobilizing an unprepared United States to fight a two-ocean war, the president and the secretary of war were swamped with difficult decisions in the aftermath of Pearl Harbor. Though managing the bomb project was an important part of Stimson's wartime work, it was not until the defeat of Germany in May 1945 that he was truly able to make it his "primary occupation."[39] Forced to divide his limited time and energy among battles on multiple fronts, the secretary engaged in a form of triage when it came to dealing with the bomb. Matters that appear mundane in retrospect, such as securing the necessary funding without revealing details to skeptical congressmen, required immediate attention if the Manhattan Project was to be successful. And while many of the diplomatic issues associated with the bomb could not be postponed (particularly the question of sharing the secret with Britain and the Soviet Union), final decisions about its wartime use could seemingly await the availability of a finished weapon.

Had Stimson been more aware of the lethal and lingering effects of nuclear radiation that had so troubled Frisch and Peierls, he might have found the time to raise moral concerns about targeting before spring 1945. On the other hand, it is also possible that what the secretary of war already knew about the effects of the nuclear weapons left him uneasy enough to want to delay the difficult choices that would attend their potential use in combat. Whatever their reasons, the inattention of high-level American leaders to the targeting question in the early years of the bomb project had important and unforeseen consequences for their later deliberations on this subject at the end of the war.

Moving Targets: Los Alamos and the Ordnance Division

In the absence of firm direction from above, important decisions about nuclear targeting were effectively delegated to the scientists and soldiers working at the top secret Los Alamos laboratory in the New Mexico desert. This was not the intention of either the civilian policymakers or the scientists themselves at the time the laboratory opened in spring 1943. But while the atomic scientists at Los Alamos did not deliberately set about to shape the targeting decision, their work nevertheless significantly narrowed the choices open to policymakers in 1945.

The most important decisions made at Los Alamos had to do with weapons design. Though the basic principles of nuclear physics remained constant, the design of the bomb itself would vary greatly depending on its intended target and means of delivery. The engineering required for a bomb designed to be exploded underwater in an enemy harbor with the intent of sinking ships was very different from a bomb exploded above an urban residential neighborhood aimed at homes and factories. There were a handful of key players involved with these issues of weapons design, including laboratory director J. Robert Oppenheimer and Commander William S. Parson, a naval officer who headed the Ordnance Division at Los Alamos.[40]

Likely in response to the Military Policy Committee's focus on a naval base as the optimal first target for the bomb, the Ordnance Division's staff, shortly after the opening of Los Alamos in 1943, set about designing nuclear weapons optimized for use against fleets and harbors. They explored the possibility of a nuclear depth charge (as originally envisioned by Frisch and Peierls in 1940) and even an atomic torpedo.[41] At the same time, Parsons and his men were also working on an alternative set of designs to be used against land targets. By December 1943, Oppenheimer became concerned that the proliferation of designs being pursued by the Ordnance Division was overtaxing its human and material resources. In response, he suggested that the technically challenging design work on an underwater weapon be "temporarily postponed." As a result of this administrative decision, work at Los Alamos shifted toward designing and building a weapon that was optimized for the destruction of cities.[42]

Though Parsons differed from most of his fellow naval officers in his strong commitment to using science in the service of the war effort, his background and training were in traditional naval ordnance. It is thus not surprising that he envisioned an atomic bomb as a very large conventional blast weapon, ignoring the radiation effects that had troubled Frisch and Peierls and briefly intrigued some American scientists.[43] Parsons, working from calculations supplied by the physicists, concluded that to maximize the bomb's blast effects, it should be detonated above the ground over an area containing many lightly built structures (wood-frame houses, for example).[44] A weapon used in this fashion would be devastating against the kinds of dwellings found in great abundance in Japanese urban neighborhoods but relatively ineffective against the kinds of hardened structures generally associated with military targets such as ships, tanks, bunkers, or even brick or concrete factory buildings.

One additional technical factor pushed Parsons and his team at Los Alamos toward favoring cities as targets. Exploding the bomb in the air to maximize blast effects created a problem: how to give the plane that dropped the bomb time to escape the blast? As the British MAUD Committee had concluded in 1941, the only way to ensure the survival of the carrying plane was to drop the bomb from a very high altitude (around thirty thousand feet).[45] This in turn raised another problem: what kinds of targets could the Army Air Forces locate and hit from such a high altitude? The answer for Parsons was an obvious one. Japanese cities not only contained a large number of wood-frame buildings susceptible to blast but were also relatively easy to find from the air and large enough so that even an inaccurate delivery would still do substantial damage. Conversely, military targets such as naval bases were more resistant to blast, more compact and thus easy to miss from thirty thousand feet, and often located in isolated areas where an errant delivery would see the bomb's effects wasted on farmlands or open ocean.[46]

This chillingly simple set of technical calculations inexorably drove weapons development in the Ordnance Division at Los Alamos toward the production of a weapon aimed at cities and civilians. By December 1944, Parsons was explicitly referring to Japanese cities as the intended target for the atomic bomb.[47] Four months later, Los Alamos scientists formally participated in selecting specific Japanese cities for nuclear destruction as part of the so-called Target Committee (discussed in more depth in chapter 5). Even before Hiroshima a handful of scientists at Los Alamos raised moral concerns about the use of the bomb against cities. The vast majority, however, focused on the technical tasks in front of them to the exclusion of all else. By the time Germany surrendered in May 1945, once and for all ending the threat of a Nazi bomb that motivated many of the physicists to join the Manhattan Project, only a single Los Alamos scientist (Joseph Rotblat) had left the project. Those who remained accelerated their work on the bombs that would eventually fall on Hiroshima and Nagasaki.[48]

Moral concerns over use against cities were explicitly rejected by the most important figures at Los Alamos. Parsons strenuously rebuked the "tender souls" who were "appalled at the idea of the horrible destruction which this bomb might wreak in battle delivery." Rejecting the idea of a noncombat demonstration in September 1944, Parsons predicted that "the reaction of observers to a desert shot would be one of intense disappointment. Even the crater would be disappointing." The only suitable dramatic demonstration of the bomb would be in use against a city "where the human and material destruction would be obvious."[49] As his admiring biographer concluded, "Throughout the studies of the bomb's killing power, Parsons remained an objective, unemotional military officer doing his job."[50]

J. Robert Oppenheimer was not a military officer. He was a brilliant, sensitive, highly cultured scientist with an affinity for philosophy, literature, Hindu religion, and leftist politics. Yet as director of wartime Los Alamos, he oversaw a single-minded drive for technical success at all costs. Oppenheimer actively endorsed use of the bomb against a city and discouraged any manifestations of dissent within the gates of Los Alamos.[51] He also joined Parsons in explicitly rejecting the idea of a noncombat demonstration. Writing to Groves in Washington, the director of the Los Alamos lab pointedly remarked, "I agree completely with all of the comments of Captain Parsons' memorandum on the fallacy of regarding a controlled test as the culmination of the work of this laboratory."[52]

The high-level officials in Washington who would ultimately bear responsibility for the use of a finished weapon do not appear to have fully understood the implications of the accretion of technical decisions about weapon design made at Los Alamos in 1943–44. This was not the result of any deliberate conspiracy on the part of those at Los Alamos to withhold information. Had he paid close attention to the reports coming from Los Alamos in this period, Stimson could not have missed the gradual evolution of the bomb into a weapon optimized for use against cities and civilians. Either he did not heed these reports or he convinced himself that decisions about targeting could be revisited at a later date. But by the time high-level civilian and military leaders in Washington did finally return to the targeting question in May 1945, Los Alamos was already on the verge of producing a weapon that would directly challenge Stimson's deeply held convictions about war, morality, and the mass killing of civilians.

"A Spiritual Revival of Christian Principles": From Los Alamos to Washington

On September 5, 1944, as Allied forces were completing the liberation of Belgium and nearing the German border, the secretary of war was frustrated and angry. "[I]t was very singular," he confided to General Marshall, "that I, the man who had charge of the Department which did the killing in the war, should be the only one who seemed to have any mercy for the other side."[53] The occasion for Stimson's sad observation was a plan circulated by Secretary of the Treasury Henry Morgenthau that called for punishing postwar Germany by destroying its industry and forcing its people "down to subsistence levels" for the foreseeable future.[54] But Stimson's lament also captured the larger dilemma that he faced in the last year of the war. Eventual Allied victory was virtually assured by fall 1944, but the timing of that victory remained uncertain in both Europe and the Pacific. Meanwhile, the war itself was growing increasingly bloody as it neared its conclusion. Even as he worried about having enough manpower to finish the job properly, Stimson remained greatly concerned about the toll that the war was taking on civilians.

Though he recognized that some civilian casualties were inevitable, to the end of the war Stimson continued to insist that deliberately targeting civilians for mass killing not only was immoral but also undermined American leadership in the war effort and the postwar world. Learning of American participation in the catastrophic bombing of Dresden in February 1945, he registered his displeasure at the "terrible and probably unnecessary" destruction and asked Marshall for an investigation. When Marshall replied with a memorandum justifying the attack, Stimson remained unmoved and asked for a further investigation. "Our policy," the secretary of war insisted, "has never been to inflict terror bombing on civilian populations."[55] But however well intentioned, Stimson's efforts to restrain the conduct of American conventional bombing had little practical effect. His failure to keep abreast of changing air force targeting priorities, his belated response to the firebombing of Dresden (and later to an even more deadly attack against Tokyo), and his apparent eagerness to accept the assurances offered by AAF leaders that "they were trying to keep [civilian causalities] down as far as possible" meant that the secretary of war's sporadically expressed concerns had no effect.[56] The decisions regarding the use of the atomic bomb, however, gave him a chance to revisit this issue.

As the time approached when a bomb would be available for use, Stimson realized that the moral and practical questions associated with nuclear weapons could not be indefinitely deferred. On March 5, 1945—the same day that he complained of the "terrible and probably unnecessary" destruction of Dresden by Allied bombers—the secretary of war had a "through and searching talk" with his personal assistant Harvey Bundy on the subject of the atomic bomb. Focusing on "certain phases of it which we hadn't gone into yet together before," Stimson acknowledged that he had put off many of the difficult practical and ethical questions associated with the new weapon. "We are up against some very big decisions," he admitted, and the "time is approaching when we can no longer avoid them."[57] Stimson was oblique in recording the details of his discussion with Bundy, noting simply that their talk "went right down to the bottom facts of human nature, morals and government, and it is by far the most searching and important thing that I have had to do since

I have been here in the office of secretary of war because it touches matters which are deeper even than the principle of the present government."[58]

An undated memorandum from Bundy's files that likely corresponds with the March 5 meeting gives some additional insight into Stimson's frame of mind in early 1945. Stirred by the "enormous implications" of the new weapon, the secretary worried that "as a result of the emotions stirred up by the war we could have never been in a worse condition to handle the impact of this discovery." Stimson was so troubled by the bomb that he floated the idea of appointing an evangelist or minister who could meet the challenge by appealing directly to "the souls of mankind and bring about a spiritual revival of Christian principles."[59] As an example of the kind of spiritual leader he was looking for to meet the atomic peril, he cited Phillips Brooks, the famous nineteenth-century Episcopal bishop who gave Abraham Lincoln's funeral oration in 1865. Nothing came of Stimson's suggestion of a religious solution to the dilemmas posed by the bomb. But as the secretary of war correctly observed, the time was fast approaching when delay was no longer a viable alternative.

This targeting question was further complicated by the death of Franklin Roosevelt on April 12, 1945, only months before the first atomic test in the New Mexico desert. Roosevelt went to his grave without having recorded any firm decision on the potential use of the bomb. The scanty evidence on FDR's thinking near the time of his death indicates that he remained uncommitted on this crucial question. At a meeting with Winston Churchill in September 1944, the president agreed to conditional language with respect to first use. The Hyde Park Aide-Mémoire, signed by Roosevelt and Churchill on September 19, stated that "when a 'bomb' is finally available, *it might, perhaps, after mature consideration*, be used against the Japanese." Four days later, Roosevelt raised with Bush "the question of whether this means should actually be used against the Japanese or whether it should be used only as a threat with full-scale experimentation in this country."[60]

According to presidential confidant Alexander Sachs (who had helped launch the American nuclear program by acting as an intermediary for Szilard and Einstein in 1939), FDR in December 1944 had decided on a noncombat demonstration of the bomb's power before unleashing it in anger against the Japanese.[61] There is no contemporary evidence to verify Sachs' claim as the president left no written instructions on the use (or nonuse) of the bomb. It is highly unlikely that Roosevelt had made *any* such decision before his death, if only because it was antithetical to his entire approach to the bomb, which hinged on maintaining maximum flexibility with respect to its potential use.

In the months between Roosevelt's death in April and the first atomic test on July 16, 1945, Stimson, Marshall, and others in Washington expressed moral and practical concerns about the use of the bomb against Japanese civilians. This in turn set off a quiet but contentious debate over the use of atomic weapons against Japanese cities that continued through August 1945. This debate would take place in the early days of a new administration led by an inexperienced former machine politician from Missouri and against a backdrop of diplomatic intrigue that focused as much on America's nominal allies as it did on the tattered remains of the Axis powers.

Chapter 4

"The International Situation"

ON THE MORNING OF APRIL 17, 1945, A SMALL GROUP OF AMERICAN
and British officers entered the German town of Stassfurt. Towns and cities
were falling to the Allied advance all across Germany in spring 1945, but this
particular operation was anything but ordinary. Stassfurt was not only well
ahead of the American and British front lines but also some fifty kilometers
east of the line that was supposed to demarcate the eventual Soviet and Western zones of occupation. This fact had alarmed the commander of the American Twelfth Army, who worried that sending an Anglo–American task force so
deep into the Soviet zone might raise diplomatic complications. General
Omar Bradley quieted his reluctant subordinate with a simple admonition:
"to Hell with the Russians."[1]

The expedition found what they were looking for in a field next to the
town's salt mine. There, in rotting barrels exposed to the elements, sat 1,100
tons of uranium. To load the materials for transport, the Anglo-American
team drafted seventy-five French and Italian men who had been working as
prison laborers. When some of the moldering barrels proved too unstable to

transport, entrepreneurial Allied officers located a paper bag factory in town where they procured sacks in which to package the loose uranium. Over the course of seven days, laborers loaded 3,210 barrels and 2,797 bags of uranium into trucks driven by African American soldiers under the command of a single white lieutenant. The uranium, paper bags and all, was driven to the town of Hildesheim (near Hannover), located safely in the Western zone of occupation, where it was unloaded by conscripted German civilians. From Hildesheim the ore was sent by air, rail, and ship to England and eventually to Oak Ridge, Tennessee, for processing. Along the way, three boxcars of uranium disappeared, leading to some anxious moments before they were recovered in a railway switching yard.[2]

According to Allied intelligence estimates, the Stassfurt ore accounted for "the bulk of uranium supplies available in Europe" and was four to five times as large as the entire estimated Soviet stockpile. Historian David Holloway concluded in *Stalin and the Bomb* that this material would have been "enormously useful to the Soviet project."[3] But the Soviets would find no traces of the uranium when they eventually arrived in Stassfurt. Following orders from Washington to "get everything we want out of there in a hurry and leave nothing behind," the Anglo-American team swept the area clean. Broken barrels were removed and burned, and fifteen barrels of paperwork were seized "to assure that no written record of the material would remain in the plant."[4]

Four days after the death of Franklin D. Roosevelt, three weeks before the end of the war in Europe, and some four months prior to the end of the Pacific war, the United States and Great Britain had plunged deep into Germany and secretly removed the largest known stock of uranium in Europe. They did so as part of a one-sided nuclear arms race originally stimulated by fears of a Nazi A-bomb. By the time of the Stassfurt operation, however, American and British intelligence had known for almost five months that the German nuclear weapons program was virtually nonexistent.[5] By spring 1945, the Soviet Union was already America's primary nuclear rival.

"After-War Control, Together with Sources of Raw Material"

Any doubt that American leaders saw the atomic bomb as a special weapon should be dispelled by a quick survey of the diplomatic history of the Manhattan Project. The very existence of this project posed important questions with respect to both wartime relations with the other Allies and postwar planning. Unlike the issues associated with the use of the bomb against Japan, these diplomatic dilemmas could not be easily deferred.

Concern over the postwar implications of the bomb was apparent as early as October 9, 1941, when OSRD director Vannevar Bush journeyed to the White House to lobby Roosevelt for an expanded American nuclear program. In the course of their meeting, Bush spoke with the president "at some length" regarding the issues of "after-war control, together with sources of raw material."[6] These two linked issues—postwar control of nuclear weapons and the raw materials needed to produce them, most notably uranium—were a consistent thread in the wartime discussions of the bomb in the United States. Nine days after Pearl Harbor, Stimson and the Top Policy Group were already discussing the implications of nuclear fission for the "international situation," including relations with America's wartime allies.[7] For most of the war, it was the diplomatic aspects of the bomb project, not its potential use against Germany or Japan, that dominated discussion at the highest levels of the American government.

The trustees of the American nuclear program were unanimous in recognizing the diplomatic challenges—and opportunities—posed by the bomb. From the start of the American program, Stimson made it clear that he believed the atomic bomb was more than just a potential weapon to be used against America's wartime enemies. The very possibility of nuclear fission posed a tremendous threat to the existence of what he often referred to as "industrial civilization." Prior to the outbreak of World War II, Stimson had lamented that man's capacity for technological innovation had outstripped "his moral and social power."[8] Arriving against the backdrop of a destructive global conflict, the prospect of nuclear weapons did nothing to ease his concerns on this score.

But while there was unanimity on the revolutionary implications of the bomb for international relations, there was no consensus on how to best plan for the nuclear future. Should the United States attempt to maintain a nuclear monopoly after the war? Might the informal exchange of information with British scientists be expanded into a formal Anglo-American agreement to control the bomb? Or should the United States attempt to negotiate a multilateral pact, including the Soviet Union, for the international control of atomic energy? American leaders struggled with these choices during World

War II. Stimson advocated all three courses—unilateral, bilateral, and multilateral—at various times between 1941 and 1945. His erratic course reflected the difficulty of reconciling a complex series of overlapping political, military, and diplomatic goals that encompassed not only the bomb but also a set of dilemmas raised by the war and the postwar settlement to follow.

On the one hand, the secretary of war sincerely believed that arms control through mutual agreement among the great powers, including the Soviet Union, was the only way to contain the threat to civilization posed by the atomic bomb. Within this context, he saw nuclear weapons as another in a long series of technological innovations that needed to be subjected to "organized self-control" at the international level.[9] By temperament, experience, and position, Stimson was ideally placed to serve as an advocate for the international control of atomic energy. But the bomb was not the only issue on Stimson's mind during World War II. The secretary of war was also concerned with both conducting the war and crafting the peace that followed. In particular, he sought a speedy victory through a direct confrontation with Nazi Germany followed by a postwar settlement in Europe and Asia that included a capitalist open door for international trade. When he encountered resistance to these ideas from America's nominal allies, Stimson was repeatedly tempted by the vision of the atomic bomb as a diplomatic "master card."[10] Complicating matters further was the difficult question of exactly *how* to go about using the atomic secret as a bargaining chip, something Stimson never successfully resolved.

Any discussion of the nuclear arms race that began during World War II must acknowledge the complex and difficult choices that faced even the most well-meaning American leaders in the years before Hiroshima. Even had Stimson consistently followed his instinct to seek a multilateral solution to the challenge posed by the bomb, it is far from certain he could have swayed Roosevelt and Truman, who closely held final decisions about the diplomatic aspects of the Manhattan Project. If American leaders had wholeheartedly embraced international control of atomic energy prior to first use of the bomb, the ultimate success of such an endeavor still would have hinged on reaching an agreement with Joseph Stalin and the Soviet Union, a difficult proposition at best. But acknowledging the difficulty of managing the bomb does not imply that a massive and mutually destructive arms race—with the United States and the USSR each possessing tens of thousands of nuclear warheads at the peak of the cold war—was inevitable. Nor does it entirely absolve American leaders for their role in contributing to that outcome.

Henry Stimson played an important and ultimately tragic role in the origins of the cold war nuclear arms race. His shifting attitude toward the bomb and the Soviet Union mirrored the growing tensions that would eventually divide Europe, and the world, into hostile armed camps living under the constant threat of a nuclear holocaust. It was Stimson who authorized the covert mission to Stassfurt in April 1945. Almost exactly five months later, in his last public act, he made a desperate plea for immediate cooperation with the Soviet Union in order to forestall a nuclear arms race. But by the time Stimson finally resolved "to control and limit the use of the atomic bomb as an instrument of war," the flickering hopes for international control had already been virtually extinguished.[11] By his own actions during World War II, the secretary of war had helped to set in motion exactly the kind of destructive international competition in armaments that he had spent much of his long public career attempting to avoid.

Anglo-American Difficulties, 1940–43

As historian Martin J. Sherwin chronicled in his pioneering work *A World Destroyed*, the roots of the nuclear arms race extend as far back as 1940–41. Stimson's involvement also dates to these early years, when the secretary of war first struggled to balance the potential short-term advantages to be gained by possessing the atomic secret with the longer-term dangers of a potential arms race.

British and American scientists began informally exchanging information on their respective nuclear efforts in September 1940, at a time when the United States lagged in basic research on the bomb. Roosevelt and Stimson initially endorsed the policy of "complete interchange with Britain on technical matters," an easy decision given the rather modest American progress in the field. Looking to formalize Anglo-American cooperation on the bomb, in October 1941 the president proposed to Churchill that "any extended efforts may be coordinated or even jointly conducted."[12] But in an early harbinger of nuclear rivalry among the Allies, the British demurred in response to the American proposal. Churchill and his key nuclear advisers, Sir John Anderson and Lord Cherwell (Frederick A. Lindemann), privately entertained hopes of leveraging their early lead in nuclear research to produce an independent British bomb. It was only in July 1942, when it became apparent that actually building the bomb during the war was beyond Britain's overtaxed resources, that Anderson reluctantly recommended accepting Roosevelt's proposal.[13]

Unbeknownst to Churchill's nuclear advisers, their counterparts on the other side of the Atlantic were developing serious reservations about Anglo-American nuclear cooperation just as the British were preparing to embrace a joint project. The American trustees of the atomic secret were well aware that Britain's contribution would become comparatively less important as the project moved from the realm of theory to the construction of vast facilities for the enrichment of uranium and the production of nuclear weapons. In October 1942, presidential science adviser Vannevar Bush concluded that there was "no reason for a joint enterprise as far as development and manufacture is concerned."[14] Stimson shared these sentiments. On October 29, the secretary of war bluntly informed Roosevelt that the United States was "doing nine-tenths of the work" and suggested that it would be "better for us to go along for the present without sharing anything more than we could help."[15] Stimson had long expressed friendly feelings for the British and had close personal connections to a number of British leaders, including Churchill. But his sympathies did not, at least initially, extend as far as sharing the production secrets of the atomic bomb.

Concern over the postwar period loomed large in the recommendations of Stimson, Bush, and James Conant to move toward unilateral control over the production of atomic weapons at the end of 1942. Neither Roosevelt nor his advisers had yet formulated a plan for the postwar control of atomic energy. In light of this uncertainty, it seemed unwise to make any wartime commitments to Britain on the bomb that might limit American options or foreclose the possibility of a broader multilateral agreement after the war. It was in the context of his discussion with Roosevelt about "meeting the ticklish situation after the war" that the secretary of war first proposed limiting cooperation with the British in October 1942.[16] Unilateral American production of the bomb undoubtedly appealed to Roosevelt as it postponed difficult decisions about postwar control and assured him freedom of action in making those eventual choices. Heeding his advisers' recommendations, the president approved a new policy of restricted interchange in December 1942. Under this directive, sharing of information with Britain on nuclear matters was sharply limited and subject to approval by General Leslie Groves on a case-by-case basis.[17]

The American attempt to buy time with which to consider a solution to the vexing diplomatic questions posed by nuclear fission was complicated by British outrage over the new policy of restricted interchange. Unlike the Americans, the British had a clear position on postwar control from the beginning: they wanted access to the production secrets of the atomic bomb for themselves while denying that knowledge to the Soviet Union. Churchill repeatedly bombarded Roosevelt and his advisers with a mix of threats and pleas for a restoration of exclusive Anglo-American nuclear cooperation.[18]

The British reaction put the president and his advisers in a difficult position. Even if they could complete the bomb without additional help, Britain was an important wartime ally whose cooperation was vital in other areas, most notably in the buildup to the invasion of western Europe. Roosevelt and Stimson also put great stock in postwar cooperation with Britain, a nation they believed would be a reliable, democratic, capitalist, pro-American bastion in a Europe devastated by war.[19] But to agree to the British demands for renewed cooperation would have important consequences for the postwar control of atomic energy. Given Churchill's strong anti-Soviet sentiments, any bilateral accord on atomic weapons with Britain would almost certainly preclude a larger multilateral agreement involving the Soviet Union.

FDR responded to the British demand for resumed cooperation with his oft-employed strategy for avoiding difficult decisions: he agreed with everybody and did nothing. In January 1943, Roosevelt asked his close confidant Harry Hopkins to assure the British prime minister that while the president "did not wish to telegraph about it," the A-bomb situation would be handled in a way that was "entirely in accord" with Churchill's wishes. Four months later, Roosevelt personally assured Churchill that "the exchange of information on Tube Alloys [A-bomb] should be resumed and that the enterprise should be considered a joint one, to which both countries would contribute their best endeavours."[20] But despite his encouraging words to the British leader, Roosevelt made no move to loosen unilateral American control over the bomb project. When Bush met with FDR in late June, the president assured him that he had "no intention of proceeding further on the matter of the relations with the British."[21] Roosevelt never informed Stimson, Bush, or Conant of his informal conversations with Churchill on resuming nuclear cooperation. Without presidential instructions to the contrary, and with the de facto trustees of the Manhattan Project still favoring unilateral American production of the bomb, Britain remained locked out of the American project through July 1943.

Fateful Decisions at London and Quebec, July–September 1943

Summer 1943 was a critical turning point in the diplomatic history of the Manhattan Project. Having been strung along with promises of renewed cooperation for seven months, Churchill was beginning to suspect that Roosevelt's soothing rhetoric masked ambivalence or even hostility to a joint Anglo-American nuclear program. Tired of waiting for action by FDR, Churchill took advantage of a visit to London by Bush and Stimson to present his case directly to the president's chief nuclear advisers.[22] The timing was fortuitous for the British prime minister. When the American secretary of war arrived in London, he was preoccupied with another important sticking point in the Anglo-American relationship, one that offered Churchill considerable leverage in the forthcoming negotiations over the bomb.

From the day he took office in the bleak summer of 1940, Stimson had looked forward to the moment when American and British troops would land in France and begin to roll back the Nazi invaders from the west. He strongly believed that the quickest road to victory—"the one straight line of finishing the war"—lay in a direct confrontation with Germany on the continent of Europe. "Geographically and historically," he insisted, an invasion of western Europe was "the easiest road to the center of our chief enemy's heart."[23] Throughout the war, Stimson insisted that all other military efforts—including the struggle against Japan—should be subordinated to the task of defeating Nazi Germany. In the short term, a second front in western Europe was vital in order to relieve some of the pressure on the Soviet Union and thus keep that beleaguered nation from either surrendering or being overrun by the Nazis. Looking ahead, Stimson realized that it was vital to make a significant military contribution to the defeat of Germany if the United States wanted to shape the postwar European economic and territorial settlement.

British bases, troops, and air and naval support were indispensable ingredients in any plan for the liberation of western Europe. The British, however, were much less eager than their American counterparts to launch a frontal attack on Nazi-occupied France. Memories of the carnage of World War I, a reluctance to

strain already thinly stretched resources, a commitment to protecting the imperial lifeline to India via Egypt, and the visceral fear of "having the Channel full
of corpses of defeated allies" led Churchill and his government to favor a more
indirect route to defeating Germany.[24] Much to Stimson's chagrin, Churchill
managed to convince Roosevelt to launch peripheral operations in North Africa
and Italy in 1942–43 rather than concentrating on an early invasion of western
Europe. Aghast at what he viewed as costly and unnecessary diversions from the
main task at hand, Stimson warned FDR in May 1943 that

> [t]he British are trying to arrange this matter so that Britain and Amer-
> ica hold the leg for Stalin to skin the deer and I think that will be a dan-
> gerous business for us at the end of the war. Stalin won't have much of
> an opinion of people who have done that and we will not be able to share
> much of the post-war world with him.[25]

Confronted with continuing British resistance to a cross-channel attack, Stimson threw himself into the task of promoting an operation he viewed as vital
to both winning the war and securing a favorable peace settlement.

It was in the midst of this contentious debate over the second front in July
1943 that Churchill personally lobbied Stimson to renew cooperation on the
atomic bomb. In a series of meetings in London, the secretary of war was
forced to choose between the short-term gains that might be had from using
the bomb as a wartime bargaining chip and the longer-term fruits of an international solution to the dangers posed by nuclear fission. Though Stimson's
account of his thinking during these crucial meetings is frustratingly vague,
the outcome was clear enough. After preliminary discussions of the second-
front issue, the prime minister on July 17 raised the question of resuming nuclear cooperation. Mindful of the importance of Anglo-American relations to
the success of the war effort, Stimson replied by offering general support for
cooperation on the bomb, assuring Churchill that he would "rather anything
should happen than a feeling of want of good faith between us."[26] Though he
could not offer any firm promises without word from the president, Stimson
privately informed Bush that he "felt very strongly that the present situation
must be altered in the direction of full interchange."[27]

At virtually the same moment back in Washington, Roosevelt independently decided to act on his previous promises to Churchill. Likely motivated

by the same concerns over fraying ties with Britain and the second-front issue, FDR on July 20 sent a telegram instructing Bush to "renew, in an inclusive manner, the full exchange of information with the British" on the bomb. This seemingly straightforward instruction was complicated, however, by an error in the telegraphic process. The directive to "renew" full interchange was translated as an instruction to "review" the issue.[28] Before the president's instructions could be clarified, Stimson had already taken part in a pivotal meeting at 10 Downing Street on July 22 in which he, Bush, and War Department aide Harvey Bundy sat down with Churchill and his nuclear advisers to hammer out an agreement governing future Anglo-American cooperation on the bomb. Though some sort of interchange was inevitable following Roosevelt's decision to finally act on the matter, it was left to the British and American negotiators in London to shape the form that that cooperation would take.

Churchill opened the July 22 meeting with a thinly veiled threat. According to Bundy's notes, the prime minister warned that "this particular matter was so important that it might affect seriously British-American relationships."[29] There is no evidence that Churchill explicitly suggested renewed nuclear cooperation as a quid pro quo for British participation in an invasion of western Europe. But coming in the midst of tense negotiations over the second front, the message was clear: if the Americans did not agree to cooperate on the bomb, they could no longer count on British cooperation in other areas. The prime minister followed this statement with his own plan for an exclusive Anglo-American nuclear partnership that would extend into the postwar period. Britain would be guaranteed "free interchange" of information, while American and British leaders would agree "not to give information to other parties without the consent of both." Churchill's bid for an Anglo-American bomb was explicitly aimed at preventing a larger multilateral agreement on atomic energy involving the Soviet Union.[30]

Reversing his previous position with respect to entangling postwar agreements, Stimson approved the prime minister's draft plan on July 22. With the secretary of war's endorsement, Churchill's plan became the basis for the Quebec Agreement signed by the prime minister and President Roosevelt on August 19, 1943. The agreement established an Anglo-American Combined Policy Committee (CPC) with the American secretary of war as its chair. Although it had no formal legal standing with respect to the postwar control of nuclear energy, the CPC clearly signaled a move away from the kind of broad, multilateral approach to the bomb that was a prerequisite to any meaningful pursuit of international control.

Why did Stimson reverse course and support an exclusive agreement on nuclear energy with Great Britain in July 1943? There is no evidence that explicitly anti-Soviet motives played a role in his thinking at London. Neither the secretary of war nor any other high-level civilian or military figure involved with the bomb on the American side had ever been particularly eager to share the atomic secret with the Soviets. Stimson, Groves, and Groves's Manhattan Project intelligence staff were aware of Soviet attempts to secure information about the nascent American nuclear effort and went to great lengths to frustrate them.[31] But Stimson's motive for withholding information from the Soviets in 1940–43 appears to have been the same one that led him initially to favor restricting interchange with Britain. His preference for unilateral American development of the bomb reflected a desire to avoid *any* entangling commitments until the president and his nuclear advisers had settled on a definitive plan for the postwar control of atomic energy.

It was the issue of wartime relations with Britain and the continuing negotiations over the second front, not postwar concerns over the Soviet Union, that appears to have motivated Stimson's reversal in July 1943. His primary motive seems to have been finding a way to prevent the nuclear issue from jeopardizing military plans for the speedy defeat of Germany. Churchill had indirectly alluded to this possibility at the start of the July 22 meeting, and when formal discussion on the bomb adjourned, the secretary and the prime minister stayed on and "had at it hammer and tongs" on the proposed cross-channel invasion of western Europe.[32] The July 1943 Anglo-American agreement on nuclear matters did not by itself guarantee a favorable outcome to the second-front debate, which was not finally resolved until Stalin, Churchill, and Roosevelt met at Tehran in late November. But Churchill's comments in London clearly signaled that securing British cooperation in such an endeavor would be greatly complicated without a prior agreement on the bomb.

In the aftermath of the London meeting, Bush attempted to convince the secretary of war that the United States should not agree to any postwar arrangement with Britain "as part of the war effort." Stimson, however, countered that it was "was quite impossible to completely separate the two in consideration."[33] This statement followed logically from his conviction that the "first necessary step in having a postwar policy is to end the war."[34] As British cooperation was vital to ending the war quickly, Stimson could justify using the atomic secret as a wartime bargaining chip as part of a broader strategy to achieve victory over Nazi Germany and thus hasten the process of postwar rebuilding. In doing so, however, he helped set a precedent that would recur in later deliberations, subordinating the possible postwar international control of nuclear energy to the more immediate needs of wartime diplomacy.

Roosevelt's motives in the Anglo–American dispute and its eventual resolution are more difficult to ascertain than Stimson's. The president shared little with his advisers on this subject and left no written account of his actions. It is possible, as Sherwin has speculated, that Roosevelt had already decided to pursue a postwar Anglo-American nuclear monopoly as a counterweight to Soviet power.[35] Certainly FDR's wartime handling of the atomic secret casts grave doubt on the charge (most recently raised by historian Wilson D. Miscamble) that the president built his hopes for postwar peace on a naïve trust in Stalin and the Soviet Union. Such trust was not evident in his decision to agree with the decidedly anti-Soviet Churchill in attempting to keep the secret of the bomb from Stalin.[36] The debate about the postwar fate of the bomb, however, was far from over.

Scientists, Statesmen, and International Control, 1944

In May 1944, Sir Ronald I. Campbell, British representative on the CPC, reported back to his superiors in London on an emerging debate within the small circle of American A-bomb insiders. The progress made by the Manhattan Project scientists toward constructing a bomb had led some on the American side to develop "a growing sense of responsibility and anxiety about their ability to play their just role in international affairs." Others, however, "thought that this weapon can be kept a tight monopoly and can thus give the maximum protection to America."[37] This debate, which pitted advocates of international control of atomic energy against those who wanted to hold on to a nuclear monopoly as long as possible, again found Stimson torn between his concerns about the destructive power of nuclear fission and the continuing lure of the atomic secret as a diplomatic tool with which to remake the postwar world.

The stimulus to revisit the international control of atomic energy came from a variety of sources in 1944. On one side were a growing number of scientists haunted by the specter of a postwar nuclear arms race. Danish physicist Niels Bohr was the first to raise the alarm. Bohr, a Nobel Prize winner and director of the Institute of Theoretical Physics in Copenhagen, commanded tremendous respect in the international physics community. Upon escaping to England from occupied Denmark and learning the full extent of the Manhattan Project in September 1943, he became greatly alarmed at the prospect of a postwar arms race. To prevent such an outcome, Bohr believed, would require an international agreement involving the Soviet Union. The success of any such effort hinged on approaching the Soviets as soon as possible, before atomic weapons were used in anger.[38]

Independently of Bohr's efforts, Roosevelt's own scientific advisers had also tentatively begun to explore the problem of postwar international control. This issue had concerned Bush and Conant from the outset of the Manhattan Project and underlay their opposition to a bilateral agreement with Britain in 1942–43. Neither man, however, had articulated a vision for how international control might work in practice. In May 1944, Conant took a first step, privately penning a draft plan that called for an international commission (including the Soviet Union) to jointly control the world's entire stock of nuclear bombs and establish rules and guidelines for the peacetime development of atomic energy.[39] In September, Conant and Bush formally presented Stimson with a series of memoranda outlining the dangers of a postwar arms race and calling for "complete international scientific and technical interchange on this subject, backed up by an international commission acting under an association of nations and having the authority to inspect."[40] These high-level concerns over an arms race in 1944 were supplemented by grassroots efforts by Manhattan Project scientists to address the issue at the Chicago Metallurgical Laboratory and, to a lesser extent, at Los Alamos.[41]

The scientists' efforts ran into strong opposition at the highest levels of the British and American governments. In response to a March 1944 memorandum suggesting an approach to the Soviet Union as part of a broader proposal for international control, Churchill added the following marginal notes: "On no account," "no," and "I do not agree."[42] The British prime minister was entirely consistent in his approach to this issue throughout the war, opposing both international control and any notification to the Soviet Union (or any other nation) of the existence of an Anglo-American bomb project.[43] A disastrous meeting between Bohr and Churchill in May did nothing to allay the prime minister's fears that the scientists advocating international control were at best misguided and at worst bordering on treason.[44]

Roosevelt was, characteristically, more ambivalent in his attitude toward international control and the Soviet Union. Supreme Court justice and Roosevelt confidant Felix Frankfurter reported the president was "worried to death" about the bomb and open to an international solution following a private meeting in early 1944. Bohr, too, came away with the impression that FDR was seriously considering an approach to Stalin after an audience with the president in August.[45] As late as February 1945, Roosevelt alarmed Churchill at the Yalta Conference by suggesting that it would be best to disclose the atomic secret to Stalin before the Soviet leader found out about it from other sources.[46]

But whatever fears FDR entertained about an arms race were not enough to trump his wartime commitment to Churchill. In September 1944, Roosevelt and the British prime minister struck a secret bargain, one that the president concealed from his own nuclear advisers. In the Hyde Park Aide-Mémoire of September 19, Roosevelt committed to keeping the atomic secret from the Soviet Union for the indefinite future. Point number one of the informal agreement definitively stated, "The suggestion that the world should be informed regarding Tube Alloys, with a view to an international agreement regarding its control and use, is not accepted." In addition, FDR pledged the United States to continue an exclusive nuclear partnership with Britain after the war and agreed with Churchill that Bohr should be investigated "to ensure that he is responsible for no leakage of information, particularly to the Russians."[47]

In light of Roosevelt's attitude, there was little Stimson could do on the fundamental question of whether or not to approach the Soviet Union. It does not follow from this, however, that he had no role to play in the behind-the-scenes drama over international control that unfolded in 1944–45. In his role as secretary of war and chair of the CPC, Stimson had substantial input into the implementation of the policies set by Roosevelt and Churchill. And as a respected elder statesman with a bipartisan record of public service, he commanded tremendous respect both inside and outside the administration. Though he could not single-handedly shift the debate on international control, he would have been a tremendously powerful ally of the advocates for such an approach. It was for just this reason that Bush and Conant approached the secretary of war in September 1944.

The president's scientific advisers had reason to believe that Stimson would be sympathetic to their cause. Though he had sided with Churchill and the British at the pivotal July 1943 meeting in London, Stimson remained deeply concerned about the long-term international problems posed by the bomb. As previously noted, he was so troubled by the implications of nuclear weapons that he eventually pondered appointing an evangelist or minister to help meet the challenge by bringing about "a spiritual revival of Christian principles."[48] On a more practical note, he met with Roosevelt as early as October 1942 to discuss "ways of meeting the ticklish situation after the war with a view to preventing [the atomic bomb] being used to conquer the world."[49] The invasion of Normandy in June 1944 and the late July breakout that sent Allied armies racing across France not only marked the successful resolution of the contentious second-front debate with Britain but also helped turn Stimson's mind toward the looming challenges of the postwar period. It was in this context that he considered the pleas of his scientific advisers for the international control of atomic energy.

The Soviet Union, Germany, and the Strategy of Quid Pro Quo, 1944–45

There was much in the approach offered by Bush, Conant, and Bohr that appealed to Stimson. The emphasis on international cooperation and arms control played directly into his long-held belief in the need to develop "organized self-control" at the international level in order to deal with dangers posed to "industrial civilization" by the rapid advance of war-making technology.[50] In a meeting with Bush in September 1944, the secretary of war agreed that an international approach to the problem of atomic fission should be carefully studied and lamented that it had been impossible to command Roosevelt's attention on the subject.[51] Though he declined to offer a formal opinion on the draft plan presented by Bush and Conant, the two scientist-administrators left encouraged by the secretary's attitude. In early 1945, Bohr conveyed to Los Alamos director J. Robert Oppenheimer his confidence that Stimson, as a former secretary of state, was "keenly alive to the international political aspects of military problems" and that "he has thought about the broader implications of the matter and is very sympathetic with the general considerations to which I have called attention."[52]

Stimson was, in fact, broadly sympathetic to the various plans for the postwar international control of atomic energy. He also understood that any meaningful form of international control would have to involve the Soviet Union. Speaking to Roosevelt in December 1944 regarding the atomic bomb project and Soviets, the secretary of war confessed to feeling "troubled about the possible effect of keeping from them even now that work."[53] The plea for international control that Stimson ultimately eventually presented to President Harry S. Truman before leaving office in September 1945 owed much to the Bush-Conant and Bohr plans of 1944. But during the crucial period from fall 1944 through the first use of the bomb in August 1945, the secretary of war not only declined to endorse an international approach but also presided over a set of policies that accelerated the budding nuclear arms race with the Soviet Union.

Why did Stimson fail to champion the international control of atomic energy when the idea was first presented to him in 1944? Bush and Conant apparently believed that the secretary was simply too mentally and physically taxed to give the issue the consideration it deserved. "He is a very wise man," Bush noted following a February 15, 1945, meeting at which the two men discussed the future control of atomic energy, "and I only wish that he had more of the vigor of youth when he is so badly needed."[54] There was some truth to Bush's characterization of Stimson as simply too busy and too exhausted to fully confront the complex diplomatic problem posed by atomic energy. It was not until late May 1945, after the end of the war in Europe, that the secretary of war was able to devote the bulk of his time to the study of this admittedly complicated and technical problem. But the most important reason for his halting approach to international control had nothing to do with issues of health or vigor. By fall 1944, Stimson's thinking about the future of the bomb had become inextricably linked to a series of issues involving the Soviet Union, Germany, and the postwar world.

From Pearl Harbor onward, Stimson had been guided by two imperatives: to win the war as quickly as possible and to lay the groundwork for a lasting peace in its aftermath. Cooperation with the Soviet Union was, he believed, crucial to achieving both of those goals. The secretary of war acknowledged that the Red Army was bearing the brunt of the military conflict in Europe with Hitler. He also understood that in eastern Europe, the Balkans, and parts of continental Asia, the United States would be relying on Soviet military power to keep the peace in the immediate postwar period.[55] While he had "no . . . love for communism or Stalin," he also saw no reason the United

States could not cooperate with the Soviet Union in matters of international security. "So far as Russia is concerned," he confided in 1940, "my views date back to a pre-Bolshevik time, when for a long period of our history, Russia was one of our most constant friends."[56]

By September 1944, as the war in Europe was reaching its climax and the debate over the international control of atomic energy was heating up in Washington, Stimson began to develop concerns about the fate of postwar Europe in general, and Germany in particular, that would decisively shift his thinking about the bomb, the Soviet Union, and international control. Postwar economic issues were foremost among his worries in fall 1944. The secretary of war strongly believed that a worldwide capitalist open door for trade and commerce was the sine qua non of any lasting peace. While the victorious Allies could keep the peace in the short term by force of arms, in the long term it was vital to remedy the root causes of war itself. Building on lessons drawn from the failure of the Versailles Treaty and the worldwide economic depression of the 1930s, Stimson became convinced that before the world could effectively outlaw war, "It must . . . be free from the thing that often starts violence—want."[57] Freedom from want, he asserted, could itself be achieved only through "equality and freedom in regard to the natural resources of the world."[58] Deeply imbued with the classical economic liberalism of Adam Smith (and its later American proponents, including Elihu Root), Stimson never questioned the assumption that capitalist free trade was the only viable means by which to achieve that goal.

The secretary of war was particularly concerned about postwar economic arrangements in Europe. Since the early 1930s, he had favored the creation of a European economic community (what he once referred to as a "United States of Europe") as a solution to the problems created by the territorial settlement at Versailles.[59] He vigorously opposed the Morgenthau Plan to deindustrialize and partition postwar Germany on both humanitarian and practical grounds. To deliberately reduce the German population "down to subsistence levels" would be "a crime against civilization itself." Imposing a "Carthaginian" peace on Germany would lead "peoples all over the world" to "suspect the validity of our spiritual tenets and question the long range effectiveness of our economic and political principles," thus compromising America's role as a postwar leader of the international community.[60]

Morgenthau privately mocked Stimson's humanitarian concerns as amounting to nothing more than a sentimental belief that "[a]ll you've got to do is let kindness and Christianity work on the Germans."[61] But there was also a more practical element to the secretary of war's critique. Stimson feared that the Morgenthau Plan would dash any hope of rebuilding a peaceful and prosperous Europe after the war.[62] Germany, with its rich natural resources and vast productive capacity, would be the linchpin of postwar economic recovery in Europe. European economic recovery was, in turn, crucial to building a lasting peace. "By such economic mistakes," Stimson summarized in a blunt letter to Roosevelt opposing the Morgenthau Plan, "I cannot help but feel that you would . . . be poisoning the springs out of which we hope that the future peace of the world can be maintained."[63]

Roosevelt backed away from the Morgenthau Plan in September 1944 after news of the internal turmoil it had created within the administration leaked to the press.[64] But the future of Germany remained very much on Stimson's mind as the end of the war in Europe appeared to draw near. His sensitivity to the issue heightened by the dispute over the Morgenthau Plan, the secretary began to fear that the Soviet Union might be unwilling to cooperate in the kind of economic initiatives that he deemed vital to the rebuilding of Europe. Should the Soviets close off economic access to the areas of Europe under their control after the war, the effects would be even more disastrous than those contemplated under the Morgenthau Plan. A closed, communist economic sphere in Soviet-occupied Germany (as well in as eastern Europe and parts of Asia) would render impossible the kind of economic recovery that Stimson believed to be a prerequisite for any lasting peace.

The secretary of war's fears were stoked by a series of meetings in October 1944 with American ambassador to the Soviet Union W. Averell Harriman. Harriman conveyed to Stimson his impressions of "the way in which the Russians were trying to dominate the countries which they are 'liberating' and the use which they are making of secret police in the process."[65] This warning not only heightened the secretary of war's fear that the Soviets were intent on developing a closed economic sphere in eastern Europe but also led him to question for the first time whether the United States could trust Stalin as a postwar diplomatic partner. Declaring that "there is nothing to choose between the Gestapo which the Germans have used and the OGPU which the Russians have historically used," Stimson concluded that the "the success of our relations with Russia" would ultimately depend on at least the partial liberalization of Soviet society.[66]

Amid his ongoing concerns over postwar economic reconstruction and emerging doubts about the Soviet Union, Stimson in late 1944 began to cast about for a diplomatic lever with which to extract concessions from America's nominal ally. He had not given up on working with the Soviet Union in the postwar period. As late as April 1945, in the midst of the rising tensions over Poland and eastern Europe, Stimson asserted that "Russia had been very good to us on the larger issues" and insisted that there was no reason for a long-term clash between the two nations.

> I felt that the only thing I could hang onto with any hopefulness was the fact that Russia and the United States had always gotten along for a hundred and fifty years history with Russia friendly and helpful. Our respective orbits do not clash geographically and I think that on the whole we can probably keep out of clashes in the future.[67]

Thus the secretary sought to walk a fine line: "persuading Russia to play ball" on economic issues he believed to be vital to postwar peace without jeopardizing continued military cooperation to defeat the Axis during the war or harming the prospect for a longer-term cooperative relationship. In this context, Stimson came to see the atomic secret as the "master card" in the high stakes negotiations over the postwar world.[68] Much as he had with the B-17 bomber in 1941, Stimson in 1944–45 embraced the bomb as a technological solution to a vexing diplomatic problem.

When Bush and Conant first approached Stimson with their proposal for international control in September 1944, he was torn between sympathy for an international approach to the challenges posed by atomic energy and concern over the need to establish a favorable (from the American point of view) relationship with the Soviet Union. Though he did not believe that these two goals were ultimately incompatible, in practical diplomatic terms there was an important choice to be made in the matter of priorities. Was finding a way to prevent a nuclear arms race so important as to take priority over other postwar goals, including a unified European economy?

By the end of 1944, the secretary of war had made up his mind: securing postwar concessions from the Soviet Union should take priority over the international control of atomic energy. As he explained in a meeting with Roosevelt on the last day of 1944: "I believed that it was essential not to take them into our confidence until we were sure to get a real quid pro quo from our frankness. I said I had no illusions as to the possibility of keeping permanently such a secret but that I did not think it was time to share it with Russia."[69] In response to renewed entreaties from Bush with regard to international control following the Yalta Conference in February 1945, Stimson reasserted that he was "still inclined to tread softly and to hold off conferences on the subject until we have some much more tangible 'fruits of repentance' from the Russians as a quid pro quo for such a communication to them."[70]

Stimson was relatively clear on what he hoped to gain in exchange for allowing the Soviet Union to participate in an international plan for the control of atomic energy. He was determined that the United States should insist on both economic access to Soviet-occupied territory in Germany, eastern Europe, and Asia and the "liberalization [of Soviet society] in exchange for S-1 [the atomic bomb]."[71] Though this was an ambitious agenda, it was circumscribed to some extent by his fundamental conservatism. Stimson had little interest in using the atomic secret to dictate the political or territorial settlement in eastern Europe. The issue of what political faction would control Poland, which would later greatly excite Harry Truman and his advisers, never concerned the secretary of war. Though strongly committed to economic liberalism and the open door, he (like Roosevelt) was willing to concede a political and territorial sphere of influence to the Soviets in eastern Europe. In response to efforts to apply the Declaration on Liberated Europe (in which Stalin at Yalta had agreed to free elections in the countries liberated from the Nazis) to the countries of eastern Europe, Stimson scrawled a dismissive note: "Good but we won't get far and I doubt whether we should get messed up in it."[72]

The question of whether Stimson's effort to use the lure of an atomic partnership to secure economic concessions (and perhaps some form of "liberalization") from the Soviet Union could have succeeded was rendered moot by a fundamental flaw in his proposed approach. As 1945 dawned, neither Stimson nor Roosevelt, who had expressed broad agreement with the idea of using the atomic secret as a bargaining chip, had defined a strategy for how, exactly, to go about obtaining the desired quid pro quo.[73] Most notably, neither man had resolved the question of how the United States could use the atomic bomb as a bargaining chip while at the same time insisting on keeping it secret. As the title character in Stanley Kubrick's 1964 cold war classic *Dr. Strangelove* pointed out, "the whole point of the Doomsday Machine is lost if you keep it a secret!" It is similarly unclear how Stimson hoped to achieve the desired "fruits of repentance" from Stalin without spilling the secret and entering into "conferences on the subject."[74]

Historian Gar Alperovitz has suggested that Stimson consciously pursued a strategy of "delayed showdown" with the Soviets, holding off negotiations with Stalin until the United States had publicly demonstrated the power of the bomb. Though the temptation to delay negotiations over the bomb grew stronger as the Manhattan Project came closer to fruition, it was not until May 1945 that Stimson explicitly embraced such a strategy (in this case, with respect to the timing of the Potsdam Conference).[75] Prior to that point, the "strategy" of delay appears to have reflected not a well-crafted master plan on the part of the secretary of war so much as a genuine uncertainty as to how exactly to use the atomic secret as a bargaining chip. For Stimson, "atomic diplomacy" never included any suggestion of either using or threatening (explicitly or implicitly) to use the bomb as a military weapon against the Soviet Union. Short of that, he was never able to craft a strategy that would extract economic and political concessions from the Soviets while preserving the foundations of a cooperative postwar relationship.

It is unclear whether Stimson's support would have made any immediate difference given Roosevelt's previous commitments to Churchill, but the secretary's halting attempts to use the atomic secret as a quid pro quo deprived the advocates of international control of a natural and powerful ally in the campaign to sway the president (and his successor). Perhaps more important, in the absence of a strategy for pursuing negotiations over international control, the secretary of war presided over a number of policies that accelerated the onset of the nuclear arms race.

"Raw Material" and the Road to Stassfurt

The top-secret mission to retrieve over a thousand tons of uranium from Stassfurt before it fell into Soviet hands is perhaps the most dramatic example of a set of pre-Hiroshima American policies that fed directly into the emerging cold war arms race. The chain of events that led Stimson to approve this operation in April 1945 originated in a combination of science, geology, geography, and diplomacy.

To exploit the possibilities of nuclear fission for military purposes required access to sufficiently large quantities of fissionable material, most notably uranium. Even if a plutonium bomb could be made to work, uranium was still necessary as a fuel in order to produce weapons-grade plutonium in a nuclear reactor. Given the uncertainty over how much uranium would be required for a chain reaction, controlling access to known "sources of raw material" was a crucial diplomatic and military goal from the beginning of the American nuclear project.[76] Wartime decisions with respect to fissionable materials, while not necessarily all-controlling with respect to postwar arrangements, were also an early practical test of how American leaders viewed the chances for international control.

As historians Gregg Herken and Robert Norris have chronicled, General Leslie Groves worked hard to monopolize control of as much uranium as possible from the beginning of his tenure as military head of the Manhattan Project in 1942.[77] Stimson was aware and approved of Groves's ore-gathering activities, but he paid only passing attention to this issue at the outset of the American program. The secretary of war's interest in the uranium question grew in 1944–45 in direct proportion to his desire to use the atomic secret as a quid pro quo in negotiations with the Soviet Union. Without defining a strategy for how such negotiations were to take place, Stimson strongly supported efforts aimed at bringing much of the world's known stocks of uranium under Anglo-American control.

In June 1944, Stimson helped oversee the creation of the Anglo-American Combined Development Trust (CDT). Building on work begun unilaterally by Groves (who was appointed chair of the new organization), the CDT's mission was to survey and gain control of "ores not within the respective territories of Great Britain, the United States of America, and the Dominion of Canada," specifically uranium and thorium.[78] Despite his genuine commitment to the principle of free trade and his oft-stated concern with assuring "equality and freedom in regard to the natural resources of the world," Stimson was not ready to support an open door for uranium.[79]

In October 1944, the secretary of war endorsed a $12.5 million check made out to Groves. The check, ostensibly for the purchase of "supplies," was intended to bankroll a secret account for the purchase of uranium on the world market. When Secretary of the Treasury Morgenthau refused to process the check without knowing what the money was for, Stimson browbeat him and even considered depositing the money in a private bank (First National) in New York.[80] Morgenthau ultimately relented, and CDT negotiators used the funds (later supplemented with additional millions of dollars) to secure exclusive contracts for materials from Brazil, the Belgian Congo, India, and the Dutch East Indies prior to the bomb's first use. In September 1944, Groves estimated in a memorandum to the secretary of war that the United States and United Kingdom would control 90 percent of the world's uranium by the end of the war, a figure he later revised to 97 percent in the aftermath of Hiroshima and Nagasaki.[81]

The existence of the CDT and its multi-million dollar slush fund did not, by itself, preclude an eventual agreement on international control of either fissionable materials or atomic weapons. In theory, American and British leaders could have bargained away control of the resources acquired by the CDT in exchange for the kinds of Soviet concessions that Stimson was seeking. Neither Roosevelt nor Churchill was so inclined, however, and in practice the CDT worked toward ensuring a postwar Anglo-American nuclear monopoly. Moreover, the very task of gathering those materials worked against Stimson's preferred solution of a quid pro quo for Soviet involvement in international control. To the extent that Stimson was eventually lured into pursuing a strategy of "delayed showdown" with the Soviet Union, the task of gathering raw materials played an important role.

Negotiations with foreign governments for control of their supplies of uranium were delicate and time-consuming and would have been greatly complicated had the Soviet Union suddenly entered the picture as an alternate suitor. It was thus in the interest of the CDT to hold off any revelation of the existence of an Anglo-American bomb project until contracts for foreign supplies of uranium were completed. Keeping the Soviets in the dark as long as possible not only simplified the task of quietly obtaining uranium on the world market but also held out the hope that the United States and United Kingdom could negotiate from strength after the war, having locked up access to the lion's share of the crucial raw materials. In practice, the delay dictated by the race to secure Anglo-American control over the world's uranium meant that there would no revelation of the atomic secret, and hence no negotiations over its future control, until after the use of the bomb against Japan.[82] Waiting until after first use in combat—while secretly working to establish monopoly control of the world's known supplies of uranium—undermined the already shaky relationship between the two emerging superpowers and fueled the postwar arms race.

If the activities of the CDT worked at cross-purposes to Stimson's own stated desire for an eventual agreement with the USSR on the bomb, his endorsement of a series of covert actions in Germany conducted by the secretive Alsos organization was a tacit admission that the arms race was already under way. The Alsos project—from a Greek word meaning "sacred grove"—had its origins in a September 1943 plan to send Allied agents into Italy in the wake of the advancing American and British armies. Their mission was to gather intelligence on the German nuclear program as well as other enemy scientific and technical projects related to the war.[83] Alsos teams, which contained a mix of Anglo-American military and scientific personnel, continued their work in France after D-Day and were vital in uncovering the fact—in November 1944—that the German atomic program had failed to proceed past the stage of basic research.[84]

As Germany collapsed in the early months of 1945, Alsos played an increasingly important role in the struggle for the postwar control of atomic energy. Though fears of a Nazi bomb had almost entirely evaporated, the fate of the German atomic scientists, their stocks of uranium, and any apparatuses they had managed to construct during the war remained unclear. German documents seized by Alsos teams in liberated France indicated that at least some of these potentially valuable resources lay outside the allotted American and British zones of occupation in Germany. Targets in the Soviet zone included the Kaiser Wilhelm Institute in Berlin, the Auer Gesellschaft uranium plant in Oranienburg, and large stores of unprocessed uranium in Stassfurt. Additional targets, including many of the German atomic scientists, were located in a zone that was soon to be occupied by the French.

Targets in the Soviet zone not easily reached by Alsos were bombed from the air. The Kaiser Wilhelm Institute had already been bombed in February 1944 as part of the effort to hamper Nazi nuclear efforts.[85] In March 1945, Groves recommended to Army Chief of Staff George C. Marshall that the German uranium plant at Oranienburg be destroyed from the air, a recommendation that Marshall approved and that was subsequently carried out by the U.S. Eighth Air Force under the command of Lieutenant General Carl A. Spaatz. A desire to deny the Soviets access to this facility after the war played an important role in the decision to attack it, as Groves revealed in his mem-oir.[86] It is unclear whether Stimson was informed of the air raid on Oranien-burg. He did, however, play an important role in a more dramatic operation inside the borders of Germany.

In February 1945, an American Alsos operative in London cabled Groves in Washington warning that "Russians have already shown possible interest TA [atomic bomb] problem and believed knowledge and raw material probably ob-tained from Germany will greatly aid them in future attempt to produce motor device."[87] In light of this, the Alsos team requested specific instructions as to how to proceed with potential targets of interest within the Soviet zone of occu-pation in Germany. Concerned with the larger diplomatic implications of con-ducting such operations, Groves consulted with the secretary of war, and both men initially agreed that "[n]o attempt should be made to enter Russian con-trolled territory in Germany." Stimson also rejected a plan to have the secretary of state negotiate a settlement with French leaders that would have allowed the United States to take over a portion of the French zone of occupation where most of the German atomic scientists and their laboratory were believed to be located. The concern in both cases was to avoid taking any steps "which would draw attention to our intense and immediate interest in the particular prob-lem."[88] But the lure of the scientists and uranium, and the fear that both might fall into Soviet hands, ultimately proved too great for Stimson to resist.

On April 6, 1945, the secretary of war approved a top-secret plan code-named "Operation Harborage." Rather than pursuing the matter through normal diplomatic channels, the United States dispatched Alsos teams to tar-gets of interest in the French and Russian zones to "get everything we want out of there in a hurry and leave nothing behind."[89] One team was dispatched to the towns of Haigerloch, Hechingen, and Talfingen ahead of the occupying French forces. There they rounded up most of the remaining German atomic scientists and discovered an incomplete atomic pile, which they disassembled and shipped westward, destroying any remaining evidence before they left.[90] Another team was dispatched to Stassfurt in the Soviet zone to secretly spirit away the uranium stored there. At Stassfurt, Alsos acted as the covert arm of the CDT, denying the Soviets access to the uranium while further increasing the Anglo-American stockpile.

There is no evidence that Stimson agonized over his role in approving the Stassfurt operation or believed it would jeopardize the chances for an eventual agreement on international control. Undoubtedly he saw the Anglo-American uranium power play as prelude to what he called "pretty rough and realistic" negotiations with Stalin over the postwar settlement and eventually the bomb itself.[91] The secretary of war did not, at the time, pause to consider the extent to which these potentially provocative incursions might further complicate prospects for a Soviet-American understanding he still believed vital to cementing a lasting peace. Not only did the covert scramble for uranium further add to the difficulty of opening negotiations over international control during the war, but it also carried the real risk of creating a serious diplomatic incident. Indeed, an Alsos team near Wismar, Germany, in early May ended up lost behind Soviet lines and escaped only with "considerable difficulty" after being interrogated by a Soviet officer.[92]

A New President Inherits the Arms Race, April 1945

Any hope that the United States might pull back from the emerging arms race suffered another blow with the death of Franklin D. Roosevelt in April 1945. On the surface, this assertion appears paradoxical. Prior to his death Roosevelt showed no inclination to share the atomic secret with the Soviets, choosing instead to embrace an Anglo-American partnership that extended into the postwar period. But by holding his nuclear cards close to the vest, FDR had ensured that he would have the flexibility to revisit the issue of international control at the close of the war. Had Roosevelt wished to escape the wartime nuclear agreements made with Churchill at Quebec and Hyde Park, he could have truthfully cited the need for congressional approval of any diplomatic arrangements that extended into the postwar period. Britain was highly dependent on American aid for postwar rebuilding and would have had little leverage to exert on the United States on nuclear issues following the conclusion of the war.

None of this implies that Roosevelt necessarily *would* have reversed his commitment to Churchill and embraced the international control of atomic weapons had he lived to the end of the war. Certainly the evidence up to his death does not point in that direction. But Roosevelt, with his deep knowledge of the diplomatic history of the bomb project, his experience in the art of coalition diplomacy, and the domestic political prowess that had allowed him to win an unprecedented four terms in office, had left himself substantial freedom of action to revisit the question of how to deal with the bomb after the war. Whether by design or simply as a byproduct of his leadership style, FDR had purchased that flexibility at the expense of a well-crafted set of formal policy directives that could guide either his advisers or his successor following his death. When Harry S. Truman was sworn in as president on April 12, 1945, he unknowingly inherited not only the Manhattan Project but also the complicated and often informal set of wartime diplomatic arrangements and decisions that had already led to a de facto arms race with the Soviet Union.

Stimson stayed on as secretary of war following Roosevelt's death and played an important role in transmitting the history and assumptions of the previous administration's nuclear policy to the new president. In spite of their differences in personality and occasional disputes over policy, Stimson greatly respected FDR as war leader. Upon learning of Roosevelt's death, he lamented the loss of both "a real personal friend" and a visionary leader whose influence would be sorely missed at a crucial time in the nation's history:

> I have never concealed the fact that I regarded his administrative procedure as disorderly, but his foreign policy was always founded on great foresight and keenness of vision, and coming at this period when the war is closing and will I feel sure be succeeded by a period of great confusion of ideas in this country, the loss of his leadership will be most serious.[93]

Any successor would have had trouble living up to the standard set by Roosevelt, but Stimson was particularly concerned about whether the failed haberdasher turned Missouri machine politician was up to the role of commander in chief.

Though Truman and the secretary of war shared in common service as artillery officers in World War I, they came from very different backgrounds. Unlike the men under whom Stimson was accustomed to serving, the new president did not hail from the kind of cosmopolitan milieu traditionally associated with "the richer and more intelligent citizens of the country."[94] Stimson biographer Godfrey Hodgson was likely correct in assessing the secretary's attitude toward Truman in April 1945 as "friendly but patronizing."[95] And though the secretary of war would ultimately develop a healthy respect for the man from Independence, Missouri, his personal and professional relationship with Truman was never as close as the one he had enjoyed with Franklin Roosevelt.

On a practical level, Stimson was particularly concerned that the new president "knew very little of the task into which he was stepping."[96] Most important of all, Truman knew nothing about the atomic bomb. Prior to 1944, the secretary of war had made it his business to ensure that Senator Truman remained ignorant on this matter. Following a series of sharp encounters with Truman during a congressional investigation into appropriations for the Manhattan Project in early 1944, the secretary of war acidly remarked that the senator was "a nuisance and a pretty untrustworthy man. He talks smoothly but he acts meanly."[97] Stimson's personal animus toward Truman cooled when the latter entered the Roosevelt administration as vice president. But even as he moved to within a heartbeat of the presidency, Truman remained in the dark when it came to the atomic secret.

At noon on April 25, 1945, Stimson, accompanied by Groves, arrived at the White House via a secret underground entrance to avoid attracting the attention of the press. Though Truman confidant James Byrnes had given the new president an informal description on the bomb project shortly after he took office on April 12, this was to be the president's first official briefing on the subject. The session was focused on what Stimson referred to as the "political aspects" of the bomb.[98] The memorandum that the secretary of war presented that afternoon was eloquent in its description of the challenges raised by the existence of the bomb project. It represented not so much a change of heart—Stimson had always worried about the postwar implications of the bomb—as much as a change in emphasis. Pulling back from the technical and military questions associated with Alsos and the CDT that had dominated his attention in the months before Roosevelt's death, the secretary of war sought to highlight the basic moral and diplomatic dilemma posed by the existence of the Manhattan Project.

"Within four months," Stimson began, "we shall in all probability have completed the most terrible weapon ever known in human history, one bomb of which could destroy a whole city." The secretary of war went on to perceptively outline the long-term diplomatic, military, and moral dilemmas posed by the bomb. Though the United States was "at present in the position of controlling the resources with which to construct and use it," he impressed upon Truman the fact that "it is practically certain that we could not remain in this position indefinitely."

> [I]t is extremely probable that the future will make it possible to be constructed by smaller nations or even groups, or at least by a large nation in a much shorter time. . . . As a result, it is indicated that the future may see a time when such a weapon may be constructed in secret and used suddenly and effectively with devastating power by a willful nation or group against an unsuspecting nation or group of much greater size and material power.[99]

Given the impossibility of maintaining an American nuclear monopoly in perpetuity, Stimson stressed that "the question of sharing it with other nations and, if so shared, upon what terms, becomes a primary question of our foreign relations," one which would need to be addressed before there could be any serious discussion of a "world peace organization." According to Groves's account of the meeting, a "great deal of emphasis was placed on foreign relations and particularly on the Russian situation."[100]

Beyond these practical questions, the secretary of war also squarely raised with Truman the moral issues that had troubled him to some degree since the inception of the project. Expanding on a theme that he had first asserted in the wake of World War I, Stimson lamented that the "world in its present state of moral advancement compared with its technical development would be eventually at the mercy of such a weapon."[101] The power of the bomb was such that it would be difficult to limit its effects to the battlefield. If not properly controlled, "modern civilization might be completely destroyed." The United States, he asserted, by virtue of its unique role in developing the atomic bomb had "a certain moral responsibility upon us which we cannot shirk without very serious responsibility for any disaster to civilization which it would further." After outlining these grave challenges, Stimson closed on an optimistic note, suggesting that if the challenges could somehow be overcome, the effort to control the bomb might provide "a pattern in which the peace of the world and our civilization can be saved."[102]

The memorandum that Stimson presented to the new president on April 25 was rich with irony and tragedy. It represented, on the one hand, the summation of a long public career dedicated to grappling with the challenges posed by war to the existence of an increasingly interdependent human civilization spread across the globe. Yet his thoughtful memorandum had already been overtaken by the facts on the ground. From the beginning of the American nuclear program, its overseers, including Stimson, had been torn between seeking a long-term international solution to the dangers of nuclear fission and the short-term diplomatic advantages that might be gained by using the bomb as a bargaining chip. Without deeply considering the consequences, the secretary of war had joined Roosevelt in embracing the atomic secret as a potential diplomatic bargaining chip. Despite talk of eventual negotiations on international control, Stimson was for all intents and purposes *already* presiding over a one-sided nuclear arms race with the Soviet Union in April 1945. Truman inherited this situation when he took office.

With Los Alamos on the verge of testing the world's first nuclear weapon, Truman and his advisers had only a few short months in which to reconsider the assumptions that had helped produce that arms race. At the same time, the new president and his advisers confronted a series of diplomatic and military decisions with respect to Japan and the culmination of the war in Pacific. For much of the war, issues relating to the diplomatic aspects of the bomb and its more immediate prospects as a weapon of war had been discussed separately, often by different groups of people in locations ranging from Washington to Los Alamos. Beginning in May 1945, these various threads came together at the highest levels of the U.S. government in a series of intense debates that shaped the dawn of the atomic age.

Chapter 5

The Ordeal of Henry L. Stimson

ON THE EVENING OF MAY 8, 1945, THE SECRETARY OF WAR ATTENDED a somber service of thanksgiving at the Presbyterian Church of the Covenant in Washington, D.C. The occasion for the special service led by pastor Dr. Albert Joseph McCartney was V-E Day, marking the surrender of Nazi Germany. For the previous five years, Stimson had devoted much of his energy toward this moment. And yet the secretary was not in a particularly celebratory mood that evening. Though he took "sober satisfaction" in the long-awaited victory, "[i]t was not," he confided to his diary, "a day of exuberance or hysterical demonstrations."[1]

As he listened to Dr. McCartney's sermon, Stimson was undoubtedly reflecting on the challenges still to come. Before going to church, the secretary of war had met with military and civilian leaders at the Pentagon to discuss the ongoing campaign against Japan. Though that nation's military defeat was now assured, there remained the tricky question of how to induce a Japanese surrender without massive bloodletting on both sides. Moreover, military victory over the Axis posed its own set of diplomatic challenges. Earlier that day,

Stimson had spoken by phone with Assistant Secretary of War John J. Mc-Cloy, who was in San Francisco representing the War Department at the international conference tasked with setting up the United Nations. The trials McCloy recounted to his boss were another reminder that the postwar settlement hung in precarious balance during the closing months of the war.[2]

Overlying these military and diplomatic dilemmas was the escalating bloodshed of the war's last year. As much as Stimson craved victory, he simultaneously worried that the indiscriminate use of force in pursuit of that goal would sow seeds of bitterness and hatred, undermining the foundations of any peace that followed. Several months before attending McCartney's V-E Day sermon, Stimson had written to the pastor to congratulate him on an article written by his son, Benjamin. Lieutenant Benjamin C. McCartney's article in *National Geographic* highlighted the efforts of American pilots to avoid damaging cultural and religious monuments in bombing the Axis-held cities of Europe.[3] While admiring the "fine spirit and care which was evidenced in your son's article," Stimson also confessed his concern "that the terrible character of modern bombing would render our people callous and brutal. I have feared that the poor people of France and Italy would therefore be unable to distinguish our work from that of the Axis brutalities which we denounce and are fighting against."[4]

It was in the context of this overlapping set of military, diplomatic, and moral concerns that Stimson confronted the atomic bomb in the wake of the Nazi defeat. Much of his busy V-E Day was taken up with discussions regarding the bomb, including the selection of members to sit on a newly created body (the Interim Committee) tasked with considering the weighty issues raised by atomic fission. In the hectic weeks following the German surrender, the secretary was unable to give his full attention to these questions. It was not until May 28, 1945, upon returning to Washington following a ten-day working vacation at his Long Island estate, that he felt prepared to tackle the issue that would dominate the remainder of his tenure in office. "I have made up my mind," Stimson confided to his diary, "to make [the atomic bomb] my primary occupation for these next few months, relieving myself so far as possible from all routine matters in the Department."[5]

Stimson's resolution to tackle the many challenges raised by nuclear weapons corresponded with a crucial period in which policymakers in Washington wrestled with the remaining questions that would fix the context of the bomb's wartime use. The choices open to Truman and his advisers had narrowed in the years since the inception of the Manhattan Project. Though Roosevelt had remained noncommittal about the use of the bomb to the end of his life, the momentum of the $2 billion project and the ongoing war with Japan made it nearly impossible for his inexperienced successor to consider not using such a weapon. Manhattan Project head General Leslie Groves later remarked that with respect to the use of the bomb, Truman was "like a little boy on a toboggan."[6] But while combat use of the bomb was probably inevitable so long as the war with Japan continued, there remained a number of important questions about *how* the bomb was to be used. In May 1945, the diplomatic issues raised by nuclear fission, including international control and relations with the Soviet Union, intertwined with the practical and moral questions posed by potential combat use of the bomb against Japan.

Decoupling the Diplomatic Track with Japan

The first of the overlapping A–bomb–related questions that Stimson confronted following his return to Washington on May 28 involved Japan. Prior to 1945, discussions about the diplomatic implications of nuclear fission had focused almost exclusively on the Soviet Union and Great Britain. Indeed, for most of the war, Stimson had paid comparatively little attention to the Pacific theater. In February 1945, following a meeting with Marshall on "the coming campaign against Japan," Stimson conceded that "I have never studied it or thought over it in the way that I had over the war in Europe."[7] But starting in early 1945 and accelerating with the end of the war in Europe, Stimson and other American policymakers faced a decision on how to integrate the atomic bomb into their diplomatic and military calculations regarding Japan.[8]

After the war, Stimson and other defenders of the A-bomb decision insisted that they had faced a stark choice between a costly invasion of the Japanese home islands and the use of the bomb against Japanese cities.[9] In spring 1945, however, it was not certain that either an invasion or atomic bombs would be necessary to compel surrender. The Imperial Japanese Navy had virtually ceased to exist following the Battle of Leyte Gulf in October 1944. American submarines were strangling and isolating Japan's home islands while Army Air Forces bombers gradually reduced its cities to ashes. Japan's increasingly precipitous military decline did not necessarily mean that surrender was imminent. The brutal battle for Okinawa (the last stepping-stone on the path to the home islands) in April–June 1945 proved that Japanese resistance could still be quite fierce. But even as the fighting on that island raged, some in the Truman administration were pondering a combination of threats and promises that might hasten Japanese surrender and achieve vital American war aims through diplomatic means.[10]

The stated policy of the Truman administration was that the United States would accept nothing less than Japan's total and unconditional surrender. Truman had inherited this formula from Roosevelt, who had publicly proclaimed Allied war aims to include "an unconditional surrender by Germany, Italy and Japan" following a meeting with Churchill at Casablanca in January 1943.[11] In practice, however, Roosevelt's own record on unconditional surrender was mixed. While he had insisted on applying that formula to Nazi Germany, Italy had been allowed to negotiate terms in September 1943 that fell short of unconditional surrender. The question in spring 1945 was whether similar flexibility ought to be granted to Japan if doing so might expedite the end of the war and save American lives.

During a review of American military strategy in the Pacific on April 25, 1945, the Joint Chiefs of Staff (JCS) recommended that " 'unconditional surrender' should be defined in terms understandable to the Japanese, who must be convinced that destruction or national suicide is not implied."[12] Several weeks later, shortly before departing for his working vacation on Long Island, Stimson received a "rather dramatic and radical" memorandum from ex-president Herbert Hoover warning that an invasion of Japan would be disastrous and suggesting that the United States should instead offer a clear set of surrender terms. Hoover's memorandum echoed ongoing discussions within the Army General Staff and the War Department's Operations Division (OPD) on clarifying or perhaps abandoning unconditional surrender. By the end of May, civilian leaders in both the War and State Departments, including Undersecretary of State Joseph Grew and Stimson deputy John J. McCloy, had determined to bring this question to the highest levels of the U.S. government.[13]

When Stimson arrived back in Washington on May 28, McCloy presented him with a memorandum urging a reconsideration of the policy of unconditional surrender. In language that mirrored the secretary of war's earlier condemnation of the Morgenthau Plan for Germany, McCloy asserted that

"Japan is struggling to find a way out of the horrible mess she has got herself into" and urged that the United States avoid seeking to impose a "Carthaginian" peace. On the subject of unconditional surrender, McCloy conveyed his belief that the United States could likely "accomplish everything we want to accomplish in regard to Japan without the use of that term." Failure to clarify and perhaps soften American terms might "hold them off to the point where we go on digging them out of caves at considerable cost to ourselves when our important objectives can be won without this attrition."[14]

On the same day, Grew (then acting as secretary of state while Edward Stettinius was attending the San Francisco Conference) suggested an even more specific change in U.S. policy. In a meeting with Truman, Grew advised that the "greatest obstacle to unconditional surrender by the Japanese is their belief that this would entail the destruction or permanent removal of the Emperor and the institution of the Throne." Grew understood that the institution of the emperor was the one unifying element of the Japanese political and military structure, "without which surrender will be highly unlikely."[15] Suggesting that a recent series of devastating attacks on Tokyo inflicted by American bombers offered a fortuitous moment to issue such a clarification, Grew pleaded for a statement guaranteeing the postwar status of the emperor. According to Grew's later account of the meeting, the president indicated that "his own thoughts had been following the same line" but asked the acting secretary to clear the proposal with Stimson, Army Chief of Staff Marshall, and Secretary of the Navy James V. Forrestal.[16] The result was an informal conference of the president's chief military and diplomatic advisers in Stimson's Pentagon office on May 29, 1945.

Stimson, motivated by a desire to end the war quickly and entirely uninterested in dictating the form of the postwar Japanese government, was sympathetic to calls for modifying American surrender terms. From the outset of American participation in the conflict, he had sought to balance the goal of "complete victory" with that of shortening the war and thus reducing both the loss of life and the burden of reconstruction that would face the victorious Allies.[17] And though he insisted on the importance of Germany's unconditional surrender, the secretary of war eagerly embraced compromises far short of that formula when it came to Hitler's partners and vassals.

The first example of Stimson's willingness to compromise on surrender terms came early in the war, prior to the public formulation of the unconditional surrender doctrine. During the course of the November 1942 landings in North Africa, Stimson strongly supported the deal struck by General Dwight D. Eisenhower with Admiral Jean Francois Darlan, commander in chief of the Vichy military forces. The so-called Darlan deal, under which the former Vichy commander was granted political authority over French North Africa in exchange for an agreement not to oppose the American landings, produced howls of outrage in the United States and Great Britain. To Stimson, however, the Darlan deal accurately reflected the priorities of the Allied war effort. Germany, not Vichy France, was the main enemy, and continental Europe, not North Africa, was the important theater of operations.[18] The secretary of war supported the Darlan deal as a way to save American lives.

Even after Roosevelt publicly proclaimed the unconditional surrender formula, the secretary of war was still eager to seek compromise outside the special case of Nazi Germany if it might shorten the war. Stimson repeatedly warned Roosevelt regarding what he laconically referred to as the dangers of "too much unconditional surrender on Italy." That nation posed little military threat by itself, and "the people of the United States," Stimson observed, were not "interested the least little bit in taking a great part in the politics of Italy." During the secret negotiations between American representatives and Italian Marshall Pietro Badoglio, the secretary of war repeatedly voiced support for a deal that allowed Italy a conditional surrender.[19]

Stimson's willingness to compromise with Italy and Vichy France reflected his judgment that the pursuit of victory needed to be tempered with an appreciation of the dangers of prolonged warfare to the fragile foundations of "industrial civilization." The secretary of war approached the problem of Japan in general and the emperor in particular with the same calculation in mind. Following any surrender, the United States would have to disarm Japan's military and seize many of its former bases in the Pacific in order to guard against any future acts of aggression. Beyond those basic requirements, he saw no need to engage in the sort of extensive reconstruction and rehabilitation that the Allies were implementing in occupied Germany. Stimson had never at any point in his career believed that the elimination of the emperor or the emperor system was necessary to check Japanese militarism. In the dying days of the war in the Pacific, he explicitly opposed any attempts to remake "the government of [Japan] as a whole in any such manner as we are committed in Germany. I am afraid we would make a hash of it if we tried."[20]

At the meeting on May 29 including Marshall, Forrestal, Grew, and State Department Far East expert Eugene Dooman, Stimson "was inclined to agree with giving the Japanese a modification of the unconditional surrender formula without the use of those words." He indicated, however, that "the timing was wrong and this was not the time to do it," a sentiment with which Marshall voiced agreement.[21] Stimson and Marshall's opposition carried the day, and the meeting adjourned without any further action taken on the question of surrender terms for Japan. This delay turned out to be highly significant in shaping the context of the bomb's use. Deliberations on surrender terms continued sporadically in the aftermath of this meeting, but by tabling the issue until an unspecified later date, Stimson and Marshall had decoupled the diplomatic track from discussion about the use of the atomic bomb at a crucial moment. In May–June 1945, American leaders made important decisions about both the use of the bomb and the invasion of the Japanese home islands without ever pausing to consider their minimum acceptable definition of victory.

Why did the secretary of war advise a delay in considering a modification of American surrender terms in May 1945? It was not any newfound commitment to the principal of unconditional surrender. The day *after* the May 29 meeting, Stimson wrote to Marshall and explicitly endorsed McCloy's suggestion that the United States should back away from insisting on an unconditional Japanese surrender.[22] In the weeks that followed, Stimson explicitly spoke in favor of allowing the Japanese to retain the emperor. Why, then, did he counsel delay at the crucial meeting on May 29?

Grew's account of the reasoning reason behind this delay was cryptic, recording simply that "for certain military reasons, not divulged, it was considered inadvisable for the President to make a statement just now."[23] Stimson later claimed that he favored a delay because "we were having considerable trouble with the Japanese in the land campaign on Okinawa and some of us were afraid that any public concession at that time might have been taken as an indication of weaknss."[24] But none of the contemporary accounts of the May 29 meeting, including Stimson's diary, mention the fighting on Okinawa as a reason for delaying a restatement of American terms. Instead we have a vague reference (in Grew's diary) to "certain military reasons, not divulged."[25] There was nothing secretive about the ongoing fighting on Okinawa and hence no reason for either Stimson or Marshall to offer such an elliptical response if this had been their primary concern. Moreover, even if such fears had made Stimson and Marshall hesitate to issue an immediate public statement on the emperor, there was no reason not to at least reach an internal consensus on the issue, agreeing on a revised set of terms that Truman could present when the time and tide of battle appeared fortuitous.

After the war, Grew and several of his former State Department colleagues were still frustrated and puzzled by the outcome of the May 29 meeting on surrender terms. Dooman privately blasted Stimson's postwar explanations for the delay, characterizing them as "disingenuous" and "sinister."[26] After a discussion with Grew in 1947, former State Department official William R. Castle (who had worked under Stimson in the Hoover administration) confided his own suspicions: "I wonder whether Stimson, with Marshall, wanted [the] war to continue long enough to give them a chance to try out the atom bomb on Japanese cities. The more I think of that performance the more I feel that it was indefensible as well as brutal."[27] But while Castle had no way of knowing it, Stimson was, in fact, far from eager to use the bomb and ultimately made a last-ditch effort behind the scenes to secure surrender without the use of this terrible new weapon.

The real explanation for Stimson's seemingly curious performance on May 29 was his continuing uncertainty over how, exactly, to integrate the atomic bomb into American diplomacy. "It was an awkward meeting," the secretary of war confided in his diary, "because there were people present in the presence of whom I could not discuss the real feature which would govern the whole situation, namely S-1 [the atomic bomb]."[28] Preoccupied with a wide range of issues relating to the use of the bomb and the shape of the postwar world, Stimson assumed that a formal decision on clarifying and perhaps softening surrender terms could wait until the bomb was closer to readiness. Once the bomb was tested and ready for use, he would presumably have a better idea of how to integrate this new weapon with diplomatic approaches to Japan.

According to McCloy, the secretary understood that the May 29 decision to delay a restatement of American terms "only postponed consideration of the matter for a time . . . for we shall have to consider it again preparatory to the employment of S-1."[29] What Stimson did not appreciate was how difficult it would be to revisit the diplomatic track with Japan after the technical and military decisions about how to use the bomb were made in the days that followed the May 29 meeting. To this extent, Stimson's strategy with respect to Japan mirrored his approach to the Soviet Union and international control. In both cases, delay would contribute to tragedies that the secretary of war would later regret.

"The Targets Suggested . . . Have Been Disapproved"

Having decided to temporarily table consideration of surrender terms on May 29, Stimson and Marshall dismissed the rest of the group while they stayed behind (with McCloy taking notes) to discuss more practical matters related to the use of the bomb. In considering "Japan and what we should do in regard to S-1 and the application of it," Stimson and Marshall returned to a set of questions about use that they had deferred in the previous years.[30] One of the subjects they discussed that afternoon was nuclear targeting and the mass killing of Japanese civilians.

Prior to May 1945, discussions of nuclear targeting had been almost entirely confined to the scientists and engineers at Los Alamos in concert with a handful of lower-level AAF officers. Driven by technical concerns, work at Los Alamos had gradually coalesced around a weapon optimized for use against cities and civilians. By December 1944, the only question so far as Ordnance Division chief William Parsons was concerned was which Japanese city would be destroyed first.[31] Beginning in late January 1945, AAF and Los Alamos personnel met with increasing frequency to discuss operational issues relating to the use of the atomic bomb, including the question of targeting. These meetings culminated in April with the formation of a group known as the Target Committee that included representatives from both Los Alamos and the AAF.[32]

The first Target Committee meeting on April 27, 1945, officially ratified the strategy of city targeting that had evolved from the work of Los Alamos and the Ordnance Division. The committee decided that in picking a target they should focus on "large urban areas of not less than 3 miles in diameter existing in the larger populated areas."[33] At a second series of meetings on May 10–11 in Oppenheimer's Los Alamos office, the Target Committee formally rejected the idea of attacking an isolated military target, concluding that "any small and strictly military objective should be located in a much larger area subject to blast damage in order to avoid undue risks of the weapon being lost due to bad placing of the bomb."[34] Operating under the same assumptions that had guided the research and development of the weapon as at Los Alamos, the AAF officers involved in selecting A-bomb targets understood the bomb primarily as a large blast weapon.[35] This logic, along with concerns over the ability of AAF planes to accurately deliver the weapon, led the committee to almost exactly reprise Parsons's earlier recommendations. The bomb would be used in a large urban area where it would be sure to destroy large numbers of lightly constructed buildings and in the process kill many Japanese civilians.

Concerns about maximizing the bomb's blast effects also dictated another recommendation that emerged from the Target Committee: that it should be used against a relatively undamaged city. The first meeting of the Target Committee rated Tokyo low on the target list because it was "now practically all bombed and burned out."[36] This inconvenient fact meant that Tokyo and other previously attacked Japanese cities lacked the abundance of light, undamaged residential and industrial structures that were the ideal targets for the bomb's blast effects. Unconcerned or uninterested in effects produced by fire and radiation, the Target Committee decided that using the bomb against an already damaged Japanese city risked producing little more than the "disappointing" crater that Parsons had warned about in arguing against a noncombat demonstration in 1944.[37]

The third and final meeting of the Target Committee on May 28, 1945, culminated in the selection of Kyoto, Hiroshima, and Niigata as targets for the atomic bomb. All three cities harbored important Japanese war industries. However, in all these cities the most significant military-industrial targets were located on the fringes of the larger urban area. Targeting these war plants risked the possibility that an inaccurate delivery might result in the bomb's exploding entirely outside the city. Moreover, even an accurate attack on one of these factories would fail to make use of the full power of the bomb as there were fewer light structures susceptible to blast on the urban fringes than in the city center. The meeting concluded with the Target Committee members' agreeing to a chilling set of recommendations that endorsed targeting densely populated urban areas at the expense of any effort to hit military-industrial targets:

> [The Target Committee agreed] not to specify aiming points, this is to be left to later determination at base when weather conditions are known.

to neglect location of industrial areas as pin point target, since on these three targets [Kyoto, Hiroshima, and Niigata] such areas are small, spread on fringes of cites and quite dispersed.

to endeavor to place the first gadget in center of selected city; that is, not to allow for later 1 or 2 gadgets for complete destruction.[38]

This was a recommendation that inevitably entailed using the bomb as a weapon for the obliteration of cities and the mass killing of civilians. And while targeting the atomic bombs in the center of Kyoto, Hiroshima, and Niigata ensured that some smaller, scattered military-industrial targets would be destroyed, it also virtually guaranteed that the most significant war industries associated with those three cities would be spared any significant damage.

Stimson and Marshall were unaware of the Target Committee's recommendations when they discussed the bomb in the secretary of war's office on May 29. Unlike the approach of Parsons and the Target Committee, Stimson's thinking about the bomb went well beyond technical efficiency. Civilian casualties were a regrettable but inevitable part of modern warfare. But to *deliberately* target civilians for mass killing not only was immoral but, by harming the international reputation of the United States, might undermine American leadership in the postwar world. Declaring that the "reputation of the United States for fair play and humanitarianism is the world's biggest asset for peace in the coming decades," Stimson repeatedly stressed that he was "anxious to hold our Air Force, so far as possible, to the 'precision' bombing which it has done so well in Europe." In a discussion with Truman on May 16, 1945, he explicitly linked his concerns over strategic bombing to the use of the atomic bomb, suggesting that "the same rules of sparing the civilian population should be applied as far as possible to the use of any new weapons."[39]

In a telephone conversation with McCloy on May 21, Stimson and his assistant secretary discussed the question of the "big bomb" and "when it should be employed and how" with specific reference to "the moral position of the United States and its responsibilities." Recounting this conversation, McCloy confided to his diary "the moral position of the U.S. weighs greatly upon [Stimson]" with respect to the use of the bomb.[40] Reflecting the concerns of the secretary of war, an outline for a presidential statement prepared by Stimson's aides on May 25 and intended for release after the use of the bomb stressed that the United States would "[c]hoose a military target like a naval base if possible so that wholesale killing of civilians will be on the heads of the Japanese who refused to surrender at our ultimatum."[41]

Concerns over the targeting of civilians surfaced again during the discussion between Marshall and Stimson on May 29. "The Secretary," McCloy noted in a memorandum summarizing the discussion, "referred to the burning of Tokyo and the possible ways and means of employing the larger bombs."[42] In the context of Stimson's explicitly stated concerns about indiscriminate incendiary attacks against Tokyo, expressed both before and immediately after the May 29 meeting, this statement strongly suggests that Stimson was troubled by the idea of using the atomic bomb against a primarily civilian target.[43] In response to Stimson's comments, Marshall offered an explicit argument against using the atomic bomb against civilians:

> General Marshall said he thought these weapons might first be used against straight military objectives such as a large naval installation and then if no complete result was derived from the effect of that, he thought we ought to designate a number of large manufacturing areas from which the people would be warned to leave—telling the Japanese that we intend to destroy such centers. . . . Every effort should be made to keep our record of warning clear. We must offset by such warning methods the opprobrium which might follow from an ill considered employment of such force.[44]

Marshall's statement, with its emphasis on limiting the conduct of war against civilians and its attention to the international reputation of the United States, mirrored Stimson's long-held concerns on this subject. These intertwined moral and practical concerns sharply diverged from the recommendation of the Target Committee, with its emphasis on the total destruction of Japanese urban areas. The next day, these divergent approaches to nuclear targeting collided in the secretary of war's Pentagon office.

At 9:20 a.m. on May 30, Harvey Bundy placed a call to General Leslie Groves to inform him that the secretary wanted to see him "right away."[45] When the general arrived at the Pentagon, he found that Stimson was intent on discussing the question of nuclear targeting. Groves had planned to submit the recommendations of the Target Committee directly to the army chief of staff at a later date and attempted to deflect Stimson's questions by declaring that "I would rather not show [the report] to him without having first discussed it with General Marshall."[46] Stimson, according to Groves's later account, reacted sharply to this attempted diversion: "Mr. Stimson said: 'This is one time I'm going to be the final deciding authority. Nobody's going to tell me what to do on this. On this matter I am the kingpin and you might just as well get that report over here.' "[47] While Stimson waited for Groves's staff to fetch the Target Committee's recommendations from his office across the Potomac, the secretary summoned Marshall to join them in a discussion of nuclear targeting.

Stimson's diary is elliptical in its description of the events of that morning, recording simply that "[w]e talked over the subject very thoroughly of how we should use this implement in respect to Japan."[48] Groves's postwar memoir described the ensuing debate as focused primarily on the targeting of Kyoto. Stimson had visited that city in the 1920s while traveling to the Philippines. Citing Kyoto's status as Japan's intellectual and cultural capital, Stimson objected to its inclusion as a target and cited his belief that the targeting decision "should be governed by the historical position that the United States would occupy after the war. He felt very strongly that anything that would tend in any way to damage this position would be unfortunate."[49] Stimson's concern with attacks on Kyoto (either conventional or nuclear) has been well documented.[50] It seems unlikely, however, that Kyoto was the only subject of conversation that morning. The underlying logic of the Target Committee's recommendation, with its narrow emphasis on technical factors and its endorsement of the deliberate destruction of an entire city, sharply contrasted with Stimson's thinking about the conduct of the war as well as Marshall's explicit suggestion that a military target should be given first priority.

A memorandum from Groves to Lauris Norstad, chief of staff of the Twentieth Air Force, written immediately after the May 30 meeting in Stimson's office, suggests that a larger controversy was brewing at the end of May 1945. "Will you please inform General Arnold," Groves wrote to Norstad, "that this AM the Secretary of War and the Chief of Staff did *not* approve the three targets we had selected, particularly Kyoto." The mention of Kyoto supports at least part of Groves's post facto account of the meeting. Yet the reference to "the *three targets* we had selected" suggests that Stimson and Marshall raised objections that went beyond the targeting of Kyoto.[51] When Norstad informed AAF Chief of Staff Henry Arnold of the decision, he omitted mention of Kyoto entirely, noting simply that "targets suggested by General Groves for 509th Composite Group have been disapproved, supposedly by the Secretary of War."[52] Thanks to Stimson's belated intervention, the entire question of nuclear targeting was suddenly thrown into doubt on the eve of the May 31 meeting of the so-called Interim Committee.

International Control, the Soviet Union, and a "Remarkable Document"

Stimson was not the only one troubled by the bomb in May 1945. On May 5, scientist-administrator James Conant wrote to the secretary of war to report "a growing restlessness" among some scientists worried about the international control of atomic energy, "particularly if use should occur before the Russians were notified of the existence of the weapon."[53] It was partially in response to these rumblings that Stimson asked Truman to establish an Interim Committee—including a number of high-level civilian advisers supplemented by scientific and industrial experts—to examine the postwar implications of atomic energy.[54] While the Interim Committee had not been intended to set policy with respect to the use of the bomb, in the midst of this bubbling dissent its deliberations helped to shape how the bomb was eventually employed.

Preparing official public releases regarding the atomic bomb and the future of nuclear energy was one of the Interim Committee's primary responsibilities. Questions about the timing of such releases, however, led to a larger debate about warnings, international control, and the Soviet Union. The minutes of the May 14 meeting (chaired by George Harrison in the absence of Stimson) indicate that at least some members of the committee assumed that the president would issue a public statement if the atomic test in New Mexico scheduled for July 1945 proved to be successful.[55] Such an announcement would have constituted an implicit warning to the Japanese prior to use. An announcement after the Trinity test also would have inevitably led to widespread public discussion over the future of atomic energy control before the bomb was used in combat. It was this latter possibility that produced an intense debate in the last two weeks of May 1945.

Leslie Groves, who was present by invitation at the May 14 meeting, violently objected to the idea of a public announcement after the Trinity test. A memorandum prepared by Groves's office following the meeting cited a number of reasons in opposing such a release, including the danger that it would allow the Japanese to prepare both militarily and politically to blunt the effects of the bomb. Whatever the merits of these arguments, the debate that followed the May 14 meeting revolved not around Japan but rather around the effect that an early announcement would have on the Soviet Union. "Release of information before use of the weapon," Groves's memorandum asserted, "could have an adverse effect on relations with our Allies."[56] There can be no doubt that the primary "Ally" that Groves had in mind was the Soviet Union and that the "adverse effect" he was most concerned about was the possibility that Stalin would demand to be included in the Anglo–American atomic partnership once he officially learned of its existence. Deeply committed to preserving an American nuclear monopoly for as long as possible, Groves also worried that "[e]arly release" of information about the existence of the bomb would complicate the ongoing secret negotiations with Belgium, Brazil, and the Netherlands being conducted by the Combined Development Trust with the aim of locking up much of the world's known supplies of uranium and thorium.[57]

Following another partial meeting of the Interim Committee on May 18, the issue of a post-Trinity test announcement was pushed into the background as debate focused on the question of what steps to take with respect to international control in general and the Soviet Union in particular. Any warning or announcement following a successful test was contingent on an agreement within the administration on how and when to approach Stalin about the bomb.[58]

Stimson's attitude on this crucial question was in a state of flux in spring 1945. Unlike Groves, the secretary of war had no illusions about the feasibility or even desirability of attempting to maintain a nuclear monopoly for very long after the war. In principle, he continued to support postwar international control of atomic energy. Nor had he given up on postwar cooperation with the Soviets in other areas. "It is a very serious matter," Stimson asserted, "for we simply cannot allow a rift to come between the two nations without endangerous [sic] the entire peace of the world."[59] Thus when Truman expressed mounting dismay over Soviet attempts to exert political control over Poland, Stimson urged restraint. In a meeting called to address the Polish question on April 23, Stimson found Truman to be "evidently disappointed at my caution and advice" on the issue. Convinced that the Polish political situation was of little concern to postwar American security, the secretary of war sought to avoid getting entangled in a dispute with Stalin over the issue.[60] Yet for all his caution, the secretary of war's belief that the atomic secret could be used as a bargaining chip in postwar negotiations—and his inability to figure out exactly *how* use it for this purpose—often led him to side tactically with hard-liners such as Groves.

On May 14, the same day that the Interim Committee was considering the question of publicity, Stimson remarked in a conversation with Marshall that "my own opinion was that the time now and the method now to deal with Russia was to keep our mouths shut and let our actions speak for words."

> The Russians will understand them better than anything else. It is a case where we have got to regain the lead and perhaps do it in a pretty rough and realistic way. . . . I told him this was a place where we really held all the cards. I called it a royal straight flush and we mustn't be a fool about the way we play it. They can't get along without our help and industries and we have coming into action a weapon which will be unique. Now the thing is not to get into unnecessary quarrels by talking too much and not to indicate any weakness by talking too much; let our actions speak for themselves.[61]

Stimson was not advocating that the bomb be used to impress the Soviet Union. But his continuing concern over postwar relations with the Soviets did affect his thinking about the context of use. Unable to figure out exactly how to use the bomb as a bargaining chip, he saw delay as an increasingly attractive strategy in spring 1945. By mid-May, he was convinced that the United States should avoid entering into any serious negotiations with Stalin until the bomb—"a royal straight flush"—was ready for use.[62] Like Groves, the secretary of war also hoped to strengthen the postwar U.S. bargaining position by allowing the CDT to secure control of additional supplies of uranium before any public disclosure.

Even as he embraced a strategy of delay, Stimson was increasingly concerned about the prospects for postwar international control. During the May 29 meeting with Marshall and McCloy on the subject of Japan and the bomb, Stimson asked Marshall to read the proposal for international control that Bush and Conant had submitted to him the previous September.[63] The next day, following his meeting with Groves on the subject of targeting,

Stimson received "a very important letter."[64] The letter in question was penned by Oswald C. Brewster, a civilian engineer attached to the Manhattan Project. As a result of his personal connection with the bomb, Brewster had become deeply concerned over its implications for the future of the world. "The possession of this weapon by any other nation, no matter how benign its intentions," Brewster concluded, "could not be tolerated by other great powers." If the United States attempted to retain sole control of the bomb, even with the best of intentions, the results would be dire. "Our elections, our foreign policy, everything we did would be viewed with suspicion and distrust. If we urged our views on the world on any subject we would be charged with threatening to use this weapon as a club. . . . We would be the most hated and feared nation on earth." Brewster's solution was as simple as it was dramatic: "This thing must not be permitted to exist on this earth. . . . With the threat of Germany removed we must stop this project." As for Japan and the war in the Pacific, Brewster stressed that with the materials already produced the United States could build a bomb for the purpose of staging a "demonstration."[65]

It would have been easy enough to ignore an unsolicited letter from a minor civilian figure within the Manhattan Project. Stimson, however, appears to have been deeply moved by what he referred to as "the letter of an honest man."[66] Brewster's clear, direct language and his emphasis on the importance of trust, morality, and the international reputation of the United States clearly appealed to Stimson, who had expressed similar sentiments throughout his own long career. After absorbing the contents of Brewster's letter on the evening of May 30, the secretary of war hurriedly forwarded it to Marshall along with a handwritten note requesting that the army chief of staff read this "remarkable document" in order to "have the impress of its logic" prior to the Interim Committee meeting the next morning.[67] As he had for much of the war, Stimson on the eve of the May 31 meeting oscillated between a sincere desire to tame the danger of the bomb through international control and the temptation of somehow using the atomic secret as a bargaining tool in postwar negotiations with Stalin.

May 31: Setting the Context of Use

The scattered and sometimes intense discussions in late May on the various questions that would determine the context of use culminated in a meeting of the Interim Committee on May 31, 1945. At 10:00 a.m., Stimson, Marshall, Groves, the regular members of the Interim Committee, and the newly created Scientific Advisory Panel, including physicists J. Robert Oppenheimer, Enrico Fermi, Arthur H. Compton, and Ernest O. Lawrence, assembled in the secretary of war's Pentagon office. Stimson opened the meeting by declaring that "this project should not be considered simply in terms of military weapons, but as a new relationship of man to the universe." He went on to warn that the bomb "must be controlled if possible to make it an assurance of future peace rather than a menace to civilization." If not, it might become "a Frankenstein which would eat us up."[68]

There appeared at the outset to be widespread support for the Bush-Conant proposal for international control of atomic weapons. Stimson, Oppenheimer, Karl T. Compton, and his brother Arthur H. Compton all spoke in favor of the idea of an international commission to control the future of atomic energy. The discussion, however, quickly foundered on the practical question of exactly how and when to approach the Soviet Union, the same dilemma that had long plagued Stimson's thinking on this issue. Both Oppenheimer and Marshall explicitly endorsed an early and direct appeal to the Soviets, with the army chief of staff going so far as to suggest that "it might be desirable to invite two prominent Russian scientists to witness the [Trinity] test."[69] But Truman's personal representative on the Interim Committee was skeptical. James F. Byrnes warned that if "information were given to the Russians, even in general terms, Stalin would ask to be brought into the partnership."

Rather than approach the Soviets prior to use, Byrnes argued, and the rest of the committee "generally agreed," that "the most desirable program would be to push ahead as fast as possible in production and research to make certain that we stay ahead and at the same time make every effort to better our political relations with Russia."[70] Byrnes thus effectively derailed any attempt to open talks with the Soviets prior to use. By implication, he also ruled out any public announcement or warning to Japan that might have risked inadvertently opening up such a discussion. In failing to agree on a plan, timetable, or even a minimum set of preconditions for negotiations with the Soviet Union, the Interim Committee endorsed the de facto policy begun by Roosevelt and Churchill of maintaining a secret Anglo-American monopoly on nuclear weapons.

Why did the Interim Committee endorse Byrnes's suggestion in spite of the fact that many of its members favored inviting the Soviet Union to join in some form of international control? Byrnes's status as the president's personal representative on the committee and his pending appointment as secretary of state undoubtedly bolstered his authority on diplomatic matters. Of those present on May 31, only Stimson and Marshall had the experience and standing to challenge Byrnes on issues of national security. Marshall made his case for a direct approach to the Soviets but apparently did not press the issue in the face of Byrnes's opposition. And though Stimson had shown a renewed interest in pursuing international control in the days leading up to the meeting, in the absence of a plan linking the atomic secret to the concessions he still sought from the Soviets, the secretary of war seems to have easily acquiesced in a decision to defer an approach to Stalin.

During an afternoon lunch break, at which time Marshall left to attend to other business, the committee informally discussed a noncombat demonstration of the bomb designed to impress the Japanese with the danger they faced.[71] Oppenheimer had already voiced his opposition to a noncombat demonstration and apparently did so again at the May 31 meeting. According to Lawrence, Oppenheimer and Groves joined in asserting that "the only way to put on a demonstration would be to attack a real target of built-up structures."[72] In advocating the use of the bomb in such a way as to maximize its blast effects against light structures, the two men were following the same logic that had guided development of the weapon at Los Alamos. In the face of this skepticism about the chances of an effective noncombat demonstration, the conversation spilled over into the start of an afternoon session that began with "much discussion concerning various types of targets and the effects to be produced."[73]

The Interim Committee minutes offer limited insight into the nature of the debate over nuclear targeting, merely recording that eventually the secretary of war offered a conclusion with which the rest of the group expressed "general agreement." Though insisting that "we could not concentrate on a civilian area," Stimson apparently joined in the consensus that an isolated target or military base would not allow for a suitably dramatic demonstration of the bomb's power. In order "to make a profound psychological impression on as many of the inhabitants as possible," the bomb would have to be used in an area where there were a large number of civilians to witness its effects. This recommendation ruled out both a noncombat demonstration and the use of the bomb against a strictly military target. It was agreed, following Conant's suggestion, that the best target would be "a vital war plant employing a large number of workers and closely surrounded by workers' houses." No warning would be given to the Japanese prior to combat use.[74]

While the notion of using the bomb against a "war plant" may have soothed the consciences of those with qualms over the targeting of noncombatants, the course of action they were recommending entailed as a basic requirement the mass killing of Japanese civilians. Why did Stimson agree to this recommendation? His long-held moral and practical concern with limiting the conduct of war and the record of his thoughts and actions in the days prior to the meeting both indicated a fundamental revulsion at the idea of using such a devastating weapon without warning against a predominantly civilian target, a sentiment shared by Marshall (who was not present for the afternoon discussion of targeting).[75] The frustratingly opaque nature of the official minutes of the May 31 meeting makes it impossible to determine why the secretary of war ultimately acquiesced in the decision to target Japanese cities and civilians. It is, however, possible to offer several plausible conjectures.

Perhaps the most important limiting factor in the May 31 discussion of targeting was the type of weapon that Los Alamos was on the verge of producing. From 1944 onward, Los Alamos scientists and engineers had been working on a bomb designed to destroy the kinds of light structures found in abundance in Japanese cities. It was a concern with maximizing the destructive effects of the type of weapon produced by Los Alamos that had led the Target Committee to recommend using "the first gadget in center of selected city" at their final meeting on May 28.[76] Though Stimson and some others on the Interim Committee were troubled by city targeting, as were some scientists connected to the Manhattan Project, their reservations could not change the fact that the bomb as designed was optimized for the destruction of cities and civilians. Given the time and money spent developing the bomb, the ongoing war in the Pacific, and the fact that Groves, Oppenheimer, and the Target Committee all endorsed use against a city, it is likely that Stimson saw the kind of mixed civilian and military-industrial target suggested by Conant, combined with the removal of Kyoto from the target list, as a lamentable but ultimately acceptable compromise.[77]

Another explanation for Stimson's decision to support the use of the bomb against Japanese cities was the so-called shock factor. In an influential article on the A-bomb decision published in *Harper's* under Stimson's name in 1947, he directly linked the decision to use the bomb without warning on Japanese cities to the need to produce "the kind of shock on the Japanese ruling oligarchy which we desired."[78] The shock factor appears to have played an important but ultimately superficial role in the May 31 deliberations. Despite the loose talk of making a "profound psychological impression" on the Japanese, there does not appear to have been any discussion about calibrating the use of the bomb to achieve specific diplomatic objectives.[79] Without an overall agreement on a diplomatic approach to Japan, including the issue of surrender terms, and without any experts on Japan present at the Interim Committee meetings, such a discussion was simply not possible. As Oppenheimer later put it, "We didn't know beans about the military situation in Japan."[80] Rather, the Interim Committee's discussion of the shock factor on May 31 appears to have focused not on "the Japanese ruling oligarchy" but rather on the effect that the bomb might have on Japanese civilians. This approach echoed a similarly superficial discussion of the psychological effects of the bomb during the course of the Target Committee's meetings at Los Alamos on May 11–12.

Technical concerns over the delivery and efficacy of the bomb had already dictated the choice of Japanese cities as targets by late 1944. It was in picking which city to attack that psychological factors came into play. The Target Committee ultimately selected Kyoto, the intellectual center and historical capital of Japan, as the best initial target in part because its inhabitants were "more highly intelligent and hence better able to appreciate the significance of the weapon." The goal was not simply to obtain "the greatest psychological effect against Japan" but also to make "the initial use sufficiently spectacular for the importance of the weapon to be internationally recognized."[81] The Target Committee apparently left unexamined the question of how incinerating and terrorizing the "highly intelligent" citizens of Kyoto might push the Japanese government into capitulation. This macabre and shallow reasoning was reflective of a greater disconnect between the planning for military operations against Japan and the diplomatic efforts to leverage military success into a Japanese surrender that characterized the last months of the war in the Pacific.

On May 31 the Interim Committee apparently embraced the Target Committee's ill-defined formulation of the bomb as a psychological weapon. The desire to make "a profound psychological impression on as many of the inhabitants as possible" clearly helped to justify the use of the bomb against cities and civilians. But as with the Target Committee's deliberations, there is no evidence that Stimson or any of the other Interim Committee members wrestled with the practical question of how the mass killing of civilians with atomic weapons might bring the Japanese government to surrender. At the May 31 meeting, the technical details of the bomb's use remained almost entirely divorced from the important diplomatic question of how—and on what terms—to end the war in the Pacific.

The ongoing conventional bombing of Japan also likely played a role in helping to validate the strategy of city targeting with nuclear weapons. The decisions at Los Alamos that had led to the design of a bomb optimized for use against cities and civilians were both independent of and predated the violent incendiary campaign against Japan begun by the AAF in March 1945. But in struggling with the question of what to do with this new weapon, the precedent set by conventional attacks on Tokyo and other Japanese cities almost certainly made it easier for the Interim Committee to consider using the weapon in the way envisioned by Parsons and the Target Committee.

A combination of self-deception and misleading information with respect to the nature of the target probably helped to seal Stimson's assent to the May 31 targeting recommendations. The self-deception came in the form of his willingness to accept that a "vital war plant employing a large number of workers and closely surrounded by workers' houses" constituted a primarily military target. Stimson's self-deception was facilitated by Groves, who apparently withheld information about the targeting of the weapon at the May 31 meeting and in subsequent discussions prior to use.

At the Target Committee meeting on May 28, it had been explicitly decided "not to specify aiming points" and "to neglect location of industrial areas as pin point target, since on these three targets, such areas are small, spread on fringes of cities and quite dispersed."[82] The 509th Composite Bomb Group subsequently adopted the Target Committee's recommendation in planning the strikes of August 6 and 9. Air crews at the 509th's forward base on the island of Tinian were allowed to select their own aiming points in order to maximize the bomb's effect on the city as a whole at the expense of hitting any particular military-industrial target.[83] Groves, however, did not correct either Stimson or Conant on May 31 (or later) when they suggested that the bomb would be employed against a specific military-industrial target rather than used in a deliberate attempt to annihilate an entire city.

The difference between the Interim Committee's May 31 recommendation on targeting and that offered by the Target Committee (and subsequently followed by the 509th in the attacks on Hiroshima and Nagasaki) was in some ways minor. Both accepted use against a city; the only difference was the aim point within the city. But to Stimson this point was likely important in that it allowed him to believe that he was not *intentionally* targeting civilians for mass killing. Moreover, as events at Nagasaki would later reveal, the seemingly academic question of aim points had real life-and-death significance for the bomb's potential victims.

"Outdoing Hitler in Atrocities"

Events proceeded rapidly following the conclusion of the marathon meeting of the Interim Committee on May 31. On June 6, Stimson met with Truman to present the committee's recommendations. The first three items on his progress report to the president that day were crucial in determining the context of the bomb's use:

1. Targets
2. Time of public statement
3. Time of statement to Russia[84]

By June 6, 1945, prior to both Truman's approval of the plan to invade Japan and the meeting at Potsdam that culminated in the final American ultimatum to the Japanese government, the top political, military, and scientific figures involved in the Manhattan Project had signaled their assent to a set of policy guidelines that would determine the use of the bomb. The United States would use nuclear weapons on Japanese cities. There would be no prior public statement or warning to Japan about the bomb. Nor would there be any attempt to enter into negotiations with the Soviet Union about postwar international control of atomic energy prior to combat use.

As he presented these recommendations to the president, Stimson exhibited a seemingly schizophrenic attitude toward the moral issues involved. In the course of the June 6 meeting, the secretary of war again raised his objections to the conventional area bombing of Japanese cities, stating his desire "to hold the Air Force down to precision bombing" if possible. Stimson offered two reasons for opposing indiscriminate attacks on Japanese cities:

> [F]irst, because I did not want to have the United States get the reputation of outdoing Hitler in atrocities; and second, I was a little fearful that before we could get ready the Air Force might have Japan so thoroughly bombed out that the new weapon would not have a fair background to show its strength.[85]

In his linkage of American area bombing to Nazi atrocities, Stimson was expressing long-held concerns about the need to restrain the conduct of the war for both practical and moral reasons. This concern was fresh in the secretary of war's mind—he had recently heard chilling private testimony from a congressional committee that had investigated Nazi war crimes in Europe, including the notorious death camps at Dachau and Buchenwald.[86] Yet after initially raising objections to city targeting with either conventional or nuclear weapons, Stimson was now apparently willing to sanction the use of indiscriminate force against Japanese civilians in the form of the atomic bomb. In response to his secretary of war's tortured logic, Truman "laughed and said he understood."[87]

Presented with a two billion-dollar weapon designed for the destruction of cities, Stimson undoubtedly hoped that, however terrible, the bomb might speed the end of the war and obviate further bombing as well as the planned invasion of the Japanese home islands.[88] Oppenheimer's rejection of a noncombat demonstration and the combination of deception and self-deception on the types of targets to be hit likely helped him to rationalize the course of action that he recommended to Truman on June 6. Ultimately, however, the position of endorsing indiscriminate nuclear killing in order to end indiscriminate conventional killing proved to be an uncomfortable one for the secretary of war. For the next two months, Stimson and others privy to the atomic secret continued to explore alternatives even as preparations for use of the bomb against Japanese cities went forward.

Chapter 6

Hiroshima and Nagasaki by Way of Potsdam

SOME OF THOSE WHO HAD BEEN PRESENT AT THE MAY 31 INTERIM Committee meeting were clearly uneasy in its aftermath. The final report of the Scientific Advisory Panel on June 16 conceded that the "opinions of our scientific colleagues on the initial use of these weapons are not unanimous." Oppenheimer, who penned the panel's final report, argued strongly for combat use against Japan. But the panel itself was badly divided on both the necessity and definition of "military use." In the months that followed, scientific dissent bubbled to the surface in the form of petitions, memoranda, and letters addressing both use against Japan and the future of international control.[1]

Interim Committee member and Undersecretary of the Navy Ralph Bard also developed reservations about the apparent consensus reached on May 31. In late June, Bard wrote a memorandum suggesting two modifications to the previously agreed-upon recommendations. First, Bard now rejected the idea of using the bomb without warning, suggesting that "Japan should have some preliminary warning for say two or three days in advance of use." Second, the Undersecretary suggested that this warning should be coupled with diplomatic efforts aimed at securing Japanese capitulation prior to use. Specifically, he urged that the United States should contact Japanese representatives and warn them not only of the bomb but also of impending Soviet entry into the Pacific war. These twin threats, coupled with "whatever assurances the President might care to make with regard to the Emperor of Japan" might present "the opportunity which the Japanese are looking for." Though he could not guarantee his proposal would induce a Japanese surrender, Bard insisted that the United States had little to lose and much to gain in making the offer.[2]

Most scholars have focused narrowly on Bard's dissent from the Interim Committee's recommendation to use the bomb against Japan without warning. But as Gar Alperovitz has observed, Bard's suggested diplomatic alternative was in many ways more significant than his narrow recommendation on the issue of warning.[3] Though the Interim Committee had spent a considerable amount of time discussing the postwar diplomatic issues associated with international control and the Soviet Union, its recommendations about use had been almost entirely divorced from the question of how to induce a Japanese surrender. In his June 27 dissent, Bard attempted to join those fragmented debates, integrating the threat of the bomb into a larger diplomatic calculus aimed at ending the war as soon as possible. In doing so, he touched on a set of concerns that increasingly occupied Stimson's mind as the clock ticked toward the first use of nuclear weapons.

"I Believe Japan *Is* Susceptible to Reason"

In the six weeks between the Interim Committee meeting of May 31 and the start of the Potsdam Conference in mid-July, which brought together the leaders of Britain, the United States, and the Soviet Union to discuss the postwar settlement as well as the continuing campaign against Japan, much of Stimson's attention was focused on possible diplomatic alternatives to ending the war. After putting off discussion of modifying American surrender terms prior to the crucial meetings that determined the context of the bomb's use in late May, the secretary of war intended to discuss the matter with the president on June 6. Specifically, he planned to raise the question of the "possible abandonment of the unconditional surrender doctrine" as part of "an overture by us" to Japan aimed at ending the war.[4] The June 6 meeting, however, was dominated by discussion of the bomb and the Soviet Union. Stimson departed without discussing surrender terms with the president, undoubtedly believing he could revisit the issue at a later date when the bomb was closer to readiness.

The secretary of war finally leaped into action on the surrender issue in the second half of June. In part he was motivated by continuing pressure from Mc-Cloy, Grew, and outsiders such as Herbert Hoover.[5] Stimson's own desire to end the war as quickly as possible also played an important role. The turning point appears to have been a June 18 meeting at the White House in which Truman met with his military and civilian advisers to discuss the possible invasion of the Japanese home islands. Much of the meeting was taken up with a confusing and inconclusive discussion of casualty estimates. Truman, who never got a straight answer on this question, concluded by giving approval for the first part of the planned invasion, Operation Olympic, scheduled to take place on southern Kyūshū in November 1945.[6] Stimson also approved the Joint Chiefs' military plans for Olympic on the eighteenth. But by contrast with his conviction that in Europe an invasion would be necessary to defeat the Nazi regime, in the case of Japan he held out hope the war could be ended "through other means."[7]

Both Stimson and his deputy, McCloy (who was also present), were apparently struck by the extent to which the June 18 discussion of the invasion was divorced from larger diplomatic efforts aimed at ending the war. While it was certainly prudent to plan for a potential invasion, it made no sense to sacrifice any more American lives if surrender could be achieved through a modest clarification or softening of terms. Stressing that "there was a large submerged class in Japan who do not favor the present war," Stimson insisted that no invasion should take place without first exploring diplomatic options for ending the war. McCloy also spoke in favor of such an approach on June 18.[8] The irony was that the same disconnect between military planning and the larger diplomatic picture had also marked the deliberations on the use of the bomb over which Stimson himself had presided in May 1945. It took the grim discussion of a potential invasion to jolt the secretary of war into rejoining the military and diplomatic efforts to end the war.

Following the June 18 meeting, Stimson pursued the diplomatic option in a series of meetings with representatives of the War, Navy, and State Departments (the so-called Committee of Three). By the end of June, he had settled on a plan that would demand Japanese surrender while simultaneously clarifying and softening American terms.[9] On July 2, he personally presented Truman with a draft statement of terms for Japan that incorporated his own ideas with those of McCloy, Undersecretary of State Joseph Grew, and others. Stressing his belief that "Japan *is* susceptible to reason," Stimson's proposal contained two important elements aimed at inducing surrender. First, he explicitly recommended that any message to Japan should include the reassurance that "we do not exclude a constitutional monarchy under her present dynasty. . . ."[10] This was the concession that Grew had insisted upon back in May, and Stimson now explicitly endorsed it in his meeting with the president.

The second important element of Stimson's plan involved the Soviet Union. At the suggestion of George Marshall, Stimson proposed that Soviet leaders might sign on to a public demand for Japan's surrender. Though Stalin had secretly pledged eventual Soviet entry into the war against Japan in his meeting with Roosevelt and Churchill at Yalta in February 1945, publicly the Soviet Union remained a nonbelligerent. A Soviet signature on an Allied warning to Japan would be tantamount to a declaration of war. This would not only complicate Japan's military situation in Manchuria, where the Red Army was staging a massive buildup following the victory against Germany, but also deal a blow to those in the Japanese government who hoped that they could use the Soviet Union to help negotiate a favorable peace agreement. Such an "additional sanction to our warning," in the shape of a Soviet signature on the Allied message would, Stimson concluded, "coordinate all the threats possible to Japan."[11] In closing, the secretary of war also reiterated his long-held belief that "[o]ur own bombing should be confined to military objectives as far as possible."[12]

The proposal that Stimson presented to Truman on July 2, 1945, represented the most comprehensive attempt by any American policymaker to leverage diplomacy in order to end the bloody war in the Pacific. The plan was not Stimson's alone—Grew, McCloy, Marshall, and (to lesser extent) Hoover, had played an important role in the genesis and evolution of the document that the secretary of war presented that day. But with its emphasis on supplementing military force with a diplomatic effort aimed at ending the killing and speeding postwar reconstruction, the July 2 proposal embodied Stimson's deeply held conviction that the pursuit of victory needed to be tempered with sensitivity to the costs of war.

The secretary of war had no way of knowing whether the combination of concessions (in the form of retaining the emperor) and threats (in the form of Soviet participation) contained in his proposal would be sufficient to secure a

Japanese surrender. Given the incomplete and sometimes conflicting intelligence information available to them, no American leader could be certain what combination of diplomatic and military actions might finally bring about Japanese surrender. But though he could not guarantee the immediate success of the diplomatic overture he presented on July 2, Stimson was certain that it was worth the attempt. "This is a matter about which I feel very strongly," he confided to his diary, "and feel that the country will not be satisfied unless every effort is made to shorten the war."[13]

Two factors on the American side complicated Stimson's diplomatic efforts in early July. The first was the attitude of the president. Though Truman was "apparently acquiescent with my attitude towards the treatment of Japan," he remained noncommittal on the specifics of Stimson's proposal, neither accepting nor rejecting the suggestion to reassure the Japanese on the postwar status of the emperor.[14] The second complicating factor was the question of how exactly the atomic bomb should figure into the diplomatic strategy outlined in the Stimson memorandum. It was his uncertainty over how to integrate nuclear weapons into the diplomatic equation that had initially led the secretary of war to delay a consideration of surrender terms at the meeting on May 29. Having finally addressed the surrender issue in his July 2 proposal, Stimson was still not sure precisely what role the bomb should play. In his meeting with Truman, Stimson frankly admitted that no diplomatic action could be taken "until we knew what was going to be done with S-1."[15]

The most important unresolved question with respect to the bomb and the Japanese war was one of timing. Should the United States offer a clarification of surrender terms *before* the use of the bomb? The secretary of war's presentation to Truman on July 2 was ambiguous on this point. The cover letter accompanying his draft message to Japan mentioned its likely release "in conjunction" with use of the bomb.[16] It was not until mid-July 1945, amid the heated atmosphere of the Potsdam Conference, that Stimson finally confronted the question of timing in a direct plea to end the war in the Pacific.

"Maneuvering for Peace" at Potsdam

Early in the morning on July 16, 1945, the blinding flash of the world's first atomic bomb illuminated the New Mexico desert. Later that day, the U.S.S. *Indianapolis* sailed from San Francisco bound for the Pacific island of Tinian with the parts for the "Little Boy" uranium bomb. Meanwhile, outside Berlin, Henry Stimson was settling in for his first full day at the Potsdam Conference. In the early afternoon, the secretary of war received an "important paper in re Japanese maneuvering for peace."[17] An intercepted and decoded Japanese cable from Foreign Minister Shigenori Togo indicated for the first time that Emperor Hirohito had expressed an interest in ending the war through negotiations. Truman privately referred to the message, with some exaggeration, as a "telegram from [the] Jap Emperor asking for peace."[18]

In the shadow of the devastated city of Berlin—a scene Stimson described in a letter to his wife Mabel as "depressing beyond words"—the secretary made a last-ditch effort to shape the use of the bomb in such as way as to conform to his deeply held beliefs about war and morality.[19] But the secretary of war's efforts were badly timed. The sheer confusion arising from the multiple vectors of policy that converged at Potsdam, as well as the chronic irresolution over many of these issues in the preceding several years, frustrated his last-minute efforts to shape the use of the bomb.

Stimson was not even an official member of the American delegation at Potsdam. His status as an informal adviser (attending at Truman's personal request) limited his access to the president, who was often occupied with the daily business of the conference.[20] At the height of the Great Depression, then Secretary of State Stimson had lamented that "the situation in the world seemed to me like the unfolding of a great Greek tragedy, where we could see the march of events and know what ought to be done, but to be powerless to prevent its marching to its grim conclusion."[21] At Potsdam in July 1945, Stimson found himself presiding over an even more dramatic tragedy, powerless to control a "Frankenstein" that he had helped to bring into the world.[22]

The combination of new information about Japanese peace feelers and the pending availability of the bomb for combat use jolted the secretary of war into action on July 16. Stimson, McCloy, and Harvey Bundy hurriedly finished a memorandum that finally offered a clear and dramatic statement of the secretary's position on the relationship between surrender terms and the use of the bomb. Invoking the same basic reasoning that had guided his earlier July 2 proposal, Stimson's Potsdam memorandum stressed the need to end the fighting as soon as possible in order to begin the urgent work of postwar reconstruction. The secretary's desire for a speedy end to the war did not, however, dull his concerns over the morality of using indiscriminate force against civilians.

Figure 7. Stimson and an unidentified woman (likely newspaper correspondent Anne O'Hare McCormick) in the ruins of Berlin, July 1945. After touring the devastated German capital, the secretary of war declared the sight to be "depressing beyond words." (Mc-George Bundy Papers, John F. Kennedy Presidential Library, Boston, Mass.)

Indeed, in his July 16 memorandum Stimson for the first time explicitly urged the president to issue a clarification of American terms *prior* to the use of the bomb. If the Japanese continued to resist after such a clarification, then, and only then, "the full force of our newer weapons should be brought to bear" along with "a renewed and even heavier warning, backed by the power of the new forces and possibly the actual entrance of the Russians in the war."[23] This put Stimson in line with Bard, who had made a similar proposal in his June 27 plea for a diplomatic approach to Japan prior to use of the bomb.[24]

There remain unresolved questions about the timing and motivation behind Stimson's July 16 memorandum. Was he jolted into action at Potsdam primarily by dread over the looming use of the bomb, hoping that perhaps the

Figure 8. Stimson and Secretary of State James F. Byrnes at Potsdam, July 1945. Byrnes was Truman's closest adviser during the conference and steadfastly resisted Stimson's pleas to include a statement on the postwar status of the Japanese Emperor in the Potsdam Declaration. (Harry S. Truman Presidential Library, Independence, Mo.)

war could be ended before it was used against Japanese cities? Or was he moved more generally by a desire to end the war as soon as possible with or without the use of the bomb? Certainly the latter explanation is consistent with the secretary's oft-stated belief that the United States should coordinate all available means—including a mixture of diplomatic threats and concessions—to end the war in expeditious fashion. There is, however, some evidence from the debate over nuclear targeting at Potsdam (discussed below) that Stimson had developed renewed concerns about using the bomb against cities and civilians. One thing is very clear: under the weight of so many other pressing matters and uncertain about the availability of the bomb, Stimson had erred in waiting until the last possible minute to finally offer his plan for integrating nuclear weapons into a larger effort to secure Japanese surrender. With only weeks before the use of the bomb, the secretary of war's diplomatic efforts were frustrated by high-level resistance at Potsdam.

The first sign of resistance to Stimson's proposal came on July 17 in a meeting with Truman's new secretary of state, James F. Byrnes. Byrnes had been sworn in on July 3 and traveled to Potsdam along with Truman, serving as the president's closest and most trusted adviser at the conference. After reading Stimson's memorandum, Byrnes informed the secretary of war that he was "opposed to a prompt and early warning to Japan."[25] Several days later, Stimson made a personal effort to raise this point with the president. On July 24 he met with Truman and "spoke of the importance which I attributed to the reassurance of the Japanese on the continuance of their dynasty." He reminded the president that "I had felt that the insertion of that in the formal warning was important and might be just the thing that would make or mar their acceptance, but that I had heard from Byrnes that they preferred not to put it in." The secretary of war loyally accepted Truman's decision, but concluded by expressing his hope that if such a statement were not included in the formal warning, Truman should at the very least watch carefully "so that the Japanese might be reassured verbally though diplomatic channels" on the matter of the emperor.[26]

The Potsdam Declaration issued on July 26, 1945, contained no guarantee or reassurance on the postwar status of the emperor. Nor was the Soviet Union invited to sign the document, despite the fact that Stalin had formally agreed to enter the war in mid-August and was eager to join in a public ultimatum to Japan.[27] While the declaration did contain a partial clarification of what unconditional surrender would entail—denying that the Allies intended to exterminate the Japanese people or permanently occupy that country—it had been stripped of the two important incentives to surrender that Stimson and others had recommended earlier in the month.[28] Without the immediate threat of Soviet entry (or the atomic bomb) and a clear statement on the postwar status of the emperor, the Potsdam Declaration was publicly dismissed by the Japanese government as representing nothing more than "a rehash of the Cairo Declaration." As historian Tsuyoshi Hasegawa has observed, the decision to release the declaration in a public broadcast, rather than through formal or informal diplomatic channels, further encouraged the belief in Japan that it was intended primarily for propaganda purposes.[29]

Why Truman failed at Potsdam to make use of the full arsenal of diplomatic threats and incentives is a matter of some mystery. While only Japanese leaders could make the final decision to surrender, it does not follow, as some historians have insisted, that American leaders had no way to influence "when and how the Pacific war would end."[30] Neither the public threat of Soviet entry nor the lure of allowing the Japanese to retain the emperor after the war were diplomatic panaceas. But diplomacy is seldom accompanied by a guarantee of success. Truman had at least two potentially useful, if imperfect, diplomatic levers that he might have employed in an effort to end the war. He deliberately declined to use either one at Potsdam.

The failure to offer any reassurance on the emperor is particularly troublesome. Nobody on the American side could guarantee that such reassurance would lead to a speedy Japanese surrender. Diplomatic cables intercepted and decrypted by the Americans in summer 1945 revealed that the Japanese government was badly divided on the issue of surrender terms.[31] But amid this uncertainty, it was widely agreed by American military and diplomatic experts that *failure* to clarify the emperor's postwar status would almost certainly delay surrender and prolong the war. According to a State Department analysis from mid-June, "[e]very evidence, without exception, that we are able to obtain of the views of the Japanese with regard to the institution of the throne indicates that the nonmolestation of the person of the present emperor and the preservation of the institution of the throne *comprise irreducible Japanese terms*."[32] It was this belief that had led Stimson to push for such a reassurance on the grounds that "the country will not be satisfied unless every effort is made to shorten the war."[33] Recognizing the "irreducible" importance of the emperor, Truman did eventually allow Hirohito to remain on the throne *after* two atomic bombs and Soviet entry into the war in early August. Why did he not follow Stimson's advice and make such an offer at Potsdam? Even if it did not produce immediate capitulation, it would at the very least have presented a clear set of terms to Japanese leaders in late July rather than forcing them to guess or intuit the American position on this pivotal question.

One possible explanation for Truman's failure was continuing opposition from some in the State Department (including Archibald MacLeish, Dean Acheson, and ex-Secretary of State Cordell Hull) who rejected retaining the emperor on the grounds that it constituted a form of appeasement and would leave the roots of Japanese militarism intact.[34] It seems unlikely, however, that the opinion of a handful of State Department officials was the key factor in Truman's decision. The fact that State Department experts on Japan were almost entirely absent from the American delegation at Potsdam is indicative of the degree to which the president and his secretary of state preferred to make this decision on their own terms.

The president and secretary of state were also little inclined to take military advice on the issue. The Joint Chiefs of Staff strongly favored retaining the emperor as the only entity capable of exercising control over the Japanese armed forces following any surrender. The chiefs were somewhat more ambiguous in their attitude regarding a public statement on this issue, leaning toward an informal reassurance of the emperor's position rather than a formal guarantee. In a meeting on July 17, the Joint Chiefs of Staff opted to tone down the language in Stimson's July 2 draft, replacing the explicit language on the emperor with a more vague promise that "the Japanese will be free to choose their own form of government." But Truman and Byrnes rejected even this modified version favored by American military leaders, leaving the Potsdam Declaration mute on the future of the emperor.[35]

Some historians have suggested that Truman and Byrnes feared that offering even an implicit reassurance on the emperor at Potsdam might have been interpreted as a sign of weakness by the Japanese, thus encouraging further resistance.[36] But it seems unlikely that Truman would have worried about Japanese perceptions of Allied weakness given the other developments at Potsdam. By the time the Potsdam Declaration was issued, Truman had received news of the successful test of the atomic bomb in New Mexico and secured a firm commitment from Stalin to enter the war in the Pacific by mid-August. These developments left the president with two powerful trump cards ready to play at short notice should the Japanese mistake a statement on the emperor for a sign of weakness.

American domestic politics and Truman's personal dislike of the Japanese emperor appear to have been the primary motives for omitting a statement on the postwar role of the emperor in the Potsdam Declaration. Truman and Byrnes feared a public backlash in the United States over any softening of surrender terms. In the midst of an ongoing war and complex diplomatic negotiations over the fate of the postwar world, domestic political concerns were never entirely absent for American leaders. In the case of the unconditional surrender formula, domestic politics appear to have played an important role for both the president and the secretary of state.[37]

There is also some evidence (albeit from several weeks after Potsdam) that Truman's personal antipathy toward the emperor left him disinclined to compromise on the issue, even if it meant prolonging the war with the further loss of American life. Notes from a meeting with Congressman Mike Mansfield on August 10 indicate that Truman objected to any "special guarantees to Hirohito" as "deeply distasteful," asserting that he was opposed to such a compromise "even if it is a face-saver for the Japs and *a life-saving device offered us.*"[38]

While Truman and Byrnes have borne the brunt of the criticism for their failure to offer a clear statement of the postwar status of the emperor at Potsdam, Stimson and Marshall also played an important (if inadvertent) role in determining this outcome. By temporarily tabling any reconsideration of American surrender terms several months earlier at the May 29 meeting, the secretary of war and army chief of staff forfeited what was almost certainly the best opportunity to join the diplomatic track with discussions over the use of the bomb. The hectic, tension-filled atmosphere of the Potsdam Conference proved to be an inauspicious place for a reasoned discussion of the unconditional surrender issue.

"Quite a Change in His Attitude toward the Russians"

Developments at Potsdam also help to explain why the Soviet Union was not invited to sign the public warning to the Japanese, as suggested by Marshall and endorsed by Stimson in late June as a way to "coordinate all the threats possible to Japan."[39] Though Truman had privately secured Stalin's pledge to enter the war against Japan by August 15, the Soviets were neither consulted about the formulation of the Potsdam Declaration nor invited to sign the final document, a fact that did not go unnoticed in Japan.[40] Stimson, who pressed Truman and Byrnes repeatedly on the issue of the emperor, was apparently untroubled by the failure to add the weight of Stalin's signature (and the accompanying threat of Soviet entry into the war) to the declaration. The secretary of war's failure to pursue this particular diplomatic avenue to ending the war was the result of his larger reevaluation of Soviet-American relations at Potsdam.

Several factors combined to shift Stimson's position on both wartime and postwar cooperation with the Soviet Union during the course of the meeting at Potsdam. One factor was his impression of the "expanding demands being made by the Russians" at the conference. After a meeting with Ambassador Averell Harriman on July 23, Stimson became convinced that the Soviets were "throwing aside all their previous restraint as to being only a Continental power and not interested in any further acquisitions, and now apparently seeking to branch in all directions."[41] Equally important, however, was his visceral reaction to the sight of the Red Army in occupied Berlin and "the atmosphere of repression that exists everywhere, and which is felt by all who come in contact with the Russian rule in Germany."[42] Though he was willing in theory to concede a Soviet sphere of influence in eastern Europe (provided they allowed some form of open door economic access), his personal experience with Soviet occupation policies led him to conclude "that no permanently safe international relations can be established between two such fundamentally different national systems."[43]

Stimson's epiphany at Potsdam with respect to the Soviet Union spilled over into thinking about ending the war with Japan. Based on a July 23 conversation with Marshall, the secretary of war concluded that "now with our new weapon we would not need the assistance of the Russians to conquer Japan."[44] At the same time, Stimson also lost interest in seeking Stalin's signature on the Potsdam Declaration, a proposal he had previously endorsed. It appears that the visceral distaste for Stalin and the Soviet system that Stimson developed at Potsdam overcame his previous commitment to employing all available diplomatic tools to end the war with Japan as soon as possible.[45]

The change in Stimson's attitude toward postwar control of the bomb was even more dramatic. Shortly prior to Potsdam, the Interim Committee, in a partial reversal of its earlier recommendation, suggested that "there would be considerable advantage, if suitable opportunity arose, in having the President advise the Russians that we were working on this weapon with every prospect of success and that we expected to use it against Japan."[46] But in a conference with British representatives at Potsdam on July 19, Stimson confessed to feeling "doubtful" about notifying the Soviets about the existence of the bomb. That same day, he expressed even more fundamental doubts about whether it was possible to cooperate at all "with a nation whose speech is strictly controlled and where the Government uses the iron hand of the secret police."[47]

In a memorandum to Truman on July 19, Stimson urged that no attempt be made to share the atomic secret with the Soviet leaders until they enacted fundamental governmental and societal reforms that would guarantee "free speech, free assembly, free press and the other essential elements of our Bill of Rights."[48] In addition to concessions involving open door economic access in Europe and Asia, Stimson was now insisting on the democratization of Soviet society in exchange for sharing the atomic secret. Though he had previously suggested that the United States might ask for some Soviet promises of liberalization in exchange for the atomic secret, he now insisted that such liberalization must take place before even entering into the most basic negotiations on the bomb. This hardening of Stimson's attitude did not go unnoticed. Former ambassador to the Soviet Union Joseph Davies (who conferred with Stimson several times at Potsdam) commented in his diary that he had "detected quite a change in his attitude toward the Russians. It was quite a contrast to the opinions he had expressed in Washington."[49]

An informal meeting between Stimson and Stalin on July 25 did little to increase the secretary's peace of mind. Upon returning from Potsdam, Stimson confessed that "he had started out entirely with the hope of the possibility of future international control but no country infected with the OGPU [secret police] would be part of an effective international control. . . . he had come back more conservative than General Groves had been and that he was quite pessimistic as to the future."[50] The secretary of war's experience at Potsdam did not make him any more enthusiastic about the use of the bomb against Japan. He had, however, shifted his thinking about the context of use as it related to international control and the Soviet Union.

The combination of confidence engendered by the success of the Trinity test and pessimism regarding Soviet intentions that characterized the secretary of war's attitude at Potsdam was widely shared among the official American delegation. Truman and Byrnes were "very greatly reinforced" by news of the success in New Mexico. Byrnes personally informed Stimson that he was "relying greatly upon the information as to S-1" in standing up to the Soviets at Potsdam. Churchill confirmed this impression, remarking to the secretary of war that after news of the test "Truman was evidently much fortified by something that had happened and that he stood up to the Russians in a most emphatic and decisive manner, telling them as to certain demands that they absolutely could not have and that the United States was against them."[51]

Confident of American power and hopeful of ending the war with Japan without Soviet military or diplomatic assistance, Truman and Byrnes made no effort to secure Stalin's signature on their warning to Japan. Byrnes, in particular, appears to have believed that the bomb would allow the United States to end the war without Soviet military *or* diplomatic assistance.[52] Truman chose to wait until the last of the Big Three meetings on July 24 before casually informing Stalin that "we had a new weapon of unusual destructive force."[53] Truman did not clarify the nature of this "new weapon" and was no doubt relieved that Stalin did not press for further details.

"Targets Previously Assigned . . . Remain Unchanged"

Truman later claimed that he had convened a major meeting of his military and civilian advisers at Potsdam to decide the question of whether or not to use the bomb against Japan. In fact, such a meeting never took place, and the scattered discussions regarding the use of the bomb at Potsdam revolved almost entirely around the question of which Japanese cities were to be targeted.[54] This issue remained a subject of occasionally intense discussion up until the very last minute. Following the initial debate over targeting in late May, Marshall had argued for making Kokura the primary target, presumably because the enormous Kokura arsenal came closest to meeting his definition of a military target.[55] Meanwhile, Groves repeatedly (and unsuccessfully) attempted to add Kyoto to the target list over Stimson's continuing objections.[56]

Perhaps frustrated by his inability to convince Truman to soften American surrender terms prior to the use of the bomb, Stimson spent his last days at Potsdam revisiting the question of targeting. On July 22, the secretary of war summoned AAF Chief of Staff Arnold for an hour-long discussion about the use of the bomb with an emphasis (as described in Arnold's diary) on "where, why and what effects." The next day, they met again to discuss targeting, including the bomb's effects on "surrounding communities." It appears that the secretary of war's long-held objection to the intentional killing of civilians had resurfaced as he pondered the bomb outside the ruins of the "dead city" of Berlin. Arnold later explained that among Stimson's concerns that day was "the killing of women and children."[57] In response to the secretary of war's insistent queries on targeting, Arnold ordered one of his aides to fly back to Washington immediately to consult with Groves and General Carl A. Spaatz (who was about to leave for the Pacific to take command of the strategic air wing charged with delivering the bomb). When Stimson badgered the AAF chief of staff about targets for a third consecutive day, Arnold demurred and told the secretary that he would simply have to await the outcome of the consultations in Washington.[58]

On July 24 Marshall and Stimson received a cable from Washington containing Groves's draft of the order authorizing the use of the atomic bomb. The directive listed four cities as potential targets for the bomb: Hiroshima, Kokura, Niigata, and Nagasaki. The first attack was to occur "after about 3 August 1945" with additional bombs to follow "as soon as made ready by the project staff."[59] The choice among which of the listed cities to strike first and the exact timing of both the initial and any subsequent attacks were to be left to the field commanders in the Pacific. No further orders would be required to drop additional atomic bombs. As to the listed targets, the cities of Hiroshima and Niigata were holdovers from the Target Committee's initial recommendations of May 28. Kokura and its massive arsenal were presumably included in response to Marshall's instructions. Nagasaki, the one new target, was added after Groves finally gave up on getting approval to attack Kyoto.

Stimson discussed the Groves directive with Truman on July 25. After this meeting, the president in his diary expressed a set of ethical concerns about the use of the weapon that mirrored those expressed earlier by Stimson and Marshall:

> I have told the Sec. Of War, Mr. Stimson to use it so that military objectives and soldiers and sailors are the target and not women and children. Even if the Japs are savages, ruthless, merciless, and fanatic, we as the leader of the world for the common welfare cannot drop this terrible bomb on the old Capitol or the new. He [Stimson] and I are in accord. The target will be a purely military one and we will issue a warning statement asking the Japs to surrender and save lives.[60]

However, when presented with a list of Japanese cities to be targeted, Truman did not insist on a "purely military" target. The president's only reaction was to agree with Stimson that Kyoto should be preserved, seemingly persuaded by the argument that "the bitterness which would be caused by such a wanton act might make it impossible during the long post-war period to reconcile the

Japanese to us in that area rather than to the Russians."[61] Contrary to claims by some historians, Truman was indeed troubled by the prospect of using nuclear weapons against Japanese civilians prior to Hiroshima, as indicated by his private insistence that "women and children" not be targeted.[62] Ultimately, however, his desire to make use of those weapons as soon as possible in order to end the war with Japan and strengthen his hand in postwar dealing with the Soviets prevented him from acting on these concerns.

In making his decision, Truman, like Stimson, indulged in self-deception encouraged by misleading information about the targets and the way they were to be attacked. The language of the target reports furnished to American leaders at Potsdam heavily emphasized the military–industrial character of the targeted cities.[63] For a president anxious about the mass killing of civilians but unwilling to delay or derail a two billion dollar project that had produced weapons optimized for use against cities, these descriptions likely offered a welcome rationalization. There is no indication that Truman or his top advisers at Potsdam were told that mission planners in the Pacific would be choosing aim points with the goal of maximizing overall destruction at the expense of damaging or destroying the major war-related industries in three of the four targeted cities (Kokura and its arsenal being the exception).

Any last-minute reservations that Truman might have entertained about city targeting were overwhelmed by the rush of events in late July. The president and his advisers had pushed the scientists at Los Alamos to speed up the Trinity test so that they would have (in Stimson's words) a "master card" in their back pocket during negotiations with Stalin at the Potsdam Conference.[64] The pressure only mounted after the successful test in New Mexico. The president was eager to use the bomb against Japan soon after the surrender ultimatum issued at Potsdam on July 26.[65] Truman and Byrnes also hoped that the speedy use of the bomb would help force a Japanese surrender "before the Russians got in."[66] The high-level push to use the weapon as soon as possible combined with anxiety about the notoriously bad summer weather over Japan ruled out any last-minute changes with respect to either the design or use of the city-busting weapons designed at Los Alamos.

On July 25, with the choice of cities finally set, Marshall sent a cable to Acting Chief of Staff Thomas T. Handy in Washington: "Reference your WAR 37683 of July 24, [the secretary of war] approves Groves directive."[67] With that brief message, the sporadic and sometimes agonized debate over the context of

Figure 9. Stimson and General Dwight D. Eisenhower at Frankfurt upon the secretary's departure from Germany, July 27, 1945. In his postwar memoirs, Eisenhower claimed that at this meeting with Stimson he expressed "grave misgivings" about the use of the bomb on the grounds that it was "no longer mandatory as a measure to save American lives." It is unclear from contemporary evidence if Eisenhower's recollections of this meeting were accurate or exaggerated in the years that followed. (Harry S. Truman Presidential Library, Independence, Mo.)

use was finally put to rest, and control of the bombs and their delivery was turned over to the 509th Composite Group on Tinian.[68] When Spaatz raised concerns that most of the proposed target cities harbored American prisoners of war, Groves, in an apparent effort to shield Stimson from having to make yet another agonizing choice about the bomb, personally cabled, "Targets previously assigned . . . remain unchanged," without consulting with the secretary of war.[69]

Stimson had no formal role in the American delegation at Potsdam, and with the dispatch of the Groves directive his work at the conference was complete.

Following approval of that directive, Stimson traveled to Munich, where he spent two days as the guest of General George S. Patton. Before beginning the return trip to the United States on July 27, Stimson stopped at the Supreme Headquarters Allied Expeditionary Force (SHAEF) in Frankfurt, where he met with General Dwight D. Eisenhower. That afternoon, over lunch, the secretary of war, Eisenhower, and General Lucius D. Clay "talked informally" about "General Groves' project."[70]

In his 1948 memoir, Eisenhower claimed that in meeting with Stimson he "expressed the hope that we would never have to use such a thing against an enemy because I disliked seeing the United States take the lead in introducing into war something as horrible and destructive as this new weapon was described to me." In a later account of this meeting, Eisenhower went even further, asserting that he expressed "grave misgivings" to the secretary of war about the use of the bomb, "whose employment was, I thought, no longer mandatory as a measure to save American lives." In response, Stimson was "deeply perturbed . . . almost angrily refuting the reasons I gave for my quick conclusions."[71]

Stimson's diary for this period, which is understandably truncated because of his demanding travel schedule, sheds no light on the nature of the July 27 discussion about the bomb. While it seems unlikely that Eisenhower fabricated his account of the conversation from whole cloth, it also seems improbable that a general known for his tact and diplomacy in dealing with civilian leaders would have spoken quite so forcefully against the bomb as he later suggested. The fact is that we simply do not know exactly what transpired between the two men that day. Nor do we know what thoughts or emotions were running through the head of the aging and exhausted secretary of war as returned home with the knowledge that nuclear weapons would soon be unleashed on the cities of Japan.

The Day After

On August 6, a lone B-29 bomber dropped an atomic bomb on Hiroshima, killing some eighty thousand people.[72] Upon receiving news of the attack, Marshall telephoned Stimson at his Washington estate. There is no record of Stimson's immediate reaction to the destruction of Hiroshima. On August 8, however, Stimson again pleaded with Truman to "proceed with Japan in a way

Figure 10. Another view of the immediate aftermath at Hiroshima by an unidentified Japanese photographer. The United States Strategic Bombing Survey (USSBS) estimated between 70,000 and 80,000 deaths at Hiroshima, though that number does not include many who later died as a result of radiation sickness or other complications. (Robert L. Capp Papers, Hoover Institution Archives, Stanford, Calif.)

which would produce as quickly as possible her surrender."[73] He urged that the president take a conciliatory approach and deplored the attitude of those still in favor of forcing an unconditional surrender upon the Japanese. The secretary of war complained that those who insisted on unconditional surrender "didn't recognize the difference between the Japanese and the Germans and [were] attempting to treat them in the way some people were trying to treat the Germans. . . . I said 'When you punish your dog you don't keep souring on him all day after the punishment is over; if you want to keep his affection, punishment takes care of itself.' It is the same way with Japan."[74]

As Stimson struggled to help end the war by diplomatic means, his own health failed him. Following what was likely a mild heart attack on the morning of August 8, Stimson was told by his doctors to leave Washington for a "complete rest." Privately, he decided that the time had come for him to resign "as soon as possible." In the interim, he prepared to leave Washington

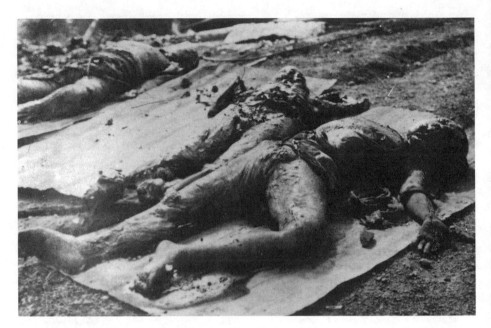

Figure 11. Casualties of the Hiroshima bombing. (Robert L. Capp Papers, Hoover Institution Archives, Stanford, Calif.)

on doctor's orders to rest and recuperate at the Ausable Club outside St. Hubert's, New York.[75] Stimson and his wife were packed and a car was waiting to take them to the airport on August 10 when news of Soviet entry into the war against Japan and the use of the second atomic bomb against Nagasaki (killing approximately another forty-five thousand people) was followed by a Japanese offer to surrender.[76] He quickly returned to his Pentagon office to read the message containing the Japanese offer before Truman summoned him to the White House to join in a major conference of civilian and military advisers.

The Japanese had offered to accept the terms outlined in the Potsdam Declaration with the sole reservation that the institution of emperor should be allowed to continue after the war.[77] It was, Stimson remarked, "the very single point that I feared would make trouble." The secretary of war repeated his earlier pleas to accept this condition in order to end the war—and the killing—as soon as possible. He railed against "uninformed agitation against the Emperor in this country mostly by people who know no more about Japan than has been given them by Gilbert and Sullivan's 'Mikado' " and insisted that the case of Japan was different from that of Germany, where unconditional surrender had been a necessary prerequisite for victory.[78]

Stimson's basic conservatism left him unmoved by those who sought to use Japan's defeat as an opportunity to remake Japanese society in the Western image. Nor did he have any interest in extracting vengeance for Pearl Harbor or Japanese atrocities during the war. The Japanese, he asserted were "naturally . . . a smiling people and we have to get on those terms with them."[79] Further delay would not only mean more lives lost but also give the Soviet Union time to "get down in reach of the Japanese homeland. I felt it was of great importance to get the homeland into our hands before the Russians could put in any substantial claims to occupy and help rule it."[80]

Though Stimson's arguments drew heavily on racist stereotypes of the Japanese and fear of the Soviet Union, his plea was also informed by humanitarian concerns. In addition to calling for a softening of American terms, the secretary of war argued that the "humane thing" would be to halt both conventional and nuclear attacks on Japanese cities while surrender negotiations continued, citing among other things the "apprehension and misgiving" created by American use of the atomic bomb.[81] Much to his frustration, the secretary of war found that there was resistance to both of these propositions. Truman continued to vacillate on the issue of the emperor, apparently driven by fear over the public reaction to any softening of American terms and his belief that Hirohito was a war criminal.[82] With the president's approval, Byrnes crafted an ambiguous response to the Japanese offer that attempted to reassure them about the postwar status of the emperor without offering an explicit guarantee. Stimson's suggestion for a cease-fire was rejected on the narrow technical ground that "we had not yet received in official form the Japanese surrender . . . and that so far as we were concerned the war was still going on."[83]

Haunted by the killing of "all those kids" at Hiroshima and Nagasaki and finding that "the thought of wiping out another 100,000 people was too horrible," Truman (as recorded in the diary of Secretary of Commerce Henry Wallace) did reassert the control over the atomic bomb that he had previously delegated to field commanders in the Pacific. No more nuclear weapons would be used against Japan without his direct authorization.[84] This undoubtedly came as a relief to Spaatz, who was preparing to deliver a third bomb if necessary. Though he would have dropped more bombs had he been so ordered,

Spaatz confided in his diary on August 11 that "[w]hen the atomic bomb was first discussed with me in Washington I was not in favor of it just as I have never favored the destruction of cities as such with all inhabitants being killed."[85]

Stimson did not record his own thoughts on what had happened at Hiroshima and Nagasaki. On August 12, 1945, the physically and mentally battered secretary of war finally left for the Ausable Club without awaiting the result of the settlement talks unfolding in Washington and Tokyo. While he was greatly relieved that the end of the war appeared to be near, Stimson was not in a celebratory mood when he departed Washington. As he had been three months earlier on V-E Day, the secretary was preoccupied with both the cost of victory and the challenges that would follow in its wake. The dawn of the atomic age saw Stimson gathering his fading energy for one last attempt to control the "Frankenstein" that he had helped to unleash upon the world.

Chapter 7

The Last Full Measure

ON THE MORNING OF SEPTEMBER 21, 1945, HENRY L. STIMSON AROSE
to perform his last act of public service. It was his seventy-eighth birthday and
his final day in office as secretary of war. After five eventful years in which he
had helped guide the United States to victory in World War II, Stimson was
on the verge of a self-described "emotional and coronary breakdown." In a
day filled with "tension and emotion," he devoted the last full measure of his
strength to a preventing another, even more terrible conflict.[1]

At the Potsdam Conference in the weeks prior to Hiroshima, Stimson had
for the first time expressed strong opposition to allowing the Soviet Union to
join in a postwar atomic partnership. Now, at a cabinet meeting on his last day
in office, he dramatically reversed his position, urging President Harry S.
Truman to immediately approach the Soviets in order to strike a deal on nuclear arms that would result in "saving civilization not for five or for twenty
years, but forever."[2] The United States, he insisted, should take the lead in
opening negotiations with Stalin even if it meant abandoning the nascent
American nuclear monopoly, halting any further work on atomic weapons,

Figure 12. On the verge of an "emotional and coronary breakdown," Stimson, accompanied by wife, Mabel, bids farewell to Army Chief of Staff General George C. Marshall and assembled officers, September 21, 1945. Prior to his departure and retirement from public life, Stimson's last official act was a dramatic plea for nuclear arms control at a meeting of Truman's cabinet. (Henry L. Stimson Papers, Manuscripts and Archives, Yale University, New Haven, Conn.)

and impounding the existing American arsenal. For Stimson it was a last, dramatic bid to control the nuclear arms race that he had helped to foster through his own actions as civilian head of the Manhattan Project.

Following the cabinet meeting, Stimson and his wife, Mabel, were chauffeured to the airport. There they were greeted by "all the general staff officers in Washington lined up in two rows, together with my immediate personal civilian staff." As the Stimsons walked past 120 generals, the largest gathering of such high-ranking officers in the history of the United States, a military band played "Auld Lang Syne" and "Happy Birthday." Following a nineteen-gun salute, Stimson shook hands with the civilian members of his War Department staff and with Army Chief of Staff George C. Marshall, to whom he had bid "a very deep emotional" farewell earlier in the day. Henry and Mabel Stimson then boarded the plane that would wing them home to Highhold, their estate on Long Island Sound.[3]

September 21, 1945, marked the last entry in the voluminous diaries that Stimson began keeping in 1909, eventually running to some ten thousand pages. His last official act that day—a plea for international cooperation in order to avoid a disastrous nuclear arms race—was a fitting capstone to a career devoted to a quiet struggle to building peace among nations. A concern with cultivating trust and instilling morality in the conduct of foreign affairs had been at the heart of his approach to national security since World War I. From the jungles of Nicaragua to the Malacañan Palace in Manila, quiet Geneva villas, and the halls of power in Washington, Stimson had labored for over three decades to promote humane alternatives to the horror of total war. All too often, however, his quest for peace was marked by failure and misfortune. There was no greater tragedy in his long career than the failure to control the use and spread of nuclear weapons in accord with his own deeply held convictions about war and morality.

"We Will with Another War End Our Civilization"

Stimson had long worked to advance the cause of international peace through arms control agreements that would build trust between nations. His 1930 plea for the elimination of submarines as weapons "particularly susceptible to abuse . . . in a way that violates alike the laws of war and the dictates of humanity" reflected both his concern with limiting the conduct of industrialized warfare (particularly against civilians) and his belief that such efforts could eventually pave the way for the elimination of war altogether.[4] He had sounded similar themes in his April 25, 1945, memorandum for Truman on the bomb and later at the May 31 Interim Committee meeting. But before he could turn these sentiments into a practical plan for the international control of atomic energy, the secretary of war had to overcome his mounting distrust of the Soviet Union.

The crucial turning point in Stimson's attitude toward the bomb, the Soviet Union, and international control came during the three-week period from

August 12 to September 3, 1945, as he recovered from the mild heart attack he had suffered in the aftermath of Hiroshima. Confined to a small cottage at the exclusive Ausable Club in upstate New York, he gradually regained his strength under a doctor's supervision. In the shadow of the Adirondacks and surrounded by the wilderness that he loved so much, the secretary of war meditated on the impact of the bombings and on the future of atomic energy. He emerged at the start of September and returned to Washington with a new dedication to preventing a nuclear arms race by making a direct approach to the Soviet Union.

Several factors combined to help Stimson overcome his distrust of the Soviet Union and embrace a far-reaching plan for the international control of atomic energy in August–September 1945. First, and most obviously, the end of the war finally freed him from having to balance long-range thinking about the bomb with the short-term demands of securing victory. Six months earlier, scientific adviser Vannevar Bush had lamented that Stimson no longer had "the vigor of youth when he is so badly needed" to address the diplomatic and moral challenges posed by the bomb.[5] Though the secretary's body was on the verge of failing him at the end of the war, peace did free his still keen mind to focus on this issue almost exclusively.

Before leaving for the Ausable Club, the secretary of war had informed Truman of his intent to retire after the imminent Japanese surrender. As he prepared to draw a close to a public career that spanned four decades and included bipartisan service under six presidents, it was inevitable that he would ponder his legacy. The issue of international control offered him a unique opportunity to revisit the lessons of the past while salvaging his reputation as a thoughtful moral internationalist. Physically removed from the pressure-cooker atmosphere of wartime Washington (though still connected to the War Department by a special scrambler phone installed in his cabin), Stimson revisited his long-held convictions about morality and trust in the conduct of international relations.

The plan for preventing an arms race that he eventually submitted to the president that September drew both implicitly and explicitly on his past experiences as a statesman and crusader for international peace. The challenge of balancing technological innovation with moral self-control was a concept that Stimson had been exploring since World War I, when he had observed firsthand the effects of industrial technology on the battlefield. During the 1930s, he had explicitly expressed his concern that "Man's technique" in the sciences had surpassed his "moral and social power" to control the resulting new technologies.[6] Stimson was also likely influenced by more recent lessons drawn from World War II. In 1941, the secretary of war had pinned his hopes for preventing war with Japan on the forward deployment of American strategic bombers to the Pacific. The failure of these high-technology offensive weapons to prevent a diplomatic and military debacle on December 7 provided a harsh lesson in the limits of deterrence.

The fallout, metaphorical and real, from the bombings of Hiroshima and Nagasaki also undoubtedly influenced Stimson's thinking in this crucial period. As part of his responsibility for overseeing the War Department's public statements on the bomb, the secretary was forced to confront a string of reports and photos dramatically illustrating the devastation unleashed on those two Japanese cities. One of the cables that Stimson presented to Truman on August 8 offered the "conservative estimate" that over one hundred thousand Japanese had died at Hiroshima.[7] Shortly afterward, reports of an "atomic plague" caused by radioactive fallout began to appear in American newspapers, raising the specter of lingering death in the ruins of Hiroshima and Nagasaki.

Though his diary contains little direct evidence on this question, it is hard to imagine that Stimson, who had long opposed targeting civilians and compared American area bombing to Nazi atrocities, was not greatly troubled by the reports he received from Japan.[8] Some indication of the bombings' effect on Stimson can be gleaned from an informal talk he gave to fellow members of the Ausable Club at a quiet V-J Day celebration on August 18. "In this war," Stimson observed, "we have been compelled to invent and unleash forces of terrific destructiveness. Unless we now develop methods of international life, backed by the spirit of tolerance and kindliness, viz: the spirit of Christianity, sufficient to make international life permanent and kindly and war impossible, we will with another war end our civilization."[9] Adding to his uneasiness were warnings from scientists, including Los Alamos director J. Robert Oppenheimer, that the bombs used against Japan might soon be dwarfed in destructive power by the "super" or hydrogen bomb.[10]

Another warning from a close aide in late August lent added urgency to Stimson's attempt to translate the principles of arms control and international cooperation into a specific plan for approaching the Soviet Union. While recuperating at the Ausable Club, he received several visits from Assistant Secretary of War John J. McCloy. In the seclusion of the quiet forest, the two friends and colleagues talked about the bomb, the Soviet Union, and the prospects for international control of atomic energy. In one of these conversations the assistant secretary relayed a disturbing piece of news:

> McCloy [had] talked the subject over with [Secretary of State James F.] Byrnes and found that he was quite radically opposed to any approach to Stalin whatever. He was on the point of departing for the foreign ministers' meeting and wished to have the implied threat of the bomb in his pocket during the conference.[11]

At a time that demanded the most patient and careful statesmanship, Stimson was dismayed that the secretary of state had apparently decided to approach postwar negotiations with the Soviet Union as if they were a Wild West showdown. The secretary of war had already resolved to tackle the issue of international control prior to this revelation, but the news about Byrnes added a new level of urgency to the endeavor.

Upon returning to Washington on September 4, Stimson met with Byrnes and found his worst fears confirmed. The secretary of state was "very much against any attempt to cooperate with Russia" and wanted "the bomb in his pocket, so to speak, as a great weapon" at the upcoming foreign ministers meeting in London.[12] The next day Stimson had an audience with Truman during which he aired his differences with Byrnes in terms that went beyond the bomb to encompass the entire conduct of postwar foreign relations. Byrnes's attempt to use the bomb as a bargaining tool, the secretary of war warned, would lead the world to "revert to power politics" in the wake of the war. International control of atomic energy, including the Soviet Union, not only was a better method of dealing with atomic energy, he insisted, but also offered the larger advantage that "we would be on the right path towards world establishment of an international world."[13] The stage was set for a showdown on international control that would serve as proxy for a larger debate over American foreign policy at the dawn of the nuclear age.

"The Only Way to Make a Man Trustworthy Is to Trust Him"

With McCloy's aid, the secretary of war had managed, during his three weeks at the Ausable Club, to hash out a rough draft of a plan for approaching the

Soviets. Realizing upon his return to Washington that he would need to offer a compelling brief for the international control of atomic energy in order to counter Byrnes, Stimson devoted his last weeks in office to polishing a memorandum to be submitted to the president.

Stimson's memorandum, which he personally presented to Truman on September 12 and subsequently defended at the cabinet meeting on his last day in office, began by addressing the apparent inconsistencies between his own pre- and post-Hiroshima position with respect to the bomb and the Soviet Union. He conceded to the president that he was "not unmindful of the fact that when in Potsdam, I talked with you about the question whether we could be safe in sharing the atomic bomb with Russia while she was still a police state and before she put into effect provisions assuring personal rights of liberty to the individual citizen." Stimson still harbored these concerns and remained dedicated to bringing about a change in the "attitude toward individual liberty" within the Soviet Union. But in a crucial reversal, he now insisted that "any demand by us for an internal change in Russia as a condition of sharing in the atomic weapon would be so resented that it would make the objective we have in view less probable." Casting the process of fostering liberty in the USSR as a long-term project, he argued that that goal was much more likely to be achieved through cooperation on the bomb than by using it as a club or bargaining chip.[14]

In laying the groundwork for his about-face on the issue of international control, the secretary of war also conceded that in "many quarters," the atomic bomb had "been interpreted as a substantial offset to the growth of Russian influence on the continent."[15] This was, in fact, precisely the point that Stimson himself had argued so strenuously in 1944–45 when he had urged first Roosevelt and then Truman to hold on to the atomic secret as a "master card" or "royal straight flush" to be employed in extracting postwar concessions in both Europe and Asia.[16] In repudiating this position after Hiroshima, he offered both practical and moral justifications for a less confrontational approach to the future of atomic energy.

On a practical level, the secretary of war argued that "if we fail to approach them now and merely continue to negotiate with them, having this weapon rather ostentatiously on our hip, their suspicions and their distrust of our purposes and motives will increase." This, in turn, would drive the Soviets into a desperate attempt to gain the bomb on their own, dashing any hopes for the "the kind of covenant we may desperately need in the future" to prevent an arms race. The quid pro quo approach, Stimson now conceded, was simply not realistic: the Soviets would not yield to atomic blackmail. Instead they would pursue the bomb on their own, and the United States would get neither the postwar concessions it sought nor an accord on atomic energy, a prediction that proved to be sadly prescient.

As an alternative, the secretary reached back to a lesson he had learned from his dealings with indigenous leaders while governor general of the Philippines in the late 1920s. "[T]he only way you can make a man trustworthy is to trust him," Stimson declared, "and the surest way to make him untrustworthy is to distrust him and show your distrust." In practice, this meant allowing the Soviets to join the Anglo-American nuclear partnership without insisting on concessions in other areas or awaiting fundamental changes within Soviet society. At most, sharing the atomic secret risked that the Soviets might be able to produce their own bomb "a little sooner than they would otherwise." But the Soviets would eventually get the bomb on their own anyway. Stimson argued that the United States had little to lose and everything to gain through an attempt to cultivate trust at this pivotal moment in world history.[17]

In light of the danger posed by the bomb, protecting and advancing the values of trust and morality in international relations were crucial to the very survival of "industrial civilization." The bomb, he insisted, was not "merely another more devastating military weapon to be assimilated into our pattern of international relations." The splitting of the atom represented nothing less than "the climax of the race between man's growing technical power for destructiveness and his psychological power of self-control and group control—his moral power."[18]

Stimson's plan for how to proceed was both simple and dramatic. The United States and Britain should immediately approach the Soviets with an offer "to control and limit the use of the atomic bomb as an instrument of war." Some of the plans floated for international control during the war had imagined the bomb's being turned over to a multinational organization such as the United Nations. Stimson rejected this as impractical, suggesting that the only way to win the trust of the Soviets was to approach them immediately and directly, without waiting for the outcome of the "loose debates" that would inevitably accompany the creation of any larger world body on atomic energy.[19] Though he remained committed to building larger international institutions over time, when it came to the crucial problems facing the postwar world, the secretary put his faith in direct and personal negotiations between the elites who represented the great powers. This, too, was a throwback to his days as secretary of state, when he had relied on personal diplomacy in hopes of overcoming the rising wave of nationalism and militarism in the early 1930s.[20]

On the crucial question of what concessions the United States and Britain should be prepared to offer in negotiations with the Soviets, Stimson was willing to travel a considerable distance to win agreement. He suggested that in addition to "stop[ping] work on the further improvement in, or manufacture of, the bomb as a military weapon," American leaders should be willing to "impound what bombs we now have in the United States" and agree that any future use of the weapon would be contingent on approval from all three governments. This amounted to a nuclear freeze and a substantial sacrifice of American sovereignty when it came to decisions about the use of nuclear weapons. And while this agreement would initially be limited to the United States, United Kingdom, and Soviet Union, Stimson saw no reason why it could not be expanded over time into a larger international structure involving the United Nations.

The plan that Stimson outlined in his memorandum to Truman and presented at his final cabinet meeting on September 21 was admittedly lacking in concrete details. He offered no specifics on how tripartite control of the bomb would work in practice. Nor did he address the crucial issue of timing. When should the United States share with the Soviet Union the technical details of the bomb's construction? At what point in the negotiations should the United States "impound" its own bombs? Should American leaders give up the bomb at the start of negotiations as a gesture of good faith or insist on holding on to it until a satisfactory agreement for international control had been reached? As the 1946–47 debate at the United Nations over the future of the bomb made clear, the timing question was one of the most difficult roadblocks in the quest for international control.[21] The secretary of war did not take a position on these questions in his September memorandum, although his critique of Byrnes's attempt to negotiate while "having this weapon rather ostentatiously on our hip" hinted at a willingness to give up exclusive control over the bomb sooner rather than later in an effort to achieve a meaningful agreement.

The lack of specifics in the plan Stimson presented on September 21 was deliberate. Having accepted as a basic premise that direct negotiations with the

USSR offered the only hope for avoiding a disastrous arms race, he was content to leave the specifics of the plan to be hammered out by Soviet and American negotiators. From his own difficult experiences at the 1930 London Naval Conference and 1932 Geneva Conference on disarmament, Stimson understood the impossibility of imposing a unilateral American plan for handling the bomb, no matter how well thought out. The specifics of any plan were bound to undergo alteration in the heat of negotiations, particularly given the highly technical nature of the subjects involved. What mattered was that the leaders involved approach the negotiations with an understanding of the gravity of the issue and a sincere desire to reach an agreement through mutual give-and-take. It was this "great principle of direct negotiations," more than any specific plan, that Stimson hoped to instill on the American side as he left office in September 1945.[22] In this respect, his approach to the atomic bomb in this period harked back to his 1930 plea that "technical arguments should be set aside in order that the submarine may henceforth be abolished."[23]

The secretary of war's impassioned bid for international control illustrated perhaps his best quality as a statesman: the ability to hold true to his core principles while remaining flexible and open-minded in considering how to implement them. Historian William Appleman Williams once observed of Stimson that he "had the relatively rare kind of courage that enabled him to modify or change his opinions on some vital issues when they were battered beyond a certain point by reality."[24] Stimson readily admitted to Undersecretary of War Robert P. Patterson that his plan for international control was "gradually formed" only after coming to the realization that "I was wrong" in seeking to hold on to the bomb as a quid pro quo in postwar negotiations with the Soviets.[25] And though the outlines of his post-Hiroshima approach were rooted in deep moral convictions and a lifetime of experience in foreign affairs, he also borrowed liberally from the ideas on international control offered by Bush and Conant in September 1944, as well as from a growing cadre of scientists concerned about the future of the bomb in summer 1945.

Stimson's long journey on international control culminated in an extraordinary session of Truman's cabinet on September 21. Before leaving the Pentagon that day, Stimson met privately with Los Alamos director J. Robert Oppenheimer, who undoubtedly gave the outgoing secretary words of encouragement as he girded for his final act of public service. Stimson then proceeded to the White House, where he received the Distinguished Service

Medal from Truman before being ushered into the cabinet room to make his presentation. Though he carried with him a copy of the memoranda he had presented to Truman, the secretary spoke extemporaneously at the meeting, delving into the history of friendly U.S. relations with Russia going back to the time of the czars and stressing his belief that the "future of world peace" hinged on a direct approach to the Soviet Union on international control. Hinting darkly about the prospects of the even more powerful hydrogen bomb, Stimson warned that a failure to control these new weapons might "put an end to the world."[26]

Bowing to Stimson's status as an elder statesman, the cabinet listened respectfully to his plea for international control of atomic energy. Several cabinet members, including Undersecretary of State Dean Acheson and Secretary of Commerce Henry Wallace, spoke in favor of a direct approach to the Soviets. And though there was substantial opposition from the military, the secretary of war left Washington that afternoon convinced that even those who had originally favored maintaining an Anglo-American nuclear monopoly "ultimately rather yielded to my views" and that "the President has decided to follow almost exactly my recommendations."[27] In fact, the chances of achieving the kind of cooperative Soviet-American relationship necessary for the international control of atomic energy were already dim and grower dimmer as Stimson boarded the plane that took him back to private life on September 21.

It would have taken extraordinary political courage on Truman's part to willingly give up the American nuclear monopoly without first extracting major concessions from the Soviet Union. As indicated by his cautious attitude toward modifying surrender terms for Japan, the newly installed president was not inclined to take such political risks. Even if Truman had been so inclined, it is not clear that Congress would have ratified such a deal. Amid a climate of postwar atomic triumphalism and growing tensions with the Soviet Union, public, press, and congressional opinion was running strongly against Stimson's plan. When news of the September 21 cabinet meeting was leaked to the press (likely by Forrestal or others in the military hostile to international control), reporters quickly latched on to the rumor that it was "warm sympathizer with Communist Russia" Henry Wallace and "his fellow travelers," not Stimson, the esteemed Republican secretary of war, who wanted "to tell Russia how to make our breed of atom bombs."[28]

It is also unlikely that the Soviets would have been receptive to international control in the wake of Hiroshima. As illustrated by the wartime disagreements between the United States and Great Britain, negotiations over the future of atomic energy were delicate and challenging under the best of circumstances. With the end of the war, the already tenuous alliance with the Soviet Union was nearing the breaking point. The American decision to employ the bomb in combat without having previously conducted exploratory discussion with Stalin on international control—a decision that Stimson had strongly supported at the time—probably doomed any slim chance for a meaningful agreement on international control involving the Soviet Union. As historian David Holloway has chronicled, in the aftermath of Hiroshima, the Soviet leader injected vast resources and renewed urgency into the Soviet nuclear program, determined to develop his own bomb at any cost.[29]

Even as the Soviets accelerated their nascent nuclear program, powerful forces within the United States government and military were pushing to maintain and extend the American nuclear monopoly. On September 15, as Stimson prepared to deliver his valedictory plea for international control, General Lauris S. Norstad, chief of staff of the Twentieth Air Force (the unit that had delivered the atomic bombs against Japan) presented Leslie Groves with a memorandum outlining a course of action radically different from that proposed by the outgoing secretary of war. Less than two weeks after Japanese leaders had signed the articles of surrender about the battleship *Missouri* in Tokyo Bay, Norstad was already looking ahead to the next war. "The United States," he argued, "must be prepared to conduct offensive operations against any other world power or combination of powers." The weapon of choice in such a conflict would be the atomic bomb.[30] Focusing specifically on the Soviet Union, Norstad and his staff drew up a target list of sixty-six cities and argued that "an optimum requirement for atomic bomb stocks would be the number necessary to obliterate all of these cities." Some larger Soviet cities were to be hit with up to six bombs to ensure their complete destruction. Whereas Stimson was clearly troubled by the precedent set at Hiroshima and Nagasaki, Norstad embraced the logic of annihilation, postulating an offensive strategy that would eventually form the core of cold war American nuclear doctrine.[31]

Leslie Groves shared Norstad's commitment to maintaining and expanding the American nuclear arsenal. The "Atomic General" had long advocated such a position and, unlike Stimson, he experienced no post-Hiroshima epiphany on the subject of international control. On the same day that Stimson presented to Truman's cabinet his plan for a direct approach to the Soviets, Groves gave a public address in which he insisted that "this weapon must be kept under control of the United States until all other nations of the world are as anxious for peace as we are."[32] Privately, Groves urged that the wartime atomic intelligence apparatus be redirected "toward learning whether scientific, technical, and industrial advances in ostensibly friendly countries throughout the world constitute an imminent military threat to the United States." By January 1946, he was suggesting a preemptive strike against any unfriendly nation that sought to develop its own nuclear weapons. So long as nuclear weapons existed, Groves concluded, the United States must have "the biggest, the best, and the most."[33]

At the September 21 cabinet meeting, Secretary of the Navy James Forrestal (who may have shared some of Stimson's reservations about the use of atomic weapons against Japanese civilians) offered strong opposition to the secretary of war's proposal for approaching the Soviet Union.[34] Forrestal, in a memorandum prepared for the September 21 meeting, likened sharing the atomic secret with Soviets to the appeasement of Hitler.[35] The irony of accusing Stimson, who had been one of the first to sound the tocsin against fascist aggression in the 1930s, of appeasement was apparently lost on the navy secretary.

The unilateral military approach suggested by Forrestal, Groves, and Norstad was not yet established as official American policy at the time that Stimson left Washington. But combined with Byrnes's inclination to "keep the bomb . . . in his hip pocket without any suggestion of sharing it with Russia," it clearly signaled a tilt toward a stance on nuclear weapons that was the very antithesis of that proposed by Stimson.[36] In an early signal of his intentions, Truman confided in an interview with congressman Mike Mansfield on August 10 that he "intended to keep the development of atomic processes—industrial and military—under strict control and possession of the governments of the U.S., Canada, and Britain. We are not giving up this ace under any consideration, even to our own industrialists."[37]

Stimson had little opportunity to shape the public debate in the immediate aftermath of the September 21 meeting. His tenure as secretary of war, culminating in the destruction of Hiroshima and Nagasaki, had taken a tremendous physical and emotional toll. Privately he described himself upon leaving office as "a pretty battered relic," and upon arriving at Highhold he was largely confined to bed on doctor's orders.[38] A little over a month after boarding the plane to leave Washington, he suffered a second heart attack that nearly killed him. Stimson's physical decline was matched by the fading fortunes of his plan for the international control of atomic energy.

As he regained his strength, Stimson entertained a roster of distinguished visitors and, when physically able, journeyed into New York City, where he retained an office in the building of his old law firm.[39] Through correspondence with insiders such as Conant, Bush, Oppenheimer, and Bernard Baruch (whom Truman appointed to head negotiations on international control at the United Nations), he kept abreast of the domestic and international debate over the future of the bomb. The news he received was not encouraging. In a public statement only weeks after Stimson left office, Truman indicated that the United States had no intention of initiating the kind of direct approach to the Soviet Union that his former secretary of war had advocated. Byrnes, meanwhile, pushed ahead with his attempts at atomic diplomacy. As Stimson had predicted, negotiating with the Soviets while "having this weapon rather ostentatiously on our hip" failed disastrously at an acrimonious meeting of foreign ministers at London.[40] With negotiations over international control seemingly stalled, Vannevar Bush wrote to the retired secretary of war in November 1945 characterizing the administration's efforts as "completely unorganized" and akin to "a chapter in 'Alice in Wonderland.' "[41]

The fading prospects for international control of atomic energy put Stimson in a difficult position. Through spring 1946 he remained firmly committed to a direct approach to the Soviet Union, and he was greatly concerned by the apparent lack of progress. But his deeply ingrained personal and professional loyalty to the Truman administration rendered the former secretary of war loath to make any public statement that might be interpreted as critical.[42] In March 1946, Stimson published a sanitized version of the memorandum that he had presented to the president and the cabinet the previous September. Though careful not to publicly embarrass Truman or Byrnes, he clearly reiterated his belief in the need for direct negotiations to deal with the threat of the bomb. The United States, he urged, "must take the lead by holding out an open hand to other nations in a spirit of genuine trust and with a real desire for a through-going cooperative effort in meeting and solving this problem."[43] After rereading his September 1945 memorandum, Stimson wrote privately to Baruch to inform him that "I find I have not changed my opinions as there expressed as to the general principles under which we should deal with this problem."[44]

In the remaining five years of his life, the aging statesman watched as cold war tensions threatened his hopes of preventing a nuclear arms race and building "an international world" out of the ashes of World War II.[45] The retired statesman also worried about his own legacy. In a final tragic irony, Stimson's most important contribution to the nuclear age in his retirement was to participate in a behind-the-scenes effort to shape the public history of the Manhattan Project. In the process, the esteemed former secretary of war helped to obscure the record of moral concerns about the bomb's use that he and others had entertained in the months and years prior to Hiroshima.

Chapter 8

"The Full Enumeration of the Steps in the Tragedy"

ON DECEMBER 12, 1946, HENRY L. STIMSON WROTE TO HIS OLD friend and confidant Supreme Court Justice Felix Frankfurter to ask a favor and make a confession. The two men had known each other for forty years, ever since Stimson selected Frankfurter at age twenty-four to assist him in the United States Attorney's office. While working together to battle corporate fraud and bust trusts during the administration of Theodore Roosevelt, they had formed a close friendship in spite of Stimson's polite—if persistent—anti-Semitism.[1] They kept up a constant correspondence to the end of Stimson's life, sharing their unique perspectives on four decades' worth of dramatic events.

On this occasion, Stimson enclosed a draft of an article entitled "The Decision to Use the Atomic Bomb." Though it was to be published under his name, the former secretary of war admitted that the enclosed article was in fact "the product of many hands." More than simply a ghostwritten account of the A-bomb decision, the article was the product of a secret effort by prominent establishment figures to shape the public and scholarly debate for decades to come. It was initiated by wartime government science adviser (and Harvard president) James Conant and built on drafts contributed by Manhattan Project head General Leslie R. Groves, Interim Committee secretary R. Gordon Arneson, and Stimson aide Harvey Bundy. War Department historian Rudolph Winnacker provided behind-the-scenes research assistance at the Pentagon. McGeorge Bundy, Harvey's son, pulled all these threads together into a polished final product.

Despite this distinguished list of silent coauthors, Stimson was troubled by the final product. "I have rarely been connected with a paper about which I have so much doubt at the last moment," he confided to Frankfurter. Stimson was particularly concerned that the story of his role in the destruction of Hiroshima and Nagasaki would appear to be at odds with his long-standing commitment to peace, law, and morality. "I think the full enumeration of the steps in the tragedy," he confessed to Frankfurter, "will excite horror among friends who theretofore thought me a kindly-minded Christian gentleman but who will, after reading this, feel that I am cold blooded and cruel and different from the man who labored for peace under Mr. Hoover." Though he was willing to make the "personal sacrifice" to his reputation by attaching his name to the article, Stimson wanted reassurance before making the final leap.[2]

Responding to his old friend's request, Frankfurter read the article twice, "slept on it two nights," and even showed it to his wife, Marion, "for her sensibilities are particularly to be trusted on the kind of issue that the present publication of your article raises." Replying on December 16, the Supreme Court Justice urged Stimson to publish the article as soon as possible. It was important, Frankfurter asserted, to combat the "sloppy sentimentality" that had led some people to question the use of the atomic bomb. Frankfurter reassured the former secretary of war that he would be vindicated in the court of history and that the article would silence the "self-righteous" critics of the bomb.[3]

Encouraged by his old friend, Stimson gave his assent to publication, and "The Decision to Use the Atomic Bomb" appeared in *Harper's Magazine* in February 1947. Public and press response was strongly positive, and the article was widely reprinted in the months that followed. Few contemporary observers detected any hint of the agony Stimson expressed privately to Frankfurter prior to its publication. But while the *Harper's* article positioned Stimson as the most visible and distinguished defender of the A-bomb, he was in reality a most uneasy apostle of the tragedy that ushered in the nuclear age.

Ultimately, the Stimson article not only enshrined several enduring myths regarding the decision to use the bomb but also, as he had feared, warped public and scholarly perception of his own ambiguous legacy in the decades to come.

"The Teachers of Our Next Generation"

The story behind the genesis of the Stimson essay has been well told elsewhere.[4] In brief, the seeds were planted by Conant, who was concerned by a small but eloquent group of critics, including prominent Protestant theologian Reinhold Niebuhr, who publicly questioned the necessity and morality of the atomic bombings. Some of the most prominent early critics of the bomb were political conservatives, including John Foster Dulles, Felix Morley (editor of *Human Events*), and David Lawrence (editor of *U.S. News*). Two days after Hiroshima, Stimson's former boss Herbert Hoover privately confided that "[t]he use of the Atomic bomb, with its indiscriminate killing of women and children, revolts my soul."[5] Finally, the publication of John Hersey's *Hiroshima* in 1946, while not a direct criticism of the decision to use the bomb, dramatically humanized the effects of the bombing on the residents of that city. The vast majority of Americans continued enthusiastically to endorse the use of the bomb against Japan in the years after the war.[6] But Conant was troubled by the thin lines of criticism that were appearing around the edges of the seemingly solid public support for the A-bomb decision.

Conant was particularly worried that the A-bomb critics, while small in number, might influence schoolteachers and college professors, whom he characterized as "sentimental and verbal minded."[7] Should educators begin to raise questions about the bomb, they might in turn influence future generations of Americans to believe that the use of the nuclear weapons against Japanese cities had been immoral and unjustified. Such a development would not only tarnish the historical legacy of the men who had presided over that use but might also lead to troubling questions about the legitimacy of nuclear weapons in America's postwar arsenal.

The latter possibility greatly concerned Conant, for he believed that a strong, unsentimental attitude toward the bomb was vital if there were ever to be an agreement on international control on atomic energy with the Soviet Union. As he explained it to Stimson:

I am firmly convinced that the Russians will eventually agree to the American proposals for the establishment of an atomic energy authority of worldwide scope, *provided* they are convinced that we would have the bomb in quantity and would be prepared to use it without hesitation in another war. Therefore, I have been fearful lest those who have been motivated by humanitarian considerations in their arguments against the bomb were as a matter of fact tending to accomplish exactly the reverse of their avowed purpose.[8]

Moved by hopes for international control—and likely by concern for his own reputation—Conant mobilized a group of A-bomb insiders to silence the critics before they could plant the seeds of doubt in the minds of the next generation.

Stimson, with his bipartisan credentials and unimpeachable reputation, was an obvious choice to serve as the self-described "victim who should do it" by lending his name to the finished product.[9] The secretary of war had harbored sincere moral reservations about the use of the bomb against Japanese civilians prior to Hiroshima. As evidenced by his confession to Frankfurter, he was still troubled by this issue. But Stimson also shared Conant's concern over both the future of international control and the possibility that "ill informed criticism" of the A-bomb decision by "the teachers of our next generation" might have "rather poisonous effects."[10]

The former secretary of war was also motivated by loyalty to his wartime colleagues, particularly to Harry Truman. Truman, clearly anxious about his own legacy, wrote to his former secretary of war on several occasions during the drafting of the essay in order to offer encouragement.[11] Quiet loyalty and devotion to service had always been hallmarks of Stimson's government career, and even in his retirement he continued to value those traits. Though he had never been as close to Truman as he had been to Franklin Roosevelt, Stimson still felt duty-bound to defend the president from charges that he had used the bomb in haste or unnecessarily. As George C. Marshall later observed, Stimson "generously took a greater share of the responsibility than was fair" in attaching his name to the article.[12]

In summer 1946, McGeorge Bundy, the twenty-seven-year-old son of Stimson's wartime assistant Harvey Bundy, moved from Harvard's Eliot House (where he was a junior fellow) into a small cottage behind the main house at Highhold.[13] It was young Bundy who took the lead in weaving together the various drafts and notes into what was to become the most influential article ever published on the atomic bomb. Henry and Mabel, who had never had children of their own, became extraordinarily fond of "Mac." Long after his work was completed, Bundy remained a frequent visitor to Highhold and carried on a constant, often feisty correspondence with the Stimsons. He not only drafted the *Harper's* article but also collaborated on the former secretary's memoir *On Active Service* (1948) as well as a number of other articles and letters offering Stimson's views on the pressing international issues of the day.[14]

At Conant's suggestion, Bundy's final draft of the A-bomb article was carefully tailored to "eliminate all sections in which the Secretary appears to be arguing his case or justifying his decision." Rather, it was to take the form of "a mere recital of the facts."[15] The facts, however, were carefully chosen to tell a particular story without appearing to be argumentative. Stripping away the agonies and complexities of the internal wartime debates over the bomb, Bundy's final draft presented a stark and simple narrative. The bomb was used to avoid an invasion of the Japanese home islands that would have cost "a million casualties, to American forces alone" and "enemy casualties . . . much larger than our own."[16] Faced with this dire scenario, American leaders had little alternative but to use atomic weapons to secure Japanese capitulation with the minimum loss of life on both sides. While the essay conveyed a tone of regret for the lives lost at Hiroshima and Nagasaki, it concluded that the use of the bomb against Japanese cities was "our least abhorrent choice" and that "no man, in our position and subject to our responsibilities, holding in his hands a weapon of such possibilities . . . could have failed to use it and afterwards looked his countrymen in the face."[17]

By positing only two choices—either an invasion or the use of nuclear weapons to induce surrender—the Stimson article presented a virtually unarguable case in favor of the bomb. It did so without ever resorting to strident rhetoric, employing crudely racist caricatures of the Japanese, or expressing satisfaction at the vengeance delivered to a hated enemy. What reasonable observer (then or now) would have preferred a horrifically bloody invasion with perhaps a million or more deaths to the quick, decisive, and comparatively bloodless end brought by two atomic bombs? Though historians have since questioned the million-casualty number floated in the Stimson essay, surely even "sentimental and verbal minded" academics could understand that the lives lost at Hiroshima and Nagasaki were only a tiny fraction of those who would have been killed had the United States gone ahead with the invasion planned for November 1945.[18] Regardless of the estimated number of casualties, no American president would have ordered such an invasion without first employing the bomb in hopes of forcing a Japanese capitulation. This simple, compelling logic yoked to Bundy's lucid writing combined to make "The Decision to Use the Atomic Bomb" stunningly effective at shaping public and scholarly understanding of the subject. Commenting on the success of the essay in stilling dissent, "Mac" Bundy privately boasted to Stimson that "we deserve some sort of medal for reducing these particular chatterers to silence."[19]

The Stimson essay remains probably the single most influential account of the use of the bomb, and many of its arguments, particularly the estimate of one million American casualties, figured prominently in the public debate over the Smithsonian's abortive *Enola Gay* exhibit in 1994.[20] But the success of the essay came at a great cost. In order to present the case for using the bomb in such a way as to ensure continued public support, Bundy and his fellow contributors deliberately stripped their narrative of any ambiguities that might raise troubling questions about the decision. The result was a misleading account that flattened the complex moral, diplomatic, and military dilemmas surrounding the development and use of nuclear weapons into a simple binary choice pitting the bomb against a costly invasion of Japan. Though rhetorically effective, this technique not only elided many important issues but also masked the painful and difficult choices facing Stimson and the other American leaders involved in the decision.

Neither Truman, Stimson, nor any other American leader ever wrestled with the question of whether it would be better to use the bomb or invade Japan. What they did question, debate, and sometime argue over were the more complex and subtle questions that made up the context of use. How should the bomb be integrated into American wartime diplomacy? What role should the Soviet Union play in the future development and control of atomic energy? Was it legitimate to use the bomb against cities and civilians? Should Japan be offered a warning? Were there opportunities to hasten the end the war, perhaps before either the bomb *or* an invasion was necessary? American leaders asked all these questions prior to Hiroshima.

Recovering the Tragedy: American Diplomacy and Japanese Surrender

One of the important choices that the Stimson essay obscured involved the debate over surrender terms for Japan. This was a tricky and potentially divisive issue for the defenders of the A-bomb decision. Several important figures within the War and State Departments had advocated abandoning the unconditional surrender formula as the war in the Pacific reached its climax in summer 1945. Stimson himself had ultimately argued in favor of clarifying American terms prior to the use of the bomb to allow the Japanese to retain their emperor. Though Truman rejected this suggestion at Potsdam and wavered on it as late as August 10, he ultimately allowed the continuation of the imperial dynasty *after* the use of two bombs, a decision that was crucial in facilitating surrender. This suggests the possibility that if American leaders had acted sooner to guarantee the status of the emperor, especially in conjunction with the public threat of Soviet entry into to conflict, they might have been able to secure a Japanese surrender at an earlier date.

Not wanting to complicate the simple choice that gave the Stimson essay such compelling rhetorical force or expose rifts within the Truman administration, Bundy did his best to acknowledge the question of surrender terms without dwelling on their larger implications. Conant had suggested ignoring the issue entirely, arguing that "the introduction of the problem of the Emperor diverts one's mind from the general line of argumentation."[21] That was not, however, a tenable strategy. Not only had Stimson personally lobbied Truman to modify the American terms, but, unlike many of the other A-bomb-related questions, the surrender issue had been widely and noisily debated within the Truman administration prior to Hiroshima. If the bomb's defenders did not address it, others privy to the surrender debate would surely raise the matter on their own.

Bundy handled the surrender debate by inserting within the essay the text of Stimson's July 2 memorandum to Truman in which he urged the president to clarify the American terms. The memorandum included the secretary of war's admonition that, "I personally think that if in saying this we should add that we do not exclude a constitutional monarchy under her present dynasty, it would substantially add to the chances of acceptance." Having acknowledged Stimson's preference for modifying unconditional surrender, Bundy disposed of the matter in laconic fashion, noting simply that the final text of the Potsdam Declaration "closely followed the above memorandum of July 2, with the exception that it made no mention of the Japanese Emperor."[22] Bundy did not elaborate or speculate on why the president had disregarded the secretary of war's advice on the emperor in issuing the Potsdam Declaration. Nor did he address the failure to secure a Soviet signature on that document as part of the effort "coordinate all the threats possible to Japan."[23]

Any apportionment of blame for the prolonged and destructive conclusion to the fighting in the Pacific must obviously fall first and foremost on Japanese leaders who continued to insist on fighting long after military defeat was assured. But American leaders must also bear some responsibility for the war's bloody denouement, culminating in the atomic destruction of two Japanese cities. There was no guarantee that a statement on the postwar status on the emperor coupled with Stalin's signature on the Potsdam Declaration would have produced a Japanese surrender prior to the use of the bomb. But it offered that possibility at least, and it did so at no cost to the United States. This was Ralph Bard's argument in his June 27 dissent, and it was one that Stimson ultimately embraced at Potsdam.

By the time the Potsdam Declaration was released, the United States had successfully tested a nuclear weapon and secured the promise of Soviet entry into the war by August 15. Had Japanese leaders mistaken a guarantee of the emperor's status for a sign of weakness, the two hammer blows provided by nuclear weapons and Soviet intervention would have quickly dispelled that notion. At the very least, an early clarification of the American attitude toward the emperor might have expedited a Japanese surrender after the use of the first bomb, perhaps concluding the war before the second bomb was used on Nagasaki. Shortening the war by even a single day would have saved not only American and Japanese lives but also those of Chinese, Vietnamese, Koreans, and other Asians engaged in the larger struggle against Japanese imperialism. This logic is frequently invoked by defenders of Truman's decision to use the bomb, but those same defenders seem unwilling to apply it when it comes to the president's failure to utilize the full range of diplomatic options to hasten the end of the war.[24] Nor is this argument simply the product of hindsight. It was in speaking of these diplomatic options that Stimson warned in June 1945 that "the country will not be satisfied unless every effort is made to shorten the war."[25]

While his share of the responsibility is considerably less than that of the heads of state who guided the major belligerents, any searching judgment of the tortured conclusion to World War II in the Pacific must also include an indictment of Stimson. In confining his discussion of surrender terms to July 1945, Bundy's essay glossed over the secretary of war's decision to defer consideration of the issue several months earlier. In rejecting Undersecretary of State Joseph Grew's May 29 plea to immediately consider a restatement of American terms, including a guarantee of the emperor, Stimson had effectively severed the diplomatic track from considerations about the bomb at a crucial moment in the decision-making process. This delay was not the result of careful deliberation on his part. Rather, it reflected a perhaps understandable desire to postpone any consideration of how to handle surrender negotiations while he awaited the fruition of the Manhattan Project. Stimson's crucial mistake was failing to anticipate the difficulty of revisiting this issue in the hectic weeks before the use of the bomb.

In the glow of victory, few people dwelled on either the surrender issue or its oblique treatment in the 1947 essay published under Stimson's name. Joseph Grew and several of his former State Department colleagues were, however, privately outraged by the strategic omissions in the *Harper's* article. Grew wrote to Stimson following the essay's publication to remind the former secretary of war of his role in torpedoing consideration of revised American terms at the May 29 meeting. "If surrender could have been brought about in May, 1945, or even in June or July, before the entrance of Soviet Russia into the war and the use of the atomic bomb," Grew lamented, "the world would have been the gainer." Stimson delayed six months before penning an evasive reply to Grew.[26] The revised version of the A-bomb essay that appeared in Stimson's 1948 memoir did give explicit credit to Grew for his advocacy on behalf of modifying American surrender terms. Without assigning blame to any particular person, his memoir also conceded that "history might find that the United States, by its delay in stating its position [on the emperor], had prolonged the war."[27] Stimson, however, never fully came to terms with his own role in the failure of diplomacy that preceded the use of the bomb against Hiroshima and Nagasaki.

Recovering the Tragedy: Targeting Civilians

The binary logic of the *Harper's* essay also obscured another important choice made by American policymakers with respect to the bomb. If the intransigence of Japanese leaders, abetted by the American delay in clarifying surrender terms, ultimately made the use of the bomb inevitable, it did not necessarily follow that it had to be used without warning against cities and civilians. Scientists working in Great Britain had raised moral concerns about the potential use of the bomb against civilians as early as March 1940, years before the start of the serious American effort to build a nuclear weapon. Prior to Hiroshima, Truman, Stimson, and Marshall all expressed a preference for avoiding nuclear attacks on the civilian population of Japan. These sentiments were later echoed by several important military figures, including General Carl A. Spaatz, General Dwight D. Eisenhower, and chief of staff, Admiral William Leahy, who after the war sharply condemned the use of the bomb against civilians. The failure to follow through on the ethical and moral concerns over the use of the bomb against Japanese cities is one of the most poorly understood incidents in the early history of nuclear weapons.[28]

The 1947 *Harper's* article published under Stimson's name contained no trace of the behind-the-scenes moral unease that had marked the American debate over city targeting during World War II. There were clear motives for this omission, given the goals of the men involved in drafting the essay. The targeting question not only was complicated (and hence liable to distract from the flow of Bundy's narrative) but also served to undermine the portrait of a united and resolute group of leaders making the only choice open to them—use of the bomb against a city without warning. But in choosing to exclude the complex, confused, and sometimes agonized history of wartime nuclear targeting from their narrative, the authors of the Stimson article helped to warp public and scholarly understanding of both the A-bomb decisions and the men and institutions that made them.

There were several missed chances on the American side to shape the targeting of the bomb so as to reduce if not eliminate civilian casualties. The first missed opportunity came in 1943–44, when Los Alamos scientists and engineers stopped work on an underwater bomb and shifted toward an airburst weapon optimized for use against cities. Though this decision was not undertaken with the intent of dictating the targeting of the atomic bomb, it had the effect of narrowing the options open to high-level policymakers when they set about considering how to use the weapon against Japan in summer 1945. The blame for this must rest largely with the policymakers themselves, including Stimson. By choosing to defer considerations about targeting until the bomb was near readiness, he forfeited the opportunity to shape the development of the weapon produced at Los Alamos. While a closer engagement with the technical developments at Los Alamos could not have guaranteed that the resulting weapon would be compatible with his own convictions about war and morality, the secretary of war's inattention in 1943–44 rendered that outcome far less likely.

Even if we discard the possibility of either a noncombat demonstration or use against a strictly military target, there were still opportunities to shape the targeting of the bomb in ways that might have reduced civilian casualties. For example, in June 1945 Marshall strongly urged that the bomb be used against the Kokura arsenal. Though not a strictly military target, Kokura was a sprawling military-industrial objective, and the resulting civilian casualties would almost surely have been less than those inflicted by targeting the bomb in the center of a residential neighborhood. This difference was dramatically illustrated at Nagasaki. When clouds prevented an attack on the Kokura arsenal, the B-29 carrying the bomb proceeded to the secondary target of Nagasaki. The original aiming point was in a residential neighborhood in the center of the city, east of the harbor. But clouds again intervened, and bombardier Thomas Beehan instead dropped the bomb in the industrial section north of the city. While the bomb used on August 9 was considerably more powerful than the one dropped three days earlier, the death toll at Nagasaki was less than half that at Hiroshima. In the grim calculus of nuclear targeting, a difference of a few miles in aiming points could have saved tens of thousands of lives.[29] This was not an academic issue to Stimson, who worried greatly prior to Hiroshima about "the moral position of the United States and its responsibilities" with respect to the use of the bomb.[30]

Stimson almost certainly did not know about the aim points within the selected cities, which were picked by the air crews on Tinian and not mentioned in the directive that he approved on July 25. The secretary of war was encouraged by the target descriptions provided by Groves and the AAF at Potsdam, all of which emphasized the military-industrial character of the cities in question, to believe there would be at least an attempt to hit a "dual target." Certainly there is no evidence that Groves or anybody else ever informed him that the aiming points in at least two of the cities (Hiroshima and Nagasaki) diverged sharply from the Interim Committee's May 31 recommendation. But if Stimson was deceived, it was a deception facilitated by his own eagerness to avoid dwelling on what was likely a difficult and unpleasant subject. Had he pressed Groves or the field commanders in the Pacific, the secretary of war could have learned the truth about the aiming points and insisted they be moved to better reflect the previous agreement on the subject. At Potsdam, however, both Stimson and Truman accepted the vague assurances that the bomb would be used against a military or military-industrial target. Stimson's failure to engage with A-bomb targeting until the last minute mirrored his troubled but largely disengaged attitude toward American conventional bombing of both Germany and Japan in 1945.

In the aftermath of the war, the escalating conventional bombing un-leashed in 1945, including the fire bombing of Tokyo that killed some hun-dred thousand Japanese on a single night in March, appeared to foreshadow the nuclear destruction of Hiroshima and Nagasaki.[31] Popular and scholarly accounts of the A-bomb attacks have often invoked the moral threshold argu-ment to suggest that American leaders had long since become inured to the mass killing of enemy civilians by August 1945. A history of racial antagonism exacerbated by the particularly brutal fighting in the Pacific from 1941 to 1945 has also been cited as explaining the willingness of American leaders to use atomic bombs against Japanese cities.[32] Stimson's case, and that of Mar-shall, Spaatz, and others, complicates this set of assumptions. While many Americans may have easily accepted, even rejoiced, in the mass killing of Japanese civilians in 1945, the secretary of war was not one of them. Stimson's tragedy was not that his moral convictions had been effaced by the brutality of the war or his own racist attitudes but rather that his failure to closely engage with the details of both conventional bombing and nuclear targeting helped facilitate actions that violated those convictions.

Recovering the Tragedy: The Myth and Reality of "Atomic Diplomacy"

Thanks to pioneering works by "revisionist" historians such as Gar Alperovitz, Martin J. Sherwin, and Barton J. Bernstein, we now know beyond a shadow of a doubt that American leaders began thinking about the long-term diplomatic impact of nuclear fission, particularly vis-à-vis the Soviet Union, from the very start of the bomb effort, years before a finished weapon was available.[33] From the birth of the Manhattan Project to the Anglo-American negotiations of

1943–44, the covert mission to Stassfurt, and the meeting at Potsdam in 1945, the handful of American leaders entrusted with the atomic secret spent far more time pondering its diplomatic ramifications than they did its military potential against Germany or Japan. There is nothing surprising or shocking about this fact. Any weapon, no matter how revolutionary, is useful for military purposes only when it is in hand and ready for delivery against the enemy. In the meantime, no responsible leader could ignore the potential impact of the bomb on either wartime diplomacy or the postwar world.

The diplomatic concerns that dominated high-level thinking about nuclear weapons in the United States during World War II were nowhere to be found in the article published under Stimson's name in 1947. Indeed, the Stimson article strategically omitted *any* references to the Soviet Union and the wartime debates within the Roosevelt and Truman administrations over international control. These omissions were neither accidental nor simply dictated by the issue of classification. As a way of lending credibility to the narrative, Bundy was allowed to excerpt several still-classified wartime documents in the text of the essay. One of these documents was Stimson's April 25 memorandum to Truman in which the secretary of war briefed the new president on the postwar implications of the bomb. The document was reproduced in full in the Stimson essay with one exception: a sentence referring to the Soviet Union was effaced. In its place were ellipses and a note indicating, "A brief reference to the estimated capabilities of other nations is here omitted; it in no way affects the course of the argument."[34] In fact, the only "other nation" mentioned in the original document was the Soviet Union. Whether or not this omission affected "the course of the argument" has become a matter of tremendous historical controversy in the decades since the initial publication of the Stimson essay.

There were multiple reasons for avoiding any reference to the Soviet Union in the Stimson essay. One of those reasons was, indeed, incidental to the argument. Stimson had no desire to embarrass Truman while negotiations over the future of the bomb still hung in the balance. Though he was increasingly pessimistic of the chances for international control, public revelations about the extent to which American leaders had attempted to deny the atomic secret to the Soviets—a wartime ally—would surely have dealt a mortal blow to the ongoing negotiations.

There was, however, another reason for Bundy and his influential coauthors to avoid this subject. Should the world learn that Stimson and other wartime leaders had seen the atomic secret as a "master card" or "royal straight flush" that might be employed in negotiations with the Soviet Union to "regain the lead and perhaps do it in a pretty rough and realistic way," it would surely raise questions about the use of the bomb against Japan.[35] Was the bomb really used solely to secure a Japanese surrender? Or were American leaders also hoping to impress the Soviet Union with American power by demonstrating the weapon in combat? Was the timing of the bombings influenced in any way by a desire to end the war in the Pacific before the Soviets could enter and thus claim some of the spoils of victory? Rather than addressing these troubling questions, Bundy and his fellow contributors sidestepped the issue entirely, avoiding any hint of atomic diplomacy by strategically excising references to the Soviet Union and the wartime debate over the future of the bomb.

Amid the general air of approval that greeted the appearance of the Stimson essay, even some casual readers were struck by the failure to address the role of the Soviet Union in American calculations about the use of the bomb. One such reader wrote to Stimson in February 1947 to take issue with the essay, claiming that "[i]t is the moral judgment of many intelligent men that the political reason the bombs were used was to prevent advantage to the Russians who were preparing to claim parts of the spoils unless the war should be ended soon enough to prevent it."[36] The retired secretary of war did not bother to respond to this charge, but the larger debate over anti-Soviet motives was only beginning. In 1948, Nobel-prize-winning British physicist P. M. S. Blackett published a controversial book in which he clamed that "the dropping of the atomic bombs was not so much the last military act of the second World War, as the first major operation of the cold diplomatic war with Russia now in progress."[37] This was a direct challenge to the narrative laid down in the Stimson article. Without access to the still-classified documents relating to the A-bomb decision, however, Blackett had no proof, and his accusations received little attention at the time of the book's publication. Stimson, having lent his name to the *Harper's* article after some private agonizing, retreated from the A-bomb debate in the last years of his life and offered neither public nor private comment on Blackett's charge.

It was not until the opening of Stimson's wartime diaries and papers to scholars in 1959 (nine years after his death) that historians finally began to unravel the carefully constructed narrative at the heart of the 1947 essay. In

1965, Cambridge-trained American historian Gar Alperovitz published *Atomic Diplomacy*, a work inspired by Blackett (who had served as one of Alperovitz's thesis advisers) but supplemented with archival research. Seizing on evidence from the Stimson papers and elsewhere, Alperovitz convincingly demonstrated that American leaders were closely attuned to the diplomatic aspects of the bomb and had come to see it as an important counterweight to Soviet power by summer 1945. Going further, Alperovitz also suggested that anti-Soviet motives had played a role not only in wartime diplomacy but also in the decision to use the bomb against Japan. By the time of the Potsdam Conference, he claimed, the main rationale for using the bomb against Japan, "was no longer military, but political." Though he hedged in discussing the decision to use the bomb, Alperovitz posited that it might have been employed against Japan "primarily to impress the world with the need to accept America's plan for a stable and lasting peace."[38]

The publication of *Atomic Diplomacy* in 1965 sharply divided the scholarly community, pitting so-called orthodox historians, who followed the line of the Stimson article in claiming the bomb was used solely to end the war with Japan, against revisionists, who emphasized anti-Soviet motives to some degree or another in explaining the decision. Beginning in the 1970s, a handful of historians, perhaps best represented by Barton J. Bernstein, attempted to find a middle ground between these two schools, emphasizing that the decision to use the bomb was not an either/or proposition. Both anti-Soviet motives *and* a genuine desire to end the war with Japan and save lives led American leaders to favor use of the bomb, making the decision, in Bernstein's words, "virtually inevitable."[39] Though this "middle ground" position has gained considerable traction, the dispute over the *Enola Gay* exhibit and the publication of a new round of books by Alperovitz and his critics in the mid-1990s indicated that passions on this issue remain high among partisans on both sides.[40]

The historiographical battle over the A-bomb in the United States, a battle that began with a preemptive strike against critics of the bomb in the form of the 1947 Stimson essay, is an interesting episode in American intellectual history. But in the heat and noise of this impassioned discussion, much has been lost. Among other things, the debate over anti-Soviet motives has obscured the larger and more tragic story of Stimson's relationship to nuclear weapons and the threat they pose to "industrial civilization."

Given our knowledge of the cold war nuclear arms race that followed, it is understandably tempting for historians to impose a teleological framework on the conduct of America's wartime atomic diplomacy with an emphasis on anti-Soviet motives. In fact, while American leaders did indeed hope to use the atomic secret for diplomatic advantage over the Soviet Union, they did so in a staggeringly haphazard fashion. Stimson, for example, supported unilateral, bilateral, and multilateral approaches to controlling the bomb at various times from 1941 to 1945. With respect to the USSR, he argued variously for using the bomb as a bargaining chip in order to gain economic and territorial concessions, withholding it altogether barring a fundamental change in the Soviet regime, and immediately welcoming Stalin into the atomic partnership without preconditions. On a practical level, the secretary of war's attempt to position the bomb as a diplomatic bargaining chip was frustrated by an inability to figure out how to barter with a weapon that he insisted on keeping secret.

Stimson, of course, never had the final word on the subject of atomic diplomacy and international control. Roosevelt and Truman, fully cognizant of the tremendous potential impact of the bomb on the postwar world, closely held their decision making on this subject, sometimes concealing it even from their closest nuclear advisers. But an examination of America's wartime atomic diplomacy reveals that virtually every American policymaker with any knowledge of the bomb shared to some degree in Stimson's conflicted and inconsistent attitude toward the future of nuclear fission. Arguably, Leslie Groves, who strongly favored unilateral American production and control of the bomb, was the only significant figure on the American side with a clear and consistent position on this issue from the beginning.[41]

Amid the confusion and uncertainty on the American side there was one consistent theme: when forced to choose between crafting a long-term solution to the danger posed by nuclear weapons and attempting to extract more immediate diplomatic concessions from the atomic secret, American policymakers repeatedly succumbed to the temptation to gain short-term advantage. None of the American leaders entrusted with the bomb were ignorant about the danger it posed to human civilization. Even Truman, who had little time to digest the significance of the bomb after taking office, privately wondered if it represented "the fire distruction [sic] prophesied in the Euphrates Valley Era, after Noah and his fabulous Ark."[42] It was, ironically, their understanding of the bomb's overriding importance in the postwar world that made it so tempting to American leaders as a wartime bargaining chip.

Whether the goal was acquiescing to the British desire for a joint program in order to smooth over transatlantic relations in 1943 or holding the atomic secret as a quid pro quo to secure an open door for American trade in Soviet-occupied Europe in 1945, U.S. leaders could not resist the lure of using the bomb to secure their desired diplomatic objectives. In Stimson's case, the intent was not explicitly anti-Soviet. With the exception of the brief period between the start of the Potsdam Conference in July 1945 and the use of the bomb in August, the secretary of war consistently held that the United States had no choice but to engage with the Soviet Union as a partner in the postwar peace, including the international control of nuclear fission. Nor is there any evidence that Stimson hoped to use the bomb against Japan in order to impress the Soviets with American power. Indeed, as evidenced by his last-ditch pleas at Potsdam, Stimson hoped to end the war before the use of the bomb.

Stimson's mistake was to believe that United States could have it all: American leaders could use the atomic secret for short-term diplomatic advantage while still cultivating a cooperative long-term relationship with the Soviet Union and eventually securing international control of atomic energy. The inevitable result of this short-sighted policy, as he belatedly realized, was to hasten the onset of a postwar nuclear arms race. And though this dangerous contest initially pitted the United States against the Soviet Union, the failure to agree on some form of nuclear arms control in the aftermath of World War II opened the door to a broader international scramble for the bomb in which any nation (or group) with great power ambitions sought its own nuclear force. The legacy of nuclear proliferation that haunts the world today has its roots in the failure to achieve control over the bomb at its birth during World War II.

It is, of course, possible to be unduly harsh in judging American leaders for their failure to better prepare for the uncertain nuclear future. These men were under tremendous pressure to win the war while simultaneously preparing to defend American interests in the postwar period. And while we know in retrospect that American leaders obtained no significant returns from their halting attempts at atomic diplomacy, the prospect was understandably tantalizing amid the complicated web of political-military problems they faced during World War II. Moreover, any realistic plan for international control would have required American leaders to fully and frankly approach the Soviet

Union with the atomic secret prior to Hiroshima, forsaking any attempt to wring diplomatic advantage out of a weapon developed at the cost of over $2 billion to American taxpayers. Not only would such a diplomatic approach have been political risky, opening up those who advocated it to charges of appeasement or even treason after the war, but there was also no guarantee that it would have succeeded in winning Soviet acquiesce. Stalin might have insisted on an independent Soviet bomb even had the United States approached him with an offer for international control prior to Hiroshima.

Acknowledging the difficulties faced by the American trustees of the bomb does not, however, absolve them of responsibility for their actions. Of all the figures in this drama, Stimson was by far the most tragic. Among the select few who were in a position to shape American nuclear policy during World War II, the secretary of war was uniquely qualified to appreciate the long-term danger posed by the bomb. Stimson's credentials as a moral statesman and his history of attempting to deal with weapons of mass destruction through international agreement led scientists of such varying backgrounds as Niels Bohr, J. Robert Oppenheimer, James Conant, and Vannevar Bush to put great faith in his leadership on international control of atomic energy during World War II. Though he was not in a position to make the final determination about the handling of the American nuclear program, Stimson's position, experience, and reputation gave him an unrivaled opportunity to shape the internal (and later public) debate over the future of the bomb.

Ultimately, it took the nuclear destruction of two Japanese cities before Stimson realized that he had made a tragic miscalculation in thinking the bomb could be used as a diplomatic bargaining chip. His impassioned plea for a direct approach to the Soviet Union in September 1945 in order "to control and limit the use of the atomic bomb as an instrument of war" was entirely consistent with a career dedicated to building trust, morality, and "organized self-control" at the international level.[43] It was also a tacit admission that the short-term quid pro quo approach to the bomb that he had embraced during the war was dangerously flawed and ultimately futile.

But for all his moral courage in confronting the looming cold war arms race, Stimson never fully accepted the degree to which his own actions had helped bring it about. By failing to directly acknowledge the consequences of his own wartime actions, even in private, Stimson opened himself up to later charges that he had been complicit in a conscious anti-Soviet conspiracy. The truth is more prosaic: under the intense pressure of a world war and deeply concerned with cementing a lasting peace in its aftermath, the secretary of war had repeatedly succumbed to the temptation of using the atomic secret as a diplomatic tool without ever figuring out exactly how to do so. The result was a failed policy that produced no meaningful diplomatic gains and contributed to the onset of the nuclear arms race.

"My Views Have Become Much More Conservative"

Stimson lived long enough after the war to see his hopes for world peace, prosperity, and security frustrated by rising tensions between the United States and the Soviet Union. In the immediate aftermath of his massive October 1945 heart attack, Stimson retreated from the public eye while he slowly recovered in the solitude of his Highhold estate on the banks of Long Island Sound. His heart condition and a severe case of arthritis (producing a pain in his legs and hips that he gamely dubbed "Johnny") limited his once vigorous outdoor lifestyle, leaving him confined to bed or a wheelchair much of the time. No longer able to ride a horse, he procured an army surplus Jeep that allowed him to roam Highhold's hundred acres at will. He shot clay pigeons, fished from the bank while perched in his wheelchair, smoked special "denictotinized" cigarettes, and stayed fit by swimming in the waters of the sound. Under doctor's orders, the teetotaling Stimson even began to drink whisky as a tonic for his ailing heart.[44]

By the time he became involved in the drafting of the *Harper's* article, disputes with the Soviets on a host of diplomatic issues (particularly in Turkey and Iran) had led Stimson to question whether a deal with Stalin on nuclear arms was still possible. In June 1946, he conceded that "the time has passed for handling the bomb in the way which I suggested to the President last summer."[45] By 1947, as the cold war began in earnest, Stimson privately confided that "[m]y views have become much more conservative with the passage of the past two years," and that it might be necessary to "stand by with all the bombs we have got and can make, and hold ourselves in readiness until Russia learns to be decent."[46]

Stimson's increasing skepticism with respect to the Soviet Union and international control reflected his general disillusionment with the tenor of postwar international relations. Though he placed most of the blame for this on the Soviet side, he did not exempt either the Truman administration or congressional Republicans from criticism for the rising tensions between the two superpowers.[47] He chastised some of his fellow Republicans for "sentiments which flavor too strongly of isolationism" and also warned that in dealing with the Soviet Union the United States should "always [be] careful to be gentlemen instead of muggers."[48] As he had thirty years earlier during America's first Red scare, Stimson expressed disdain for those who sought to fight radicalism abroad with repression at home or to criminalize political dissent. He was particularly scornful of Senator Joseph McCarthy, whom he privately dismissed as "a little junket from Wisconsin."[49] In March 1950, years before the Republican establishment finally abandoned McCarthy, Stimson in a letter to the *New York Times* sharply condemned the "noisy antics" of the Red-baiters in Washington, an effort he hoped would "spank the pants of Senator McCarthy of Wisconsin."[50]

Stimson's critique of McCarthy and his rejection of a preventative war against the Soviet Union—an idea he denounced as "criminal and futile folly"—illustrated the extent to which his own brand of conservatism differed from that of the more vitriolic anti-Communists within his own party.[51] Amid a rising Red scare, he sought to anchor American foreign policy—and international relations as a whole—to a set of moral and legal principles that transcended the current dispute with the Soviet Union. "The thing that I would never consent to," he repeatedly insisted, "would be to debauch our standards because the Russians have theirs. . . . I say Bolshevism is a passing episode in the world which should not be allowed to alter the character of the United States."[52] Reluctantly conceding that the world conditions did not allow for international control of nuclear energy at the present time, Stimson placed his hopes for the future in patient diplomacy built on the bedrock principles that had long shaped his view of America's role in the world. Morality and law were the first principles to which the aging statesman returned as he grappled with the dangers of the nuclear age in the twilight years of his life.

"Skillful Technicians without Morals"

In the last year of World War II, Stimson had suggested to his aide Harvey Bundy that only through "a spiritual revival of Christian principles" could mankind meet the challenge posed by nuclear weapons, a sentiment he reiterated in the immediate aftermath of Hiroshima and Nagasaki.[53] Morality rooted in religious conviction remained at the heart of Stimson's approach to the bomb as the prospects of international control faded following his retirement from government. In April 1946 he wrote to Reverend Howard M. Lehn affirming his belief that the "only solution which I can see for the terrible problems which we are now facing must come through a recognition of the authority of our Lord in the universe and the inculcation and development of the sprit taught by Jesus Christ."[54] In his postwar writings and private conversations, he presented the challenge facing the world not as a contest against Communism but rather as a race to match mankind's technical progress, exemplified by the atomic bomb, with the moral self-control necessary to preserve an increasingly "brittle" human civilization. "If we are going to evolve into a group of skillful technicians without morals," Stimson asserted, "the evolution of mankind is pretty grim."[55]

Though inspired by faith, Stimson understood that faith alone was not a remedy for the dangers of the nuclear age. He had never embraced religious dogma, asserting rather that faith should serve as an inspiration to develop practical solutions to the problems of the world.[56] Reaching back to his legal education at the knee of Elihu Root, Stimson sought to promote "a combination of steps, each of which may seem small and humble but the aggregate of which produces the new system of law."[57] Rather than directly addressing the challenge of nuclear weapons through international control, from 1947 onward he sought to promote the development of international law that would both limit the conduct of future wars and provide a kind of moral education that might eventually lead to the abolishment of war altogether.

As an example of the legal-moral approach to the problems posed by war and technology, Stimson highlighted the International Military Tribunal and the trials of Nazi war criminals at Nuremberg as nothing less than "the best piece of international work that has been done since the war."[58] The judgment at Nuremberg would, Stimson believed, serve several important functions in shaping the peaceful development of the postwar world. In addition to facilitating the rehabilitation of postwar Germany by punishing top Nazi leaders, the trials would also serve a more broadly educative function by graphically illustrating the damage that such lawless men could inflict upon their people and their neighbors if left unchecked.

Most important, as far as Stimson was concerned, the Nuremberg trials represented "a long step forward towards establishing a rule of law in this world."[59] He was particularly pleased with the convictions on the charge of "planning . . . or waging . . . a war of aggression in violation of international treaties," which he saw as a vindication of both the spirit and the letter of the Kellogg-Briand Pact, which he had unsuccessfully defended as secretary of state under Herbert Hoover in the early 1930s.[60] He insisted that "in the judgment of Nuremberg there is affirmed the central principle of peace—that the man who makes or plans to make aggressive war is a criminal."[61] In doing so, he reached back to Root's long-held conviction that war would one day be declared criminal conduct rather than a legitimate tool of state policy.[62] Stimson believed that the convictions on the charge of aggressive war, combined with the work being done by the United Nations to implement the ideals enshrined in the Nuremberg Charter, would go a long way toward making good his 1932 promise to "make the [Kellogg-Briand] Pact a living force of law in the world."[63]

Not all American observers shared Stimson's belief that the Nuremburg proceedings represented an important step forward in the development of international law. In response to an article by the former secretary of war defending the International Military Tribunal, the *Chicago Tribune*, which had never forgiven him for helping Franklin Roosevelt lead the United States into World War II, responded with a vicious editorial suggesting that "if his own statement of the appropriateness of the Nuremberg law is correct, Stimson should be hanged as a war criminal."[64]

Stimson gave no indication that he was troubled by either his ill-tempered critics or the looming challenges posed by the cold war. But for all the confidence that he evinced in the general trend of "moral progress" in the aftermath of World War II, the atomic bomb continued to cast a dark shadow over the aging statesman's hopes in his last years. Even as he hoped to contain the bomb through the gradual development of legal and moral standards, the weapon itself, he admitted, was so dangerous that it threatened mankind "to the point of extinction." In a grim defense of his belief in moral progress in the face of a possible nuclear catastrophe, Stimson privately suggested that there could still be "a law of moral progress even if there were few left to profit by it."[65]

To the end of his life, Stimson remained optimistic that the principles that he had stood for during his public career—trust, morality, and law—would outlast the tensions brought about by the cold war and the nuclear arms race. Writing to another former Roosevelt and Truman cabinet member, Harold Ickes, in October 1947, he mused on the task that the United States faced as it attempted to guide the rebuilding of the postwar world under the shadow of increasing tensions with the Soviet Union. "It's probably a long job with many difficulties and disappointments," Stimson conceded, "but I am confident that a satisfactory end will come."[66] Stimson himself would not live to see that end. His heart finally gave out on October 20, 1950. Stimson died at the age of eighty-three while a new generation of American leaders was grappling with the legacy of World War II and the new challenges of the cold war.

Conclusion

"A Grave and Continuing Responsibility"

ON AUGUST 20, 1966, UNDERSECRETARY OF STATE GEORGE W. BALL paid tribute to a man under whom he had served in the War Department during World War II.[1] At a speech in Groton, Connecticut, Ball praised Henry L. Stimson as "a distinguished American" and "a man of rare vision" who "understood, as few have done before or since, the basic issues of war and peace." In an address that ranged from the war in Vietnam to the future of America's role in the world, Ball gave special praise to Stimson as "the first to urge international agreement to control atomic weapons so that they might never have to be used again." Ball went on to quote with approval the former secretary of war's admonition that "[u]pon us as the people who first harnessed and made use of this force, there rests a grave and continuing responsibility for leadership, turning it toward life, not death."[2]

The occasion of Ball's tribute was the commissioning of a nuclear submarine, the U.S.S. *Henry L. Stimson* (SSBN 685). When it departed on its first patrol, the *Stimson* carried with it a deadly cargo of sixteen nuclear-tipped Polaris missiles, a combined destructive force 853 times more powerful than the

Figure 13. The commissioning of the U.S.S. *Henry L. Stimson* (SSBN 655), August 20, 1966. Sixteen years after his death, Stimson, who had previously argued for both nuclear arms control and the abolition of submarines, was memorialized in the form of a nuclear ballistic missile submarine carrying a destructive payload more than 800 times greater than the Hiroshima bomb. Not visible in this photo are the Playboy bunny logos later painted inside the launch tubes by the *Stimson*'s crew. (United States Naval Institute)

bomb that devastated Hiroshima.[3] In the event of a nuclear war, these missiles would have been part of a massive barrage that U.S. planners estimated would result in as many as 525 million enemy deaths, a vast number of them civilians.[4] Stimson, who had argued for the abolition of submarines in the 1930s and sought to halt the spread of nuclear weapons after World War II, was memorialized by a nuclear submarine that embodied the technological arms race he had so desperately hoped to avoid. In a further irony, given his reputation for prudishness, the covers of the launch tubes housing the ship's Polaris missiles were decorated by the *Stimson*'s crew with large replicas of the Playboy bunny logo.[5]

Stimson's Legacy

The commissioning of the U.S.S. *Henry L. Stimson* is a striking example of the extent to which important elements of Stimson's legacy were warped or forgotten in the decades after his death in 1950. Many commentators have stressed Stimson's role in exhorting Americans to shrug off isolationism in order to play a more active role on the world stage. He has been lionized as "the original anti-appeaser" and "the American Churchill" for his timely and prescient exhortations to confront German and Japanese aggression during the 1930s.[6] Greater American involvement on the international scene and an awareness of the danger posed by outlaw nations bent on military aggression are undoubtedly important elements of Stimson's legacy. World War I had convinced him that American security and prosperity ultimately could not be divorced from the affairs of the world's other industrialized nations. In such a delicately interconnected world, Stimson concluded, "American isolation is an economic fantasy."[7] The changes wrought upon human society by the industrial revolution required a correspondingly revolutionary change in the way that the American people understood the place of their nation in the world.

But while historians and policymakers have focused on Stimson's call for greater international engagement on the part of the United States, they have often missed what he had to say about the form and content of that engagement. Drawing on sources as diverse as philosopher John Fiske, lawyer and international jurist Elihu Root, and crusading reverend Charles Parkhurst, as well as his own experiences and convictions, Stimson consistently sought to bring the weight of the United States to bear in moving the world toward a peaceful international order rooted in law and morality. His preferred tools in advancing that cause were international law, arms control, and the cultivation of mutual trust between world leaders.

Stimson's conservatism was neither bellicose nor slavishly dedicated to preserving the status quo. At home, he believed it was necessary to tame the unfettered capitalism of Gilded Age America to better distribute its benefits. He applied a similar logic to the conduct of American foreign policy. Convinced that "poverty in one part of the world usually induces poverty in other parts," Stimson believed that the United States, as a powerful, prosperous, and secure nation, had a special responsibility to take the lead in ensuring "equality and freedom in regard to the natural resources of the world."[8]

Though a vocal proponent of the "white man's burden" and a defender of American imperialism in the 1910s and 1920s, he ultimately rejected the notion that the United States could impose its values on the rest of the world at the barrel of gun. Stimson preferred, as he put it to Herbert Hoover, to rely on "American education, guidance, and advice, and a genuinely brotherly attitude towards those nations who need it."[9]

Stimson was never a pacifist. There were times, most notably the two world wars, when he accepted the need for force to protect the "kind of world which we have been trying to create and the methods of freedom and self-government" against aggressive, lawless nations such as Nazi Germany.[10] But even in fighting those wars, Stimson remained committed to upholding law and morality, limiting as much as possible the destruction inflicted on noncombatants. He also kept his eyes fixed on what he believed the United States was fighting for—namely, the establishment of "methods of international life, backed by the spirit of tolerance and kindliness, viz: the spirit of Christianity, sufficient to make international life permanent and kindly and war impossible."[11]

Stimson's legacy of quiet behind-the-scenes service was continued by the men whom he mentored during his lengthy career. Many of the so-called Wise Men who dominated the American foreign policy establishment after World War II, including John J. McCloy, Robert Lovett, and McGeorge Bundy, looked to "the Colonel" as their model in trying to chart America's course in the cold war.[12]

On October 18, 1962, Lovett was hurriedly summoned to the White House by president John F. Kennedy. Upon arriving, he met with Bundy, who was then Kennedy's national security adviser. Bundy wanted advice as the president and his advisers secretly deliberated over how to respond to the recent discovery of Soviet nuclear missiles in Cuba. Spying a picture of Stimson on Bundy's desk, Lovett declared, "Mac, I think the best service we can do to President Kennedy is to try to approach this as Colonel Stimson would."[13] Bundy agreed, and the secret White House meetings that determined U.S. policy during the Cuban missile crisis have often been hailed as a model of calm, reasoned decision making in international crisis. Kennedy's decision to reject an immediate air strike or invasion of Cuba in favor of a more moderate response in the form of a blockade almost certainly prevented an even greater atomic tragedy in October 1962.[14] The Nuclear Test Ban Treaty of 1963 that Kennedy negotiated with Soviet leader Nikita Khrushchev in the aftermath of the crisis represented the first tentative step toward the kind of international solution to the challenge of nuclear weapons that Stimson had proposed in September 1945.

Not all of the values and precedents that Stimson bequeathed to the Wise Men were admirable. His Victorian code of conduct contained within it racism, sexism, and elitism that are justifiably repugnant to modern eyes. He never entirely lost the belief that the American people were "ignorant as babies about their foreign relations" and that it was the responsibility of the "richer and more intelligent citizens of the country" to take the lead in shaping policy and guiding public opinion.[15] To this well-bred, male, Anglo-Saxon Protestant elite would fall the task of resolving the challenges posed by "industrial civilization" in conjunction with similar elites in other industrialized nations who shared the same basic set of values and concerns. Not surprisingly, his "brotherly attitude" toward lesser-developed nations often took the form of a condescending paternalism that still retained traces of the white man's burden.

The combination of elitism, secrecy, and unwavering loyalty to the president that marked Stimson's approach to the conduct of foreign policy was among the most dangerous and least laudable aspects of his legacy. His example encouraged the formulation of policy in secret guided by unelected and largely unaccountable elites whose loyalty to the president sometimes trumped their own moral and practical judgments. While the secret meetings that helped craft U.S. policy in the Cuban missile crisis are a positive example of Stimson's preferred approach to foreign policy decision making, on other occasions that approach failed, with disastrous results. As national security adviser to President Lyndon B. Johnson, "Mac" Bundy played a leading role in another American tragedy: the war in Vietnam. Bundy biographer Kai Bird concludes that while Bundy "had private qualms about the war, these were questions he felt compelled to keep to himself." Like his mentor Henry Stimson, "Mac saw it was his duty to loyally defend the president and his war."[16]

In another sad and ironic example, George Ball was privately the most skeptical of Johnson's advisers when the president decided to escalate the Vietnam war in 1964–65. In a prescient series of memoranda, Ball cast doubt on the ability of escalating force to win the conflict, argued against bombing North Vietnam, and suggested that a negotiated settlement might be preferable to continued American military involvement.[17] But much as Stimson had with respect to using the atomic bomb, Ball voiced his dissent inconsistently in private and was entirely silent in public. In his August 22, 1966, address commemorating the former secretary of war, Ball praised Johnson's handling of the war, giving no hint of his private reservations.

"When the Righteous Sin"

The atomic bomb was the ultimate test of Stimson's abilities as a moral states-man. It was a test he ultimately failed for reasons that were all too human. Since World War I, he had warned of the dangerous temptation to employ high-technology weapons "in the way that is most effective for immediate pur-poses, regardless of consequences."[18] And yet when confronted by the bomb, Stimson himself fell victim to this very temptation. The secretary of war did not discard his deep convictions about war, law, and morality when he took office in June 1940, or later when he took charge of the Manhattan Project. But in succumbing to the lure of the atomic secret as a diplomatic tool, delaying pursuit of a diplomatic approach to the war in the Pacific, and failing to pay at-tention to the details of nuclear targeting, Stimson contributed to a brutal and tragic act with lingering human and diplomatic consequences. This judgment is not merely the product of post facto morality on the part of critical histori-ans; it was the logical conclusion of his own convictions. Stimson himself feared that the "full enumeration of the steps in the tragedy" would besmirch his reputation as "a kindly-minded Christian gentleman" who had "labored for peace" for much of his long career.[19]

It may seem unfair to dwell at such length on Stimson's role in the atomic tragedy of August 1945. After all, many people bore responsibility for the use of the bomb, and some of them would appear far more culpable than the aging and tired secretary of war. American leaders would probably not even have pursued atomic weapons during World War II if they had not feared a nuclear-armed Nazi Germany. Even then, there would have been no opportunity for the United States to use them in combat had not Japanese leaders insisted on prolonging the fighting into summer 1945, long after that nation's military defeat was assured. And, of course, the ultimate decisions about the development and use of these weapons lay in the hands of the American president, not the secretary of war.

Despite these caveats, there is an important reason for focusing on Stim-son's role in this affair, one that Lewis Mumford eloquently captured in a 1958 essay on the bomb and its legacy:

This utter collapse of moral values, this breakdown in the elementary code needed to preserve even animal species from extinction, first occurred under a decision made by a public servant of the highest probity and personal rectitude, Secretary Henry L. Stimson. Doubtless this fact made it easier for other presumably virtuous people to close their minds to the implications of our catastrophic moral collapse; for when the righteous sin, they add the force of their virtue to all the evil that they do.[20]

Mumford understood that Stimson's failure was not simply an isolated historical tragedy. It had momentous consequences that reverberated long after the great statesman went to his grave.

The first use of nuclear weapons took place without warning on primarily civilian targets. It also took place without any consultation between the two emerging superpowers and without any plan for the postwar international control of this destructive force. These decisions, in which Stimson played an important part, together formed the foundational acts of the nuclear era. J. Robert Oppenheimer, who himself played a pivotal if ambivalent role in the unfolding drama of the nuclear arms race, observed in November 1945 that, "[t]he pattern of the use of atomic weapons was set at Hiroshima. They are the weapons of aggression, of surprise, and of terror. If they are ever used again, it may well be by thousands or by tens of thousands."[21]

When George Ball commissioned the U.S.S. *Henry L. Stimson* in August 1966, its missiles added to a stockpile that included 32,040 nuclear warheads.[22] That number, the cold war peak of the American nuclear build up, represented a form of institutionalized insanity that had its origins in the failure to control the use and spread of the bomb at the dawn of the atomic age. It was probably impossible to put the nuclear genie back in its bottle after 1945. But there was neither logic nor safety in the process whereby the United States and Soviet Union together held tens of thousands of nuclear weapons as they stood on the precipice of war in October 1962. The most hawkish of analysts would be hard-pressed to justify such overkill, a deadly redundancy that carried with it tremendous monetary, environmental, and human costs.[23]

By 2006 the American arsenal had shrunk to the more "reasonable" level of approximately 10,000 warheads, still far beyond the modest requirements of nuclear deterrence.[24] Under President George W. Bush, the United States has actually expanded its nuclear ambitions with plans for a new generation of "usable" tactical weapons.[25] Meanwhile, contemporary conservative and neo-conservative American policymakers have emulated Stimson's elitist and sometimes arrogant approach to foreign relations while abandoning his commitment to law, morality, and peace as the bedrock of international life, with disastrous consequences at home and abroad.

Nuclear proliferation, another legacy of the early failure to control the bomb, threatens national, regional, and global security as nations such as Iran seek entry into the nuclear club. The spread of nuclear technology to "rogue nations" and the difficulty of safeguarding the outsized, aging Soviet and American arsenals both raise the danger of nuclear terrorism. In his April 25, 1945, memorandum to Truman, Stimson presciently warned that "the future may see a time when such a weapon may be constructed in secret and used suddenly and effectively with devastating power by a willful nation or group against an unsuspecting nation or group of much greater size and material power."[26] That danger is far greater today than it was when Stimson issued his warning some sixty years ago.

Amid the still-potent threat of nuclear annihilation, there exists in the United States a widespread historical ignorance about the events that ushered in the atomic age. Though scholars have produced hundreds if not thousands of monographs and articles on the A-bomb decision, the vast majority of these are still contesting the same narrow terrain laid out by Stimson, Bundy, and their silent coauthors in the 1947 *Harper's* essay. Outside the academy, the situation is even more dire. The Smithsonian's plans for the *Enola Gay* exhibit in 1994–95 stimulated an emotional and partisan debate that offered little insight into the complex and tragic choices made by American leaders about the bomb during World War II. More recently, one of the nuclear engineers responsible for designing a new generation of American nuclear weapons at the Lawrence Livermore National Laboratory dismissed a reporter's question about Hiroshima and Nagasaki by replying, "I haven't especially studied those two tests."[27] This continuing ignorance is dangerous to our future survival. As the British physicist P. M. S. Blackett observed, "All attempts to control atomic energy involve predications about the course of future events. . . . Inaccurate views as to the historical facts of their first use are a poor basis on which to plan for the future."[28]

Stimson's story by itself does not hold the key to understanding the past and future of nuclear weapons. This is a rich, complex topic that demands continuing scholarly engagement at the national and international levels, looking across borders and within the domestic sphere as we strive to understand both the A-bomb decision and the arms race that followed.[29] But as we work to come to terms with our nuclear past and present, both the wisdom and failures of Henry L. Stimson remain instructive. In a dangerous world we would do well to learn from the mistakes of a thoughtful, moral man who presided over the tragic opening of the nuclear age.

Notes

Introduction

1. August 8, 1945, Henry Lewis Stimson Diaries (microfilm edition), Manuscripts and Archives, Yale University Library (hereafter cited as Stimson Diary).

2. J. Samuel Walker, *Prompt and Utter Destruction: Truman and the Use of Atomic Bombs Against Japan* (Chapel Hill, N.C., 1997), 86. The immediate deaths at Hiroshima were likely somewhat lower than this initial estimate. A postwar study by the United States Strategic Bombing Survey (USSBS) placed the number at somewhere between seventy and eighty thousand people. But neither the August 8 estimate nor the postwar USSBS numbers include long-term fatalities due to radiation effects, which would surely result in a higher total. For a discussion of the varying estimates of deaths at both Hiroshima and Nagasaki see Barton J. Bernstein, "Truman and the A-Bomb: Targeting Noncombatants, Using the Bomb, and His Defending the 'Decision,' " *Journal of Military History* 62, no. 3 (July 1998): 565–56 n. 43.

3. "Memorandum of Conference with the President," August 8, 1945, Stimson Diary.

4. "Memorandum for the Press," August 9, 1945, Stimson Diary.

5. Stimson Diary, August 10, 1945; August 10, 1945, James V. Forrestal Diary, microfilm section, Navy Publication and Printing Service Office (NPPSO), Naval District, Washington, D.C. Forrestal joined Stimson in calling for an end to both nuclear and conventional bombing of Japan.

6. At the bottom of an August 10 memorandum from Manhattan Project head General Leslie R. Groves outlining the timetable for the next atomic strike against Japan, army chief of staff, General George C. Marshall penned the note, "It is not to be released over Japan without express authority from the President." Groves, "Memorandum to Chief of Staff " [with handwritten notation by Marshall], Correspondence ("Top Secret") of the Manhattan Engineer District, 1942–46, microfilm publication M1109, file 25, National Archives.

7. Fearing that "area bombing may complicate the situation" with respect to the Japanese surrender, Spaatz on August 11 independently called off all such attacks by American strategic bombers (though precision bombing of specific military-industrial targets continued). When Army Chief of Staff Marshall found out about Spaatz's decision, he worried that the press would conclude that the bombing halt had been ordered from Washington. He was particularly concerned that if Spaatz resumed operations against Japan, it would appear to be a signal from Washington that surrender talks had failed. Thus Marshall ordered Spaatz not to fly any more missions until he could discuss the matter further with the president and the secretary of war. Presented with a fait acompli by Spaatz and Marshall, Truman on August 11 consented to a halt of bombing operations against Japanese cities. On August 13, however, while awaiting word on whether the Japanese would accept the clarification of American terms offered, Truman instructed Marshall to resume the bombing of Japanese cities ("the President directs that we go ahead with everything we've got"). This resulted in conventional bombing raids on August 14 in which 45 percent of the city of Kumagaya was burned to the ground, as was 17 percent of the city of Isezaki. Larry I. Bland, ed., *The Papers of George Catlett Marshall*, vol. 5, *The Finest Soldier, January 1, 1945—January 7, 1947* (Baltimore, 2003), 266–67, 271; Wesley Frank Craven and James Lea Cate, *The Army Air Forces in World War II*, vol. 5, *The Pacific: Matterhorn to Nagasaki* (Washington, D.C., 1983), 732–33; Kit C. Carter and Robert Mueller, *United States Army Air Forces: Combat Chronology, 1941–1945* (Washington, D.C., 1991), 688.

8. "Memorandum for the President," September 11, 1945, Stimson Diary. The secretary of war's September 21 presentation on his last day in office drew heavily on the memorandum that he submitted to Truman on the eleventh.

9. Drew Pearson and Allen Roberts, *Washington Merry-Go-Round* (New York, 1931), 112 ("the human icicle"); "The Reminiscences of Harvey H. Bundy," Oral History Research Office, 145, Columbia University ("a Puritan"); *New York Herald Tribune*, October 21, 1950 ("New England conscience").

10. The assertion regarding divorced persons appears in Godfrey Hodgson's *The Colonel: The Life and Wars of Henry Stimson, 1867–1950* (New York, 1990), 16.

11. Stimson to Theodore Roosevelt ("richer and more intelligent"), September 2, 1910, Henry Lewis Stimson Papers (microfilm ed.), reel 19, Manuscripts and Archives, Yale University Library (hereafter cited as Stimson Papers). Transcript of an interview between Stimson and McGeorge Bundy (on his opposition to women's suffrage), May 30, 1946, Stimson Papers, reel 136. See also Henry L. Stimson, *Suffrage Not a Natural Right* (New York, 1915).

12. Stimson to Frank McIntyre, January 12, 1928 ("might be a Hebrew"), Stimson Papers, reel 74; Stimson interview with McGeorge Bundy, July 8, 1946 ("lesser breeds"), Stimson Papers, reel 136.

13. Robert Lovett to McGeorge Bundy, October 18, 1947, McGeorge Bundy Papers, box 8, John F. Kennedy Presidential Library, Boston.

14. Evan Thomas with Thomas M. DeFrank and Ann McDaniel, "The Code of the WASP Warrior," *Newsweek*, August 20, 1990, 33.

15. David Schmitz, *Henry L. Stimson: The First Wise Man* (Wilmington, Del., 2001), 3.

16. Charles Beard to Herbert Hoover, December 23, 1945, Post-Presidential Individual File, box 14, Herbert Hoover Presidential Library, West Branch, Iowa.

17. Pearson and Roberts, *Washington Merry-Go-Round*, 124.

18. Statement of Henry L. Stimson at dinner given in his honor by Squadron A, January 24, 1947, Waldorf Astoria, Stimson Papers, reel 132.

19. Stimson quoted in *New York Times*, August 9, 1932, 2.

20. The first substantial work on Stimson was his autobiography, cowritten with McGeorge Bundy: Henry L. Stimson and McGeorge Bundy, *On Active Service in Peace and War* (New York 1948). Thoughtful and well-written, it focuses largely on Stimson's role as secretary of war in World War II. Other works on Stimson include Richard Nelson Current's brief and harshly critical *Secretary Stimson, a Study in Statecraft* (New Brunswick, 1954) and Elting Elmore Morison's lengthy and adulatory *Turmoil and Tradition: A Study of the Life and Times of Henry L. Stimson* (Boston, 1960). Both

Morison's and Current's works were published before the bulk of Stimson's diaries and papers were publicly available (though Morison as an authorized biographer had access to most of his personal materials) and well before the relevant A-bomb documents were declassified. Journalist Godfrey Hodgson's *The Colonel: The Life and Wars of Henry Stimson, 1867–1950* (New York, 1990) is a readable journalistic account but lacking in depth, particularly for the period prior to 1940. Schmitz, *Henry L. Stimson* is a brief but useful overview of Stimson's career from the *Biographies in American Foreign Policy* series. Readers beset with insomnia may consult Sean Malloy, "The Reluctant Warrior: Henry L. Stimson and the Crisis of 'Industrial Civilization,' " (PhD diss., Stanford University, 2002) for a lengthy treatment of his life and career.

21. Stimson Diary, September 5, 1944 ("mercy for the other side"); Stimson to Harry S. Truman, May 16, 1945, Stimson Diary ("fair play and humanitarianism").

22. Stimson Diary, November 6, 1941.

23. Ibid., May 31, 1945.

24. A complete bibliography of relevant writings on the bomb could itself easily comprise a book. I will cite many of the relevant texts in the notes of this book, but readers interested in the development of the literature as a whole are directed to four articles that together trace the first sixty years of A-bomb historiography: Barton J. Bernstein, "The Atomic Bomb and American Foreign Policy: An Historiographical Controversy," *Peace and Change* 2 (Spring 1974): 1–16; J. Samuel Walker, "The Decision to Use the Bomb: A Historiographical Update," *Diplomatic History* 14, no. 1 (Winter 1990): 97–114; Barton J. Bernstein, "The Struggle over History: Defining the Hiroshima Narrative," in *Judgment at the Smithsonian: The Bombing of Hiroshima and Nagasaki,* ed. Philip Nobile (New York, 1995): 127–256; J. Samuel Walker, "Recent Literature on Truman's Atomic Bomb Decision: A Search for Middle Ground," *Diplomatic History* 29, no. 2 (April 2005): 311–34. The introductory essays (pp. 4–116) in Michael Kort, *The Columbia Guide to Hiroshima and the Bomb* (New York, 2007), also provide an overview of the historiographical debate, albeit one that appears slanted toward the "orthodox," or probomb, position.

25. An excellent English-language overview of the recent scholarship based on research in Soviet and Japanese archival sources can be found in the essays in Tsuyoshi Hasegawa, ed., *The End of the Pacific War: Reappraisals* (Stanford, 2007). The most important recent work in this area is Hasegawa's *Racing The Enemy: Stalin, Truman, and the Surrender of Japan* (Cambridge, Mass., 2005), with an ensuing roundtable discussion by several noted historians at http://www.hnet.org/~diplo/roundtables/#hasegawa. Also see Richard B. Frank, *Downfall: The End of the Imperial Japanese Empire* (New York, 1999); Sadao Asada, "The Shock of the Atomic Bomb and Japan's Decision to Surrender—A Reconsideration," in *Hiroshima in History: The Myths of Revisionism,* ed. Robert James Maddox (Columbia, Mo., 2007), 25–58.

26. Truman gave the go-ahead for the invasion of Kyūshū (Operation Olympic) following a meeting on June 18, 1945. The invasion was scheduled to begin in November 1945. However, alarming intelligence reports about growing Japanese strength on Kyūshū led many important military leaders to reconsider the wisdom of Operation Olympic by early August. Even if the bomb had not been used and other factors (such as a Soviet declaration of war or the effects of the continuing American blockade) had not led to Japanese capitulation, it is doubtful that Truman would have gone through with Olympic as planned in light of what American intelligence had discovered that summer. Frank, *Downfall,* 211–13; Frank, "Ketsu Gō," in Hasegawa, *The End of the Pacific War,* 80–86; Barton J. Bernstein, "The Alarming Japanese Buildup on Southern Kyushu, Growing U.S. Fears, and Counterfactual Analysis: Would the Planned November 1945 Invasion of Southern Kyushu Have Occurred?" *Pacific Historical Review* 68, no. 4 (November 1999): 561–609; Donald J. MacEachin, *The Final Months of the War With Japan: Signals Intelligence, U.S. Invasion Planning, and the A-bomb Decision* (Washington, D.C., 1998). None of these authors offer a definitive answer to the counterfactual question of what Truman would have done with respect to Olympic had the war continued into fall 1945. All, however, are skeptical that he would have continued with the operation in light of the information already in hand by August 1945. For a review of the heated controversy over casualty estimates for the planned invasion of Japan, see Walker, "The Decision to Use the Bomb," 315, 322–27.

While this debate is intellectually and methodologically interesting, I do not believe it casts any significant light on the A-bomb decision itself, which did not hinge on any particular casualty estimate, high or low.

27. With the exception of a handful of works by Barton J. Bernstein and Martin J. Sherwin, the vast majority of the scholarship on the bomb focuses on the period from Roosevelt's death in April 1945 to the end of the war in the Pacific.

28. Gar Alperovitz, *Atomic Diplomacy: Hiroshima and Potsdam: The Use of the Atomic Bomb and the Confrontation with Soviet Power* (New York, 1985), 50. On Byrnes see David Robertson, *Sly and Able: A Political Biography of James F. Byrnes* (New York, 1994), and Robert L. Messer, *The End of An Alliance: James F. Byrnes, Roosevelt, Truman, and the Origins of the Cold War* (Chapel Hill, N.C., 1982).

29. Norris's biography is by far the best work available on Groves. Robert S. Norris, *Racing for the Bomb: General Leslie R. Groves, the Manhattan Project's Indispensable Man* (South Royalton, Vt., 2002).

30. Groves, for example, was repeatedly overruled by Stimson and Truman on the issue of targeting the Japanese city of Kyoto. Norris, *Racing for the Bomb*, 386–88.

31. On Bush and Conant see James G. Hershberg, *James B. Conant: Harvard to Hiroshima and the Making of the Nuclear Age* (Stanford, 1993); G. Pascal Zachary, *Endless Frontier: Vannevar Bush, Engineer of the American Century* (Cambridge, Mass., 1999).

32. On Marshall, see Forrest C. Pogue's four-volume series, *George C. Marshall* (New York, 1963–87).

33. Stimson to Felix Frankfurter, December 12, 1946, Stimson Papers, reel 116.

34. Of all the critical scholars of Truman's decision, the most subtle is probably Barton J. Bernstein. Though Bernstein has suggested that the decision to use the bomb was "virtually inevitable," his work has also explored some of the questions surrounding the context of use, most notably on the issue of the targeting of civilians. Bernstein, "Understanding the Atomic Bomb and the Japanese Surrender: Missed Opportunities, Little-Known Near Disasters, and Modern Memory," *Diplomatic History* 19, no. 2 (Spring 1995): 227–73. See also Bernstein, "Truman and the A-Bomb."

35. Alperovitz first outlined this thesis tentatively in *Atomic Diplomacy*, which was subsequently revised and expanded in 1985 and 1994. He took up the subject again in *The Decision to Use the Atomic Bomb* (New York, 1995). For a vitriolic critique of Alperovitz's early work see Robert James Maddox, "*Atomic Diplomacy*: A Study in Creative Writing," *Journal of American History* 59, no. 4 (March 1973): 925–34. For a more recent attack on Alperovitz see Maddox, "Gar Alperovitz: Godfather of Hiroshima Revisionism," in Maddox, *Hiroshima in History*, 7–23.

36. The best volume on the World War II origins of the cold war arms race remains Martin J. Sherwin, *A World Destroyed: Hiroshima and Its Legacies* (Stanford, 2003). The original 1975 edition of this book was the first to fully document the extent to which Anglo-American leaders grasped the diplomatic significance of the bomb—particularly vis-à-vis the Soviet Union—years before Hiroshima. Another pioneering study of this subject is Barton J. Bernstein, "The Uneasy Alliance: Roosevelt, Churchill, and the Atomic Bomb, 1940–1945," *Western Political Quarterly* 29, no. 2 (June 1976): 202–30. For an excellent history of the early years of the cold war arms race see Gregg Herken, *The Winning Weapon: The Atomic Bomb in the Cold War, 1945–1950* (New York, 1980).

Chapter 1. The Education of Henry L. Stimson

1. *Los Angeles Times*, February 12, 1930, 1.

2. "Speech Delivered by the Chairman of the American Delegation, Henry L. Stimson at the Plenary Session of the Conference, London, February 11, 1930," Henry Lewis Stimson Diaries (microfilm ed.), Manuscripts and Archives, Yale University Library (hereafter cited as Stimson Diary).

3. Ibid.

4. *Los Angeles Times*, February 12, 1930, 1.

5. This account of Stimson's early life and schooling is largely drawn from Elting Elmore Morison, *Turmoil and Tradition: A Study of the Life and Times of Henry L. Stimson* (Boston, 1960), 19–38.

While too adulatory to be useful on matters of policy, Morison's authorized biography is an unparalleled source for both the early years of Stimson's life and the social world that he inhabited.

6. Ibid., 27.

7. Ibid., 41.

8. *New York Times*, March 14, 1892, 1; *Chicago Daily Tribune*, February 15, 1892, 3.

9. On Parkhurst see Warren Sloat, *A Battle for the Soul of New York: Tammany Hall, Police Corruption, Vice, and Reverend Charles Parkhurst's Crusade against Them, 1892—1895* (New York, 2002).

10. Interview between McGeorge Bundy and Henry Stimson, May 27, 1946, Henry Lewis Stimson Papers (microfilm ed.), reel 136, Manuscripts and Archives, Yale University Library (hereafter cited as Stimson Papers).

11. Ibid.

12. Morison, *Triumph and Turmoil*, 43–45.

13. Stimson interview with McGeorge Bundy, June 4, 1946, "Historic Law of Basic Moral Problems," Stimson Papers, reel 136. Also see John Bonnett, "Jekyll and Hyde: Henry L. Stimson, *Mentalité*, and the Decision to Use the Atomic Bomb on Japan," *War in History* 4, no. 2 (April 1997): 178.

14. Richard W. Leopold, *Elihu Root and the Conservative Tradition* (Boston, 1954), 189.

15. Ibid., 197.

16. Ibid., 35.

17. Robert Bacon and James Brown Scott, eds., *Addresses on International Subjects by Elihu Root* (London, 1916), 156–57.

18. Ibid., 395.

19. Ibid., 160.

20. Stimson to General James A. Drain, June 27, 1911, Stimson Papers, reel 7. Stimson extensively chronicled his western adventures in a self-published 1949 volume entitled *My Vacations*. Also see his letters from the early 1890s in reels 150–52 of the Stimson Papers. The story of having a mountain named after him is in a letter to Mabel White, September 30, 1891, Stimson Papers, reel 151.

21. Stimson to John Leipe, February 15, 1905, Stimson Papers, reel 3; Stimson to Illinois Surety Company, September 13, 1911, Stimson Papers, reel 6; Stimson, *My Vacations*, 175–79.

22. Morison, *Turmoil and Tradition*, 95.

23. Stimson to Gifford Pinchot, September 2, 1910, Stimson Papers, reel 19. On Stimson and the strike at Cornell Dam see Stimson, *My Vacations*, 118–20. For a general account of the strike, see *New York Times*, April 16–20, 24–25, 1900.

24. Stimson to Lewis W. Welch, November 17, 1910, Stimson Papers, reel 6.

25. Stimson, "Socialists' Rights," *New York Herald Tribune*, January 16, 1920.

26. Stimson to Everett P. Wheeler, April 7, 1913, Stimson Papers, reel 32 ("dilution of the suffrage"); Stimson to Theodore Roosevelt, September 2, 1910, Stimson Papers, reel 19 ("richer and more intelligent citizens").

27. Stimson Diary, February 18, 1916.

28. For the cartoon in question see *New York Times*, November 6, 1910, SM 16.

29. The sole piece of evidence pointing to Stimson's embracing war at this early stage of his career comes from a quote in Morison's biography in which Stimson purportedly remarked sometime in the 1880s or 1890s that a war would be "a wonderfully good thing for this country" in that it would "lift men out of selfish, individual work." Morison, *Turmoil and Tradition*, 40. Though several Stimson biographers have since quoted this remark, Morison himself does not provide a date or citation for this partial quotation. Moreover, a close reading of this section of Morison's account suggests that the statement was not contemporary but rather a later reflection by Stimson on this period in his life. Whatever the genesis of this particular quotation, it does not stand up to the much larger body of contemporary evidence indicating that Stimson in the 1890s had little interest in war for either himself or the United States. For two uncritical uses of the Morison quotation see Schmitz, *Henry L. Stimson: The First Wise Man* (Wilmington, Del., 2001), 11, and Godfrey Hodgson, *The Colonel: The Life and Wars of Henry Stimson, 1867–1950* (New York, 1990), 43.

30. For more on the relationship between gender, masculinity, and the Spanish-American War see Kristin L. Hoganson, *Fighting for American Manhood: How Gender Politics Provoked the Spanish-American and Philippine-American Wars* (New Haven, 1998).

31. In the introduction to his 1947 memoir, Stimson admitted that the Spanish-American War had "caught me napping" and that "the thought of preparing oneself for possible military service hardly entered my head." Henry L. Stimson and McGeorge Bundy, *On Active Service in Peace and War* (New York, 1948), xx.

32. Stimson to Alden Sampson, August 8, 1898, Stimson Papers, reel 1.

33. Stimson to Gifford Pinchot, July 1, 1898, Stimson Papers, reel 1.

34. Stimson Diary, February 14, 1932.

35. *New York Times*, December 25, 1899, 10; May 5, 1902, 5.

36. Stimson to George Wharton Pepper, July 14, 1898, Stimson Papers, reel 1. Also see Stimson to Lloyd McKim Garrison, May 4, 1900, Stimson Papers, reel 2.

37. Stimson interview with McGeorge Bundy, July 8, 1946, Stimson Papers, reel 136.

38. Henry Stimson to Lewis Stimson, August 3, 1911, Stimson Papers, reel 25.

39. Ibid.

40. Stimson to Dr. Charles H. Parkhurst, February 21, 1913, Stimson Papers, reel 31.

41. On Stimson's missions in the developing world during the 1920s, see Michael J. J. Smith, "Colonialism in Southeast Asia: Henry L. Stimson and the Pro-Consulship in the Philippines," *Michigan Academician* 12, no. 2 (1979): 137–53; Charles E. Frazier, Jr., "Colonel Henry L. Stimson's Peace Mission to Nicaragua," *Journal of the West* 2, no. 1 (1963), 66–84; Paul H. Boeker, ed., *Henry L. Stimson's American Policy in Nicaragua: The Lasting Legacy* (New York, 1991).

42. Stimson Diary, January 6, 1929.

43. Stimson to Lyman P. Hammond, June 16, 1932, Stimson Papers, reel 83.

44. Henry Stimson, "Report of the Secretary of War," December 4, 1911, *War Department Annual Reports* (Washington, D.C., 1912), 7; Tami Davis Biddle, *Rhetoric and Reality in Air Warfare: The Evolution of British and American Ideas about Strategic Bombing, 1914–1945* (Princeton, 2002), 49.

45. Stimson, "Report of the Secretary of War," 11.

46. Stimson to Theodore Roosevelt, November 2, 1911, Stimson Papers, reel 9.

47. Stimson, *My Vacations*, 128, 124.

48. George Wharton Pepper to George Roberts, January 17, 1949, Stimson Papers, reel 121.

49. Henry Stimson to Lewis Stimson, February 13, 1913, Stimson Papers, reel 31.

50. Stimson to Root, April 22, 1914, Stimson Papers, reel 35.

51. Stimson to John C. H. Lee, June 30, 1914, and Stimson to John M. Palmer, June 30, 1914, Stimson Papers, reel 36.

52. "Address to the National Security League, Carnegie Hall, June 14, 1915," Stimson Papers, reel 130.

53. Henry Stimson to Lewis Stimson, June 3, 1917, Stimson Papers, reel 49.

54. Stimson wrote approvingly to Wilson in April 1917, declaring that "the real issue of the war was between Prussian autocracy and democracy which you so admirably epitomized in your address to Congress when you stated: 'The World must be made a safe place for democracy.' " Stimson to Woodrow Wilson, April 17, 1917, Stimson Papers, reel 48.

55. Stimson and Bundy, *On Active Service*, 91–98. For more on Stimson's brief stint "over there," see Stimson, "Artillery in a Quiet Sector," *Scribner's Magazine*, June 1919, 709–16.

56. Statement of Henry L. Stimson at dinner given in his honor by Squadron A, January 24, 1947, Waldorf Astoria, Stimson Papers, reel 132.

57. Stimson to Samuel B. Clarke, December 20, 1918, Stimson Papers, reel 51.

58. Stimson Diary, February 27, 1933.

59. Handwritten notes on the League Covenant dated March 21, 1919, Stimson Papers, reel 130.

60. Stimson to William H. Taft, March 6, 1919, Stimson Papers, reel 51.

61. Stimson to Sir George Montague Harper, February 11, 1919, Stimson Papers, reel 51.

62. *Foreign Relations of the United States, 1928* (Washington, D.C.) 1:155 (hereafter cited as *FRUS*). On Kellogg-Briand (also known as the Pact of Paris), see Harold Josephson, "Outlawing War: Internationalism and the Pact of Paris," *Diplomatic History* 3, no. 4 (Fall 1979): 377–90.

63. Stimson to George Wharton Pepper, March 5, 1919, Stimson Papers, reel 51; Henry Stimson, "Bases of American Foreign Policy during the Past Four Years," *Foreign Affairs* 11, no. 3 (April 1933): 384.

64. "Address to the Officers of the Army War College," January 5, 1931, Stimson Papers, reel 131.

65. Ibid. Stimson did not dwell on the troubling exception to this trend: Andrew Jackson's defiance of the Supreme Court in *Worcester v. Georgia* (1832).

66. Stimson to Herbert Hoover, November 18, 1929, Stimson Diary.

67. Robert H. Ferrell, *American Diplomacy in the Great Depression: Hoover-Stimson Foreign Policy, 1929–1933* (New Haven, 1957), 41.

68. Diary of William R. Castle, February 14, 1933, Herbert Hoover Presidential Library, West Branch, Iowa (hereafter cited as Castle Diary). Hoover in his memoirs made only a veiled reference to Stimson's mental and physical capacity, noting that in 1929 he was "not in good health" and that as a result the president was "obliged to take over more duties in this field [foreign relations] than otherwise would have been the case." Herbert Hoover, *Memoirs: The Cabinet and the Presidency* (New York, 1952), 336.

69. Stimson Diary, November 8, 1930. On the World Court, also see ibid., September 24, October 3, and December 11, 1930.

70. "Address to the Officers of the Army War College," January 5, 1931, Stimson Papers, reel 131.

71. *FRUS, 1929*, 3:5.

72. The only notable work focusing exclusively on the London Naval Conference is Raymond O'Connor, *Perilous Equilibrium* (Lawrence, Kans., 1962). Also see O'Connor, "The 'Yardstick' and Naval Disarmament in the 1920s," *Mississippi Valley Historical Review* 45, no. 3 (December 1958): 441–63, for more background on the events preceding the London Naval Conference.

73. Henry Stimson, *Democracy and Nationalism in Europe* (Princeton, 1934), 28.

74. "Address to the Permanent International Association of Road Congresses," October 6, 1930, Stimson Papers, reel 131.

75. "Memorandum for the President," September 11, 1945, Stimson Diary.

76. "Memorandum of Conversations with Signor Grandi on July 9, 11 and 12 and with Mussolini on July 12, 1931," Stimson Diary.

77. Stimson to Lyman P. Hammond, June 16, 1932, Stimson Papers, reel 83.

78. *Public Papers of the Presidents of the United States: Herbert Hoover, 1930* (Washington, D.C., 1976), 39.

79. *FRUS, 1933*, 4:493.

80. Stimson Diary, June 1, 1931; Stimson interview with McGeorge Bundy, June 14, 1946, Stimson Papers, reel 136; Stimson and Bundy, *On Active Service*, 188. Stimson shut down the Black Chamber in 1929 and promptly forgot about the matter until Herbert Yardley created a stir by publishing a book recounting his code-breaking exploits while at the State Department. Stimson Diary, June 1, 1931. Also see Herbert O. Yardley, *The American Black Chamber* (Laguna Hills, Calif., 1931).

81. Stimson Diary, April 17, 1932.

82. Ibid., February 20, 1928.

83. Ibid., October 9, 1931.

84. "Mr. Hoover's Foreign Policy and the Commercial Welfare of the United States," October 1, 1932, Stimson Papers, reel 132.

85. Stimson Diary, January 26 ("thousand to one") and February 18, 1932 ("the only police force").

86. For more on Stimson and Manchuria see Paul H. Clyde, "The Diplomacy of 'Playing No Favorites,' " *Mississippi Valley Historical Review* 35, no. 2 (September 1948): 187–202; Richard N. Current, "The Stimson Doctrine and the Hoover Doctrine," *American Historical Review* 59, no. 3 (April 1954), 513–42.

87. Castle Diary, January 24, 1933.

Chapter 2. The Road to Pearl Harbor

1. Stimson to Ramsay MacDonald, December 4, 1932, Henry Lewis Stimson Papers (microfilm ed.), reel 83, Manuscripts and Archives, Yale University Library (hereafter cited as Stimson Papers). The title of this chapter is borrowed from a book of the same name by Herbert Feis, who worked under Stimson in the State Department. Herbert Feis, *The Road to Pearl Harbor: The Coming of the War between the United States and Japan* (Princeton, 1971).

2. The dinner was held at the house of Harvey Bundy. Those attending included Stimson, Arthur Ballantine, James Grafton Rogers, and their respective spouses. March 4, 1933, Henry Lewis Stimson Diaries (microfilm ed.), Manuscripts and Archives, Yale University Library (hereafter cited as Stimson Diary).

3. Stimson to Herbert Hoover, April 10, 1933, Stimson Papers, reel 84.

4. Henry Stimson, "Bases of American Foreign Policy during the Past Four Years," *Foreign Affairs* 11, no. 3 (April 1933): 391–92.

5. "Outline of Princeton lectures," n.d. [circa March or April, 1934], Stimson Papers, reel 132.

6. Henry Stimson, *Democracy and Nationalism in Europe* (Princeton, 1934), 79.

7. Ibid.

8. Stimson to Wellington S. Tinker, December 21, 1936, Stimson Papers, reel 92.

9. "Memorandum of talk with James G. Rogers," n.d. [circa March or April, 1934], Stimson Papers, reel 132; "Fourth Lecture," n.d. [circa April 1934], Stimson Papers, reel 132.

10. Stimson to Cordell Hull, August 30, 1937, Stimson Papers, reel 94.

11. Stimson, "America's Interest in the British Navy," June 18, 1940, Stimson Papers, reel 132.

12. *New York Times*, March 7, 1939, 16.

13. Stimson, "America's Interest in the British Navy."

14. Max Freedman, ed., *Roosevelt and Frankfurter: Their Correspondence, 1928–1945* (Boston, 1967), 524.

15. Stimson, "America's Interest in the British Navy."

16. *New York Times*, January 11, 1940, 4.

17. Of the three, McCloy was unique in having come from somewhat humble origins. This group was supplemented in summer 1943 by the addition of New York Life Insurance president George L. Harrison (himself a Yale, Skull and Bones, and Harvard Law alumnus). On McCloy and Bundy, see Kai Bird, *The Chairman: John J. McCloy and the Making of the American Establishment* (New York, 1992); Bird, *The Color of Truth: McGeorge Bundy and William Bundy, Brothers in Arms* (New York, 1998). On Lovett and Harrison, see Walter Isaacson and Evan Thomas, *The Wise Men: Six Friends and the World They Made: Acheson, Bohlen, Harriman, Kennan, Lovett, McCloy* (New York, 1988). On Under Secretary of War Patterson see Keith E. Eiler, *Mobilizing America: Robert P. Patterson and the War Effort, 1940–1945* (Ithaca, 1998).

18. Robert Lovett to McGeorge Bundy, October 18, 1947, McGeorge Bundy Papers, box 8, John F. Kennedy Presidential Library, Boston.

19. "The Reminiscences of Harvey H. Bundy," Oral History Research Office, 111, Columbia University (hereafter cited as HHB Oral History). Deck tennis (also known as tennequoits) was one of Stimson's favorite pastimes. The game, which involved tossing small rings over a net, apparently originated on ocean liners during the nineteenth century. It is likely that Stimson picked up the game as a child during the family's frequent ocean voyages to Europe. He later had a deck tennis court laid out at Woodley, his Washington estate.

20. Senate Committee on Military Affairs, *Hearings before the Committee on Military Affairs on Nomination of Henry L. Stimson to Be Secretary of War*, 76th Cong., 3d Sess., July 2, 1940, 7.

21. Stimson Diary, December 19, 1940.

22. Ibid., August 11, 1932.

23. Ibid., January 17, 1933.

24. Ibid., September 26, 1940.

25. Ibid., April 24, 1941.

26. Stimson to Roosevelt, May 24, 1941, Stimson Papers, reel 103.

27. "Historical Memorandum as to Japan's Relations with the United States Which May Have a Bearing Upon the Present Situation," October 2, 1940, Stimson Diary.

28. Stimson to Nelson T. Johnson, November 6, 1940, Stimson Papers, reel 102.

29. Stimson Diary, April 20, 1931.

30. G. Pascal Zachary, *Endless Frontier: Vannevar Bush, Engineer of the American Century* (Cambridge, Mass., 1999), 106, 126.

31. The only full-length work on Loomis is a celebratory biography by Jennet Conant, *Tuxedo Park: A Wall Street Tycoon and the Secret Palace of Science That Changed the Course of World War II* (New York, 2002).

32. Wesley F. Craven and James Lea Cate, eds., *The Army Air Forces in World War II:* vol. IV, *Men and Planes* (Chicago, 1955), 204.

33. Stimson Diary, April 23, 1941. Apparently it was Army Air Forces General Carl A. Spaatz, who would later reluctantly oversee the dropping of atomic bombs against Japan, who first suggested to Marshall the deterrent power of the B-17 in 1941. Kenneth P. Werrell, *Blankets of Fire: U.S. Bombers over Japan during World War II* (Washington D.C., 1996), 40.

34. Stimson Diary, September 12, 1941. Also see Stimson to Roosevelt, October 21, 1941, Stimson Diary.

35. Larry Bland, ed., *The Papers of George Catlett Marshall*, vol. 2 (Baltimore, 1986), 676–78.

36. Stimson Diary, October 28, 1941.

37. Ibid., November 25, 1941.

38. HHB Oral History, 260–61.

39. Stimson Diary, December 7, 1941.

40. Henry Stimson, "The Decision to Use the Atomic Bomb," *Harper's* (February 1947): 106.

41. Stimson Diary, June 2, 1942.

Chapter 3. "A Most Terrible Thing"

1. November 6, 1941, Henry Lewis Stimson Diaries (microfilm ed.), Manuscripts and Archives, Yale University Library (hereafter cited as Stimson Diary); "Report to the President of the National Academy of Sciences by the Academy Committee on Uranium," November 6, 1941, Bush-Conant File Relating to the Development of the Atomic Bomb, 1940–45, Records of the Office of Scientific Research and Development, record group 227, microfilm publication M1392, file 1, National Archives (hereafter cited as Bush-Conant).

2. Historian Michael Gordin has suggested that "many planners and influential politicians considered the atomic bomb to be, at least in some degree, an 'ordinary weapon' " prior to its use against Hiroshima. Though intelligently argued, Gordin's contrarian thesis simply does not hold true for any of the important decision makers within the Roosevelt or Truman administrations from 1941 to 1945. While a handful of lower-level military planners may have seen the bomb as "just another weapon," neither Roosevelt, Truman, Stimson nor any of the key higher-level military, political, or scientific figures who advised them on the bomb shared this belief. Michael Gordin, *Five Days in August: How World War II Became a Nuclear War* (Princeton, 2007), 7, 108.

3. Vannevar Bush, "Memorandum for Dr. Conant," December 16, 1941, Bush-Conant, file 2.

4. Stimson Diary, December 16, 1941.

5. Henry Stimson, "The Decision to Use the Atomic Bomb," *Harper's* (February, 1947): 98.

6. Robert P. Newman, "Hiroshima and the Trashing of Henry Stimson," *New England Quarterly* 71, no. 1 (March, 1998): 22. The moral threshold argument is widely accepted by A-bomb scholars who often differ on other major interpretive points. For a skeptical examination of this argument see Sean Malloy, " 'The Rules of Civilized Warfare': Scientists, Soldiers, Civilians, and American Nuclear Targeting, 1940–1945," *Journal of Strategic Studies* 30, no. 3 (June 2007): 475–512. For more examples of the moral threshold argument see Samuel Walker, "The Decision to Use the Bomb: A Historiographical Update," *Diplomatic History* 14, no. 1 (Winter 1990): 106; Tami Davis Biddle, *Rhetoric and*

Reality in Air Warfare: The Evolution of British and American Ideas about Strategic Bombing, 1914–1945 (Princeton, 2002), 270, 288; Robert S. Norris, *Racing for the Bomb: General Leslie R. Groves, the Manhattan Project's Indispensable Man* (South Royalton, Vt., 2002), 380; Gordin, *Five Days in August*, 7–8, 10–11, 18; Wilson D. Miscamble, *From Roosevelt to Truman: Potsdam, Hiroshima, and the Cold War* (New York, 2007), 246; Richard B. Frank, *Downfall: The End of the Imperial Japanese Empire* (New York, 1999), 254, 257; Lawrence Freedman and Saki Dockrill, "Hiroshima: A Strategy of Shock," in *From Pearl Harbor to Hiroshima: The Second World War in Asia and the Pacific, 1941–1945*, ed. Saki Dockrill (New York, 1993), 196; Michael S. Sherry, *The Rise of American Air Power: The Creation of Armageddon* (New Haven, 1987), 341; David M. Kennedy, "Crossing the Moral Threshold," *Time*, August 1, 2005, 50; A. C. Grayling, *Among the Dead Cities: The History and Moral Legacy of the World War II Strategic Bombing of Civilians in Germany and Japan* (New York, 2005), 78.

7. Otto Frisch and Rudolf Peierls, "Memorandum on the Properties of a Radioactive Superbomb," March 19, 1940, in Robert Serber, *The Los Alamos Primer: The First Lectures on How to Build an Atomic Bomb*, edited with an introduction by Richard Rhodes (Berkeley, 1992), 81.

8. Ibid., 81–82.

9. The code name MAUD was not an acronym but rather was derived from the name of an English governess employed by physicist Niels Bohr. James G. Hershberg, *James B. Conant: Harvard to Hiroshima and the Making of the Nuclear Age* (Stanford, 1993), 148.

10. The MAUD reports, reprinted in Margaret Gowing, *Britain and Atomic Energy, 1939–1945* (London, 1964), 396, 398.

11. Ibid., 396, 407.

12. Ibid., 86–87.

13. "Report of National Academy of Sciences Committee on Atomic Fission," May 17, 1941, Bush-Conant, file 1.

14. J. Robert Oppenheimer to Enrico Fermi, May 25, 1943, Papers of J. Robert Oppenheimer, box 33, Library of Congress (hereafter cited as Oppenheimer Papers). Conant biographer James Hershberg noted that "Conant's qualms about going first appear to have been not moral scruples but worries about the practical obstacles of uniformly or efficiently distributing radioactive particles or gas over enemy territory." Hershberg, *James B. Conant*, 201. For more on radiological warfare see Barton J. Bernstein, "Radiological Warfare: The Path Not Taken," *Bulletin of the Atomic Scientists* 41, no. 7 (August 1985): 44–49; Bernstein, "Oppenheimer and the Radioactive Poison Plan," *Technology Review* 88, no. 4 (May/June 1985): 14–17; Norris, *Racing for the Bomb*, 297–98.

15. *New York Herald Tribune*, October 13, 1939. Stimson to William Allen White, October 24, 1939, Henry Lewis Stimson Papers (microfilm ed.), reel 99, Manuscripts and Archives, Yale University Library (hereafter cited as Stimson Papers). Also see letter to Dr. Alfred E. Stearns on the same date for similar sentiments.

16. Stimson to William Allen White, October 24, 1939, Stimson Papers, reel 9. Also see his letter to Dr. Alfred E. Stearns on the same date for similar sentiments.

17. Kuter quoted in Richard G. Davis, "Operation 'Thunderclap': The US Army Air Force and the Bombing of Berlin," *Journal of Strategic Studies* 14 (March 1991): 94. On the origins of American precision bombing doctrine see Stephen L. McFarland, *America's Pursuit of Precision Bombing, 1910–1945* (Washington D.C., 1997); Sherry, *The Rise of American Air Power*, 49–61; Conrad Crane, *Bombs, Cities, and Civilians: American Air Power Strategy in World War II* (Lawrence, Kans., 1993), 9–10, 22.

18. Stimson Diary, September 11, 1941.

19. Ibid., September 2, 1942; ibid., October 15, 1943; Stimson to Lt. Gen. Carl Spaatz, February 13, 1945, Formerly Top Secret Correspondence of Secretary of War Stimson, record group 107, box 10, National Archives II, College Park, Md. (hereafter cited as "Safe File").

20. Elting Elmore Morison, *Turmoil and Tradition: A Study of the Life and Times of Henry L. Stimson* (Boston, 1960), 618.

21. "Report to the President of the National Academy of Sciences by the Academy Committee on Uranium," November 6, 1941, Bush-Conant, file 1.

22. Stimson to Roosevelt, April 29, 1942, "Safe File," box 14. For more on Stimson's involvement in the American biological warfare program see the "Biological Warfare" folder in "Safe File," box 2. Also see Barton J. Bernstein, "America's Biological Warfare Program in World War II," *Journal of Strategic Studies* 11, no. 3 (September 1988): 292–317.

23. Franklin D. Roosevelt to Vannevar Bush, March 11, 1942, Bush-Conant, file 2.

24. Quebec Agreement, August 19, 1943, Harrison-Bundy Files Relating to the Development of the Atomic Bomb, 1942–46, Records of the Office of the Chief of Engineers, record group 77, microfilm publication M1108, file 3, National Archives (hereafter cited as Harrison-Bundy).

25. Stimson Diary, December 18, 1940.

26. Harvey H. Bundy, "Memorandum for the Secretary," September 10, 1942, Harrison-Bundy, file 5; Stimson Diary, September 10, 1942.

27. General William D. Styer represented the army and Admiral William R. Purnell served as the navy's representative. Memorandum "A," September 23, 1942, Harrison-Bundy, file 1.

28. Robert Jungk, *Brighter Than a Thousand Suns: A Personal History of the Atomic Scientists* (New York, 1970), 87.

29. "Draft of a Letter to the President to Be Signed by Dr. Bush," n.d., Bush-Conant, file 5. This phrase also appears in an August 21, 1943, report by Leslie R. Groves, "Present Status and Future Program," Harrison-Bundy, file 6.

30. Leo Szilard to Vannevar Bush, May 26, 1942, Bush-Conant, file 2.

31. This discovery was made by the Alsos team (a covert Anglo-American operation to uncover intelligence on the Nazi nuclear effort), discussed in more depth in chapter 4. Samuel Goudsmit, *Alsos* (New York, 1947), 71. On Werner Heisenberg and the German nuclear program see Mark Walker, *Nazi Science: Myth, Truth, and the German Atomic Bomb* (New York, 1995); Thomas Power, *Heisenberg's War: The Secret History of the German Atomic Bomb* (New York, 1993).

32. *In the Matter of J. Robert Oppenheimer: Transcript of Hearing before Personnel Security Board and Texts of Principal Documents and Letters* (Cambridge, Mass., 1970), 731.

33. Vannevar Bush to James Conant, June 17, 1943, Bush-Conant, file 3; Norris, *Racing for the Bomb*, 281–95.

34. Bush to Conant, January 18, 1943, Bush-Conant, file 18. During the cold war, U.S. leaders considered but ultimately rejected preemptive nuclear strikes against the Soviet Union and China to prevent those nations from developing nuclear weapons capabilities of their own. On the early cold war debate over preemptive nuclear strikes see Marc Trachtenberg, " 'A Wasting Asset': American Strategy and the Shifting Nuclear Balance, 1949–54," *International Security* 13 (Winter 1988/89): 5–49.

35. Leslie R. Groves, "Policy Meeting," May 5, 1943, Correspondence ("Top Secret") of the Manhattan Engineer District, 1942–46, microfilm publication M1109, file 23, National Archives (hereafter cited as Groves "Top Secret"). It is also possible, as some historians have speculated, that the Military Policy Committee was contemplating a form of deterrence by withholding use against the only other nation likely to achieve nuclear capability during World War II. There is no direct evidence for this assertion, however, and Hitler would have appeared to be the very model of an undeterrable "rogue" leader. For the deterrence argument see Martin J. Sherwin, "How Well They Meant," *Bulletin of the Atomic Scientists* 41, no. 7 (August 1985): 10; Arjun Makhijani, " 'Always' the Target?" *Bulletin of the Atomic Scientists* 51, no. 3 (May/June 1995): 26. Japan did have a small-scale nuclear weapons program during the war, albeit one that never came close to fruition. See John Dower, " 'NI' and 'F': Japan's Wartime Atomic Bomb Research," in *Japan in War and Peace* (New York, 1993), 55–100.

36. Conant to Bush, May 26, 1942, Bush-Conant, file 16. The first American scientific study of the potential effects of an atomic bomb was conducted by George B. Kistiakowsky and offered as an appendix to the November 6, 1941, report by Compton and the National Academy of Sciences. Kistiakowsky's report did not take into consideration either radiation effects or the moral concerns over civilian deaths initially raised by Frisch and Peierls. Confining his report to technical details of the bomb's blast effect, he indicated that because of the varying effects of shock waves in air and water,

an underwater bomb was likely to have greater "destructive action" than a similar bomb exploded in the air or on the ground. In a follow-up report in late December, Kistiakowsky offered damage projections for both land and sea use of atomic weapons. This second report was slightly more optimistic about causing damage to land targets but retained a heavy emphasis on underwater use, estimating that a uranium bomb dropped in a deep harbor would "cause 'lethal' damage to any ship at a distance of at least one thousand and possibly three thousand feet. G. B. Kistiakowsky, "The Probable Destructive Action of Uranium Fission Bombs," appendix B to "Report to the President of the National Academy of Sciences by the Academy Committee on Uranium," November 6, 1941, Bush-Conant, file 1; G. B. Kistiakowsky, "The Destructive Action of Uranium Bombs," December 26, 1941, Bush-Conant, file 2.

37. Groves, "Policy Meeting," May 5, 1943, Groves "Top Secret," file 23.

38. Bush, "Memorandum of Conference with the President," June 24, 1943, Bush-Conant, file 10.

39. Stimson Diary, May 28, 1945.

40. Parsons had previously worked on other secretive military projects, including radar and proximity fuses. The only biography of Parsons is Al Christman's celebratory *Target Hiroshima: Deak Parsons and the Creation of the Atomic Bomb* (Annapolis, 1998).

41. The development of the underwater (or UW) bomb project can be traced in the following documents, received by the author from the Los Alamos National Laboratory (LANL) after a request filed under the Freedom of Information Act: William S. Parsons to J. Robert Oppenheimer, November 17, 1943, "Performance of Gadget, as Estimated October 28, 1943"; Parsons to Ordnance Group Leaders, December 27, 1943; Oppenheimer to Parsons, December 27, 1943, "Design Schedule for Overall Assemblies." See Malloy, " 'The Rules of Civilized Warfare,' " for a lengthier treatment of these issues. Barton J. Bernstein briefly discussed the underwater weapons program at Los Alamos in his review of a recent biography of William Parsons. Bernstein, "The Making of the Atomic Admiral: 'Deak' Parsons and the Modernizing of the U.S. Navy," *Journal of Military History* 63, no. 2 (April 1999): 418. Also see Bernstein, "It's History—The Quest for an Atomic Torpedo," *San Francisco Chronicle*, August 5, 1997, A19; David Hawkins, *Project Y: The Los Alamos Story, Part I: Toward Trinity* (Los Alamos, 1961), 88, 121, 191, 196.

42. Oppenheimer to Parsons, "Design Schedule for Overall Assemblies." Low-level theoretical work on the UW program continued in the Water Delivery section of the Ordnance Division until at least February 1945, though work on a deliverable underwater weapon appears to have ceased sometime in early 1944. The idea was revived after the war, and the efficacy of an underwater nuclear blast was dramatically demonstrated by Test Baker at Bikini Atoll in July 1946.

43. For more on the lasting impact of failure to address the implications of damage caused by fire, see Lynn Eden, *Whole World on Fire: Organizations, Knowledge, and Nuclear Weapons Devastation* (Ithaca, 2004).

44. Parsons to Groves, May 19, 1944, Groves "Top Secret," file 5F.

45. 509th Composite Group, Mission Planning Summary, 2, n.d. [circa August 1945], Records of the 509th Composite Group, microfilm reel B0679, Air Force Historical Records Agency, Maxwell Air Force Base, Ala. Also see Groves to Marshall, "Atomic Fission Bombs—Present Status and Expected Progress," August 7, 1944, Groves "Top Secret," file 25M.

46. Parsons to Groves, September 25, 1944, Papers of William S. Parsons, Library of Congress (hereafter cited as Parsons Papers).

47. Parsons to Purnell (via Groves), December 12, 1944, Groves "Top Secret," file 5D.

48. Joseph Rotblat, "Leaving the Bomb Project," *Bulletin of the Atomic Scientists* 41, no. 7 (August 1985): 16–19. Also see Charles Thorpe, "Against Time: Scheduling, Momentum, and Moral Order at Wartime Los Alamos," *Journal of Historical Sociology* 17, no. 1 (March 2004): 44.

49. Parsons to Groves, September 25, 1944, Parsons Papers.

50. Christman, *Target Hiroshima*, 164.

51. According to physicist Robert Wilson, Oppenheimer attempted to discourage him from holding a meeting at Los Alamos to discuss ethical concerns over the use of the bomb. Gregg Herken,

Brotherhood of the Bomb: The Tangled Lives and Loyalties of Robert Oppenheimer, Ernest Lawrence, and Edward Teller (New York, 2002), 364 n. 79; Kai Bird and Martin J. Sherwin, *American Prometheus: The Triumph and Tragedy of J. Robert Oppenheimer* (New York, 2005), 287.

52. J. R. Oppenheimer to Leslie Groves, October 6, 1944, Oppenheimer Papers, box 36.

53. Stimson Diary, September 5, 1944.

54. "Suggested Recommendations of Treatment of Germany from the Cabinet Committee for the President," *Foreign Relations of the United States, The Conference at Quebec, 1944* (Washington, D.C.), 97.

55. Stimson Diary, March 5, 1945. For Marshall's response and Stimson's further comments see Larry I. Bland, ed., *The Papers of George Catlett Marshall*, vol. 5, *The Finest Soldier, January 1, 1945–January 7, 1947* (Baltimore, 2003), 79–80. The Stimson quote on "bombing civilian populations" is from the *New York Herald Tribune*, February 23, 1945.

56. Stimson Diary, June 1, 1945; Crane, *Bombs, Cities, and Civilians*, 6.

57. Stimson Diary, March 5, 1945.

58. Ibid.

59. Undated, handwritten note, Harrison-Bundy, file 7.

60. Hyde Park Aide-Mémoire, September 19, 1944, Harrison-Bundy, file 3 (emphasis added); Vannevar Bush, "Memorandum to Dr. Conant," September 23, 1944, Bush-Conant, file 19.

61. For Sachs' post facto account of this meeting see Nat S. Finney, "How F.D.R. Planned to Use the A-Bomb," *Look*, March 14, 1950.

Chapter 4. "The International Situation"

1. John Lansdale, "Capture of Material" (draft), July 10, 1946, Leslie R. Groves, Correspondence ("Top Secret") of the Manhattan Engineer District, 1942–46, microfilm publication M1109, file 7F, National Archives (hereafter cited as Groves "Top Secret"); Leslie Groves, *Now It Can be Told: The Story of the Manhattan Project* (New York, 1962), 237–38.

2. Lansdale, "Capture of Material"; Groves, *Now It Can be Told*, 237–38; U.S. Military Attaché, London, England to Groves, April 26, 1945, Boris T. Pash Papers, box 2, folder 4, Hoover Institution Archives, Stanford, Calif. (hereafter cited as Pash Papers); Major J. C. Bullock, "Target 'Wirtschaftliche Forschungsellschaft' (WIFO)," May 9, 1945, Pash Papers, box 4, folder 2.

3. Groves, "Memorandum for the Secretary of War," April 23, 1945, Groves "Top Secret," file 25M. The Soviets sent their own teams into Germany looking for scientists and raw materials but for the most part found that the British and Americans had beaten them to it. David Holloway, *Stalin and the Bomb* (New Haven, 1994), 111.

4. Bullock, "Target 'Wirtschaftliche Forschungsellschaft' (WIFO)"; Major Francis J. Smith, "Memorandum for the Files," April 7, 1945, Groves "Top Secret," file 7F.

5. When the Anglo-American Alsos nuclear intelligence team examined captured scientific papers in the French town of Strasbourg in November 1944, they discovered that the "evidence at hand proved definitely that Germany had no atom bomb and was not likely to have one in any reasonable time. . . . they were about as far as we were in 1940, before we had begun any large-scale efforts on the atom bomb at all." Samuel Goudsmit, *Alsos* (New York, 1947), 71.

6. Bush, "Memorandum for Dr. Conant," October 9, 1941, Bush-Conant File Relating to the Development of the Atomic Bomb, 1940–1945, Records of the Office of Scientific Research and Development, record group 227, microfilm publication M1392, file 2, National Archives (hereafter cited as Bush-Conant).

7. Bush, "Memorandum for Dr. Conant," December 16, 1941, Bush-Conant, file 2.

8. "Outline of Princeton lectures," n.d. [circa March or April 1934], Henry Lewis Stimson Papers (microfilm ed.), reel 132, Manuscripts and Archives, Yale University Library (hereafter cited as Stimson Papers).

9. Henry Stimson, *Democracy and Nationalism in Europe* (Princeton, 1934), 79.

10. May 15, 1945, Henry Lewis Stimson Diaries (microfilm ed.), Manuscripts and Archives, Yale University Library (hereafter cited as Stimson Diary).

11. "Memorandum for the President," September 11, 1945, Stimson Diary.

12. Franklin Roosevelt to Winston Churchill, October 11, 1941, Premier Files of Winston Churchill (microfilm ed.), 3/139/8A, Public Record Office, London, England (hereafter cited as Prem); Vannevar Bush, "Memorandum for Dr. Conant," October 9, 1941, Bush-Conant, file 2. The best treatments of the Anglo-American negotiations over atomic energy during World War II are Septimus H. Paul, *Nuclear Rivals: Anglo-American Atomic Relations, 1941–1952* (Columbus, Ohio, 2000), and Martin A. Sherwin, *A World Destroyed: Hiroshima and Its Legacies* (Stanford, 2003), 67–114. Also see Barton J. Bernstein, "The Quest for Security: American Foreign Policy and International Control, 1942–1946," *Journal of American History* 60, no. 4 (March 1974): 1003–44; Bernstein, "The Uneasy Alliance: Roosevelt, Churchill, and the Atomic Bomb, 1940–1945," *Western Political Quarterly* 29, no. 2 (June 1976): 202–30; James G. Hershberg, *James B. Conant: Harvard to Hiroshima and the Making of the Nuclear Age* (Stanford, 1993), 172–93.

13. Churchill to Roosevelt, December 1941, Prem 3/139/8A; John Anderson to Churchill, July 31, 1942, Prem 3/139/8A. For more on British thinking in this period see Paul, *Nuclear Rivals*, 24–30.

14. Bush to Conant, "Some Thoughts on the S-1 Project," October 26, 1942, Bush-Conant, file 9.

15. Annex 5, "Diplomatic History of the Manhattan Project," Harrison-Bundy Files Relating to the Development of the Atomic Bomb, 1942–1946, Records of the Office of the Chief of Engineers, record group 77, microfilm publication M1108, file 109, National Archives (hereafter cited as Harrison-Bundy).

16. Ibid.

17. Sherwin, *A World Destroyed*, 73; Robert S. Norris, *Racing for the Bomb: General Leslie R. Groves, the Manhattan Project's Indispensable Man* (South Royalton, Vt., 2002), 327.

18. Warning that "the Russians, who are peculiarly well equipped scientifically for this kind of development may well be working on the Tube Alloys [atomic bomb] project somewhere beyond the Urals and making great progress," Anderson urged Churchill in April 1943 to "make every possible effort to bring about an effective co-operation between the United States and ourselves." John Anderson to Churchill, April 29, 1943, Prem 3/139/8A. On Churchill's pleas for renewed cooperation see Sherwin, *A World Destroyed*, 76–85.

19. Stimson Diary, September 7, 8, 1943.

20. Prime Minister to Sir John Anderson, May 26, 1943, Prem 3/139/8; "Lord President's Minute," January 18, 1943, Prem 3/139/8A.

21. Bush, "Memorandum of Conference with the President," June 24, 1943, Bush-Conant, file 10.

22. Stimson was in London as part of a tour of American bases in Britain and North Africa. Bush had traveled to London separately to coordinate research with the British on antisubmarine efforts.

23. Stimson to Roosevelt, June 19, 1942, Stimson Diary; Stimson Diary November 7, 1942.

24. "Brief Report on Certain Features of Overseas Trip," n.d. [July 1943], Stimson Diary.

25. Stimson Diary, May 17, 1943.

26. Churchill to Anderson and Cherwell, July 18, 1943, Prem 3/139/8A.

27. Bush to Conant, July 23, 1943, Bush-Conant, file 10.

28. Roosevelt to Bush, July 20, 1943, Harrison-Bundy, file 109; Sherwin, *A World Destroyed*, 85. In Washington, Conant wrote to Bush, noting, "You and [Stimson] on the one hand and F.D.R. on the other seem to have arrived at the same conclusion independently." Conant to Bush, August 3, 1943, Bush-Conant, file 10. For speculation on Roosevelt's motives and a possible link to the second-front debate see Paul, *Nuclear Rivals*, 47–48, 53; Hershberg, *James B. Conant*, 188–89.

29. Bundy, "Memorandum of Meeting at 10 Downing Street on July 22, 1943," Harrison-Bundy, file 47.

30. Ibid.

31. Norris, *Racing for the Bomb*, 253–79; Groves, August 21, 1943, "Present Status and Future Program," Harrison-Bundy, file 6; Stimson Diary, September 9, 1943.

32. "Brief Report on Certain Features of Overseas Trip," n.d. [circa July 1943], Stimson Diary.

33. Bush, "Memorandum for the Files," August 4, 1943, Bush-Conant, file 10.

34. "Conference between Henry Lewis Stimson and the Council of Bishops of the Methodist Church," February 26, 1943, Stanley K. Hornbeck Papers, box 401, Hoover Institution Archives, Stanford, Calif.

35. Sherwin, *A World Destroyed*, 79, 89, 91, 104.

36. Wilson D. Miscamble, *From Roosevelt to Truman: Potsdam, Hiroshima, and the Cold War* (New York, 2007). Miscamble acknowledges Roosevelt's decision not to divulge information on the bomb to the Soviets but credits Churchill's powers of persuasion for this result (p. 75). But if, as Miscamble suggests elsewhere in pungent language (p. 55) when discussing the 1943 Tehran meeting, Roosevelt's "main priority centered on gaining Stalin's friendship, which he sought at Churchill's expense with all the good sense of an immature teenage male trying to impress a member of the opposite sex," it seems odd that he would agree to the British leader's explicitly anti-Soviet pleas to withhold the atomic secret. Yet FDR sided with Churchill on the bomb not only at Quebec but also in a later meeting at Hyde Park in 1944. I agree with Miscamble's assessment (p. 75) that "FDR for the most part postponed decisions on this issue . . . while awaiting the successful test of a weapon." I would add, however, that Roosevelt's decision to hold the atomic secret in his back pocket until the bomb was ready for combat use tends to undercut Miscamble's thesis, which hinges on a naïve, gullible Roosevelt easily manipulated by the more canny Soviet dictator.

37. Ronald I. Campbell to John Anderson, May 31, 1944, Prem 3/139/11A

38. Ibid., 96–97. On Bohr see Abraham Pais, *Niels Bohr's Times: In Physics, Philosophy, and Polity* (New York, 1991).

39. Hershberg, *James B. Conant*, 198–99.

40. Bush and Conant to Stimson, September 30, 1944, Harrison-Bundy, file 69.

41. For an example of such concerns at Chicago see the Compton Report, November 18, 1944, Harrison-Bundy, file 59. On unease at Los Alamos see, Gregg Herken, *Brotherhood of the Bomb: The Tangled Lives and Loyalties of Robert Oppenheimer, Ernest Lawrence, and Edward Teller* (New York, 2002), 364, n. 79; Kai Bird and Martin J. Sherwin, *American Prometheus: The Triumph and Tragedy of J. Robert Oppenheimer* (New York, 2005), 287.

42. John Anderson to Churchill, March 21, 1944, Prem 3/139/2.

43. "Even six months," he insisted in opposing any disclosure to foreign powers, "will make a difference should it come to a showdown with Russia, or indeed with [Free French leader Charles] de Gaulle." Draft of Churchill to Foreign Secretary, March 25, 1945, Prem 3/139/6. This line was deleted from the final version of the memo.

44. In a note to Cherwell in September 1944, the British prime minister suggested that "Bohr ought to be confined or at any rate made to see that he is very near the edge of mortal crimes." Churchill to Cherwell, September 20, 1944, Prem 3/139/8A.

45. Felix Frankfurter, "Strictly Private," April 26, 1945, Papers of J. Robert Oppenheimer, box 34, Library of Congress (hereafter cited as Oppenheimer Papers); Sherwin, *A World Destroyed*, 100, 109.

46. Specifically, Roosevelt feared the French would learn of the Anglo-American project and then disclose the secret to the Soviet Union. Churchill to Foreign Secretary, March 25, 1945, Prem 3/139/6.

47. "Hyde Park Aide-Mémoire," September 19, 1944, Harrison-Bundy, file 3.

48. Undated, handwritten note, Harrison-Bundy, file 7. Judging from the context and content, this document likely corresponded to a conversation between Bundy and Stimson on March 5, 1945.

49. Annex 5, "Diplomatic History of the Manhattan Project," Harrison-Bundy, file 109.

50. "Outline of Princeton lectures," n.d. [circa March or April, 1934], Stimson Papers, reel 132; Stimson, *Democracy and Nationalism in Europe*, 79.

51. Bush, "Memorandum for Dr. Conant," September 25, 1944, Bush-Conant, file 10.

52. The note in question was appended to Felix Frankfurter, "Strictly Private," April 26, 1945, Oppenheimer Papers, box 34." Though unsigned, from the context it is clear that the author of the note was Bohr.

53. Stimson Diary, December 31, 1944.

54. Bush, "Memorandum for Dr. Conant," February 15, 1945, Bush-Conant, file 37.

55. Stimson Diary, November 4, 1943; October 13, 1944; May 17, 1943. On Stimson's willingness to accept a Soviet sphere of influence (and perhaps territorial concessions) in eastern Europe and the eastern Mediterranean, see Stimson Diary, January 11 and June 21, 1944.

56. Stimson to Dorothy Thompson, August 12, 1940, Stimson Papers, reel 102; Stimson to John Spencer Muirhead, March 24, 1939, Stimson Papers, reel 97.

57. Stimson Diary, April 4, 1944; "Conference between Henry Lewis Stimson and the Council of Bishops of the Methodist Church," February 26, 1943.

58. Stimson Diary, June 2, 1942.

59. "Memorandum of talk with James G. Rogers," n.d. [circa March or April, 1934], Stimson Papers, reel 132.

60. "Memorandum for the President," September 15, 1944, Stimson Diary.

61. "Telephone Conversation—September 5, 1944 at 11:25 A.M.," Henry Morgenthau, *Morgenthau Diary (Germany)* (Washington, D.C., 1967), 1:521. *FRUS, The Conference at Quebec, 1944*, 97 ("down to subsistence levels").

62. I use the term "Morgenthau Plan" here to refer to a loose set of proposals for postwar Germany that included partition into multiple states, partial or full deindustrialization of the German economy, and extensive efforts at de-Nazification, including social and educational reforms and the internment and possible execution of many Nazi officials. *FRUS, 1943*, 1:542; *FRUS, Conferences at Cairo and Tehran, 1943*, 253–54, 600, 602–3; Morgenthau, *Morgenthau Diary*, 1:415, 436.

63. "Stimson Memorandum," September 5, 1944, Stimson Diary.

64. For more on the Morgenthau Plan dispute see Eleanor Roosevelt, *The Roosevelt I Remember* (New York, 1949), 334–35; David M. Kennedy, *Freedom from Fear: The American People in Depression and War, 1929–1945* (New York, 1999), 803–4; Steven Casey, *Cautious Crusade: Franklin D. Roosevelt, American Public Opinion, and the War against Nazi Germany* (New York, 2001), 184–89; Robert Dallek, *Franklin Roosevelt and American Foreign Policy, 1932–1945* (New York, 1979), 472–75, 477.

65. Stimson Diary, October 23, 1944.

66. Ibid.

67. Ibid., April 16, 1945; April 2 ("been good to us").

68. Stimson Diary, May 15, 1945 ("master card"); Stimson to Truman, May 16, 1945 ("play ball"), Stimson Diary.

69. Stimson Diary, December 31, 1944.

70. Ibid., February 13, 1945.

71. Ibid., February 15, 1945.

72. Stimson's handwritten comment on "Memorandum, proposed items for the agenda," n.d. [circa April 1945], Formerly Top Secret Correspondence of Secretary of War Stimson, record group 107, box 3, National Archives II, College Park, Md. (hereafter cited as "Safe File"). Gar Alperovitz claimed in *Atomic Diplomacy: Hiroshima and Potsdam: The Use of the Atomic Bomb and the Confrontation with Soviet Power* (New York, 1985) that Stimson shared Truman's concern over the Polish issue but simply sought to delay a confrontation until after the bomb had been tested. There is, however, no evidence to support this claim. While Stimson clearly foresaw the need for a "showdown" (in Alperovitz's words) on economic access to Soviet-controlled eastern Europe, he remained consistently uninterested in dictating the form of the Polish government or in contesting Soviet political (as opposed to economic) influence in eastern Europe. Ibid., 108. On Stimson's lack of interest in Poland see Stimson Diary, January 11, 1944; April 23, 1945.

73. Stimson Diary, December 31, 1944; February 15, 1945.

74. Ibid., February 13, 1945.

75. On Alperovitz's claims with respect to Stimson and a "delayed showdown," see Alperovitz, *Atomic Diplomacy*, 89–139; Alperovitz, *The Decision to Use the Atomic Bomb* (New York, 1995), 142–45. The major focus of both of these works is on the period from Roosevelt's death until the end of the war, which likely accounts for Alperovitz's conclusion that Stimson was deliberately pursuing a strat-

egy of delay. Had he focused on the period before spring 1945, he might have reached a more nuanced conclusion with respect to Stimson's position on the bomb as a bargaining chip.

76. Bush, "Memorandum for Dr. Conant," October 9, 1941, Bush-Conant, file 2.

77. Gregg Herken, *The Winning Weapon: The Atomic Bomb in the Cold War, 1945–1950* (New York, 1980), 101–2; Norris, *Racing for the Bomb*, 326–27.

78. Though most of the effort on the Anglo-American side was focused on uranium, the naturally occurring element thorium was also considered important as a potential fuel for nuclear fission. "Agreement and Declaration of Trust," June 13, 1944, Harrison-Bundy, file 48.

79. Stimson Diary, June 2, 1942.

80. Stimson aide George Harrison was a director of First National and offered to make the necessary arrangements. It was determined, however, that such an action would be illegal. Groves, "Memorandum to the Files," October 17, 1944, Groves "Top Secret," file 9B; Groves, "Memorandum to the Secretary of War," October 27, 1944, Groves "Top Secret," file 9B; Stimson Diary, October 17, 21, 1944. For more, see Norris, *Racing for the Bomb*, 336–37.

81. The trust tried, but failed, to secure control of major uranium deposits in Sweden. For a copy of the check made out to Groves and more on the complicated and secret arrangements undertaken by the trust, see the Groves "Top Secret" papers, file 9B. For more on the trust see Herken, *The Winning Weapon*, 102–13; Norris, *Racing for the Bomb*, 335–43; Sherwin, *A World Destroyed*, 104–5; Groves, *Now It Can Be Told*, 170–84; Richard G. Hewlett and Oscar E. Anderson, *A History of the United States Atomic Energy Commission: The New World 1939–1946* (University Park, Pa., 1962), 285–88.

82. An undated, handwritten memorandum in Stimson's War Department "Safe File" (likely produced shortly before the July 1945 Potsdam Conference) illustrates the link between the work of the CDT and the decision to delay opening negotiations with Stalin over the fate of the bomb. In a list of items to be considered in making such a decision, Stimson highlighted the discovery of a large amount of uranium in Sweden, material not yet locked up by the CDT. In the same document, he also outlined the timetable for the conclusion of the CDT's negotiations with Brazil and the Dutch East Indies, indicating that the completion of these arrangements was an important factor in his thinking about the timing of any negotiations over postwar control. Stimson, "Left Over from Japan & S1," "Safe File," box 11.

83. Norris, *Racing for the Bomb*, 285.

84. Goudschmidt, *Alsos*, 71; Norris, *Racing for the Bomb*, 301.

85. Norris, *Racing for the Bomb*, 293–94.

86. Groves, *Now It Can Be Told*, 231. On the destruction of the Auer Gesellschaft Works see "Memorandum to General Groves," March 6, 1945; Groves, "Memorandum to the Chief of Staff," March 7, 1945; Marshall to Spaatz, March 7, 1945; Spaatz to Marshall, March 19, 1945, all in Groves "Top Secret," file 7C. Also see Norris, *Racing for the Bomb*, 302. The Soviets apparently understood the motivation behind the American decision to bomb the plant. Some of the equipment from the Auer plant survived the bombing and was eventually seized by the Soviets for use in their own atomic project. Holloway, *Stalin and the Bomb*, 111, 178.

87. U.S. Military Attaché [Captain Horace T. Calvert], London to War Department, February 1, 1945, Harrison-Bundy, file 55.

88. Groves to Calvert, London, February 3, 1945, Harrison-Bundy, file 55; Norris, *Racing for the Bomb*, 302; Major Francis J. Smith, "Memo to File," April 6, 7, 1945, Groves "Top Secret," file 7B.

89. Smith, "Memorandum for the Files," April 7, 1945, Groves "Top Secret," file 7B.

90. Werner Heisenberg, the head of the German program, was captured on May 2 in the town of Urfeldt. Norris, *Racing for the Bomb*, 304–6.

91. Stimson Diary, May 14, 1945.

92. Major H. K. Calvert, "Visit to Wismar," n.d. [covering events of May 4, 1945], Pash Papers, box 2, folder 4.

93. Stimson Diary, April 12, 1945.

94. Stimson to Theodore Roosevelt, September 2, 1910, Stimson Papers, reel 19.

95. Godfrey Hodgson, *The Colonel: The Life and Wars of Henry Stimson, 1867–1950* (New York, 1990), 316. Also see the Stimson Diary for April 12 and 13, 1945.

96. Stimson Diary, April 12, 1945.

97. Ibid., March 13, 1944.

98. Ibid., April 25, 1945.

99. "Memorandum Discussed with the President," April 25, 1945, Stimson Diary.

100. Ibid.; Leslie Groves, "Report of Meeting with the President," April 25, 1945, Groves, "Top Secret," file 20.

101. Stimson, "Memorandum discussed with the President," April 25, 1945, Stimson Diary.

102. Ibid.

Chapter 5. The Ordeal of Henry L. Stimson

1. May 8, 1945, Henry Lewis Stimson Diaries (microfilm ed.), Manuscripts and Archives, Yale University Library (hereafter cited as Stimson Diary).

2. "Telephone Conversation between the Secretary of War and Mr. McCloy in San Francisco," May 8, 1945, Henry Lewis Stimson Papers (microfilm ed.), reel 128, Manuscripts and Archives, Yale University Library (hereafter cited as Stimson Papers).

3. Benjamin C. McCartney, "Return to Florence," *National Geographic Magazine* 87, no. 3 (March 1945): 257–96. McCartney was killed in action before the article was published.

4. Stimson to Rev. Dr. Albert Joseph McCartney, February 19, 1945, Stimson Papers, reel 112.

5. Stimson Diary, May 28, 1945.

6. Groves quoted in Peter Wyden, *Day One: Hiroshima and After* (New York, 1984), 135.

7. Stimson Diary, February 27, 1945.

8. Though its focus is split between the USSR, Japan, and the United States, Tsuyoshi Hasegawa's *Racing the Enemy: Stalin, Truman, and the Surrender of Japan* (Cambridge, Mass., 2005) is probably the best single source on the debate within the American government over surrender terms in 1945. Also see Dale M. Hellegers, *We, the Japanese People: World War II and the Origins of the Japanese Constitution* (Stanford, 2001), 1–158; Gar Alperovitz, *The Decision to Use the Atomic Bomb* (New York, 1995), 31–79; Richard B. Frank, *Downfall: The End of the Imperial Japanese Empire* (New York, 1999), 214–21.

9. The original and most influential statement of this orthodox defense of the bomb was Stimson, "The Decision to Use the Atomic Bomb," *Harper's* (February 1947): 97–107. For more contemporary restatements of this position see Robert James Maddox, *Weapons for Victory: The Hiroshima Decision* (Columbia, Mo., 2004); Robert Newman, *Truman and the Hiroshima Cult* (East Lansing, Mich., 1995).

10. Stimson Diary, August 10, 1945.

11. *Foreign Relations of the United States, The Conferences at Washington, 1941–1942, and Casablanca, 1943* (Washington, D.C.), 837 (hereafter cited as *FRUS*).

12. Joint Chiefs of Staff 924/15, April 25, 1945, box 169, section 12, record group 218, National Archives II, College Park, Md.

13. Herbert Hoover Memorandum, May 15, 1945, Formerly Top Secret Correspondence of Secretary of War Stimson, record group 107, box 8, National Archives II, College Park, Md. (hereafter cited as "Safe File"); Stimson Diary, May 16, 1945. The question of Japan, the atomic bomb, and the need to clarify surrender terms came directly to Stimson's attention as early as May 1, 1945, at a meeting of the Committee of Three (which included representatives from the War, Navy, and State Departments). It was not until later that month, however, following prodding from McCloy and Grew, that Stimson began to consider the matter. "Minutes of the Meeting of the Committee of Three," May 1, 1945, "Safe File," box 3. For more on discussion within army and the War Department on this issue see Hasegawa, *Racing the Enemy*, 78–79; Kai Bird, *The Chairman: John J. McCloy and the Making of the American Establishment* (New York, 1992), 242.

14. McCloy, "Memorandum for Colonel Stimson," May, 28, 1945, "Safe File," box 8.

15. Grew, "Memorandum of Conversation with the President," May 28, 1945, enclosed in Grew to Stimson, February 12, 1947, Stimson Papers, reel 116. On the background to Grew's meeting with

Truman, including dissent within the State Department on the issue of the Japanese emperor, see Hasegawa, *Racing the Enemy*, 80–82.

16. Joseph Grew to Stimson, February 12, 1947, Stimson Papers, reel 116.

17. Stimson to Roosevelt, March 15, 1944, Stimson Papers, reel 109. Richard Frank has asserted that Stimson's willingness to modify unconditional surrender in spring–summer 1945 represented an "evolution of his thinking," citing the secretary's January 1945 opposition to such a proposal by the chief of naval operations, Admiral Ernest J. King. Frank, *Downfall*, 409n; Stimson Diary, January 22, 1945. But Stimson's qualms in January almost certainly reflected his hesitancy to publicly abandon that formula with respect to *Germany*, not Japan. See the account of Stimson's thinking on this issue in the entry for January 16, 1945, in James V. Forrestal Diary, microfilm section, Navy Publication and Printing Service Office (NPPSO), Naval District, Washington, D.C. (hereafter cited as Forrestal Diary), which is entirely focused on the question of Germany and unconditional surrender. The secretary of war was consistently willing to consider terms short of unconditional surrender for Italy and Japan. On King's objections to unconditional surrender with respect to Germany see Raymond G. O'Connor, *Diplomacy for Victory: FDR and Unconditional Surrender* (New York, 1971), 54, 86.

18. Stimson Diary, November 18, 1942; David M. Kennedy, *Freedom from Fear: The American People in Depression and War, 1929–1945* (New York, 1999), 582–83; Robert Dallek, *Franklin D. Roosevelt and American Foreign Policy 1932–1945* (New York, 1979), 364–66. For a more complete account of the Darlan deal and Roosevelt's flirtations with the Vichy regime see William L. Langer, *Our Vichy Gamble* (New York, 1947).

19. Stimson Diary, June 14 ("politics of Italy"), July 1("too much unconditional surrender"), 1943. Also see Stimson to Roosevelt, September 20, 1943, Stimson Diary.

20. Stimson, "Memorandum for the President: The Conduct of the War with Japan," enclosed in Stimson to James F. Byrnes, July 16, 1945, Stimson Papers, reel 113.

21. Others present included the director of the Office of War Information (OWI), Elmer Davis, and Judge Samuel Rosenman, counsel to the president. Stimson Diary, May 29, 1945; Forrestal Diary, May 29, 1945.

22. Stimson, "Memorandum for the Chief of Staff," May 30, 1945, "Safe File," box 8.

23. Grew Diary, May 29, 1945, reprinted in Grew, *Turbulent Era: A Diplomatic Record of Forty Years, 1904–1945* (Cambridge, Mass., 1952), 1434.

24. Stimson to Joseph Grew, June 19, 1947, Eugene H. Dooman Papers, box 2, Hoover Institution Archives, Stanford, Calif. (hereafter cited as Dooman Papers).

25. Grew, *Turbulent Era*, 1434.

26. Eugene Dooman to Joseph Grew, June 30, 1947, Dooman Papers, box 2.

27. February 9, 1947, The Diary of William R. Castle (microfilm of original), Houghton Library, Harvard University.

28. Stimson Diary, May 29, 1945.

29. John J. McCloy, "Memorandum of Conversation with General Marshall May 29, 1945, 11:45 AM," "Safe File," box 12.

30. Stimson Diary, May 29, 1945.

31. "Character and strength of buildings in different parts of the city" and the "Contour of the ground" were the factors that Parsons suggested would be most important in selecting cities for destruction. William Parsons to William Purnell (via Leslie Groves), December 12, 1944, Correspondence ("Top Secret") of the Manhattan Engineer District, 1942–46, microfilm publication M1109, file 5D, National Archives (hereafter cited as Groves "Top Secret").

32. AAF Target Committee members were Brigadier General Lauris R. Norstad, Colonel William P. Fisher, Colonel Paul W. Tibbets, Dr. David M. Dennison, and Dr. Robert Stearns. Manhattan Project representatives included Dr. John von Neumann, Dr. R. Bright Wilson, Dr. William Penny, Dr. Norman F. Ramsey, Colonel Lyle E. Seeman, and Major Jack Derry (who wrote the summary notes after each meeting).

33. Jack Derry, "Notes on Initial Meeting of the Target Committee," April 27, 1945, Groves "Top Secret," file 5D.

34. Derry, "Summary of Target Committee Meetings on 10 and 11 May 1945," Groves, "Top Secret," file 5D.

35. One of the important criteria used by the committee in selecting a target was that it "be capable of being damaged effectively by a blast." Ibid. When Norstad asked the AAF's Joint Target Group (JTG) to suggest targets in Japan that would be susceptible to such a weapon, they responded by reiterating that "[l]arge blast bombs . . . are most effective against light industrial and residential structures. . . . They are relatively ineffective against heavily constructed buildings, single or multi-story." Norstad to Director, Joint Target Group, April 28, 1945; Director, Joint Target Group to Norstad, May 5, 1945, both in Groves "Top Secret," file 5D.

36. Derry, "Notes on Initial Meeting of the Target Committee."

37. Parsons to Groves, September 25, 1944, Parsons Papers.

38. Derry, "Minutes of Third Target Committee Meeting—Washington, 28 May 1945, Groves, "Top Secret," file 5D.

39. Stimson to Truman, May 16, 1945, Stimson Diary.

40. Diary of John J. McCloy, May 21, 1945, John J. McCloy Papers, box DY1, folder 17, Amherst College Library, Amherst, Mass. (hereafter cited as McCloy Diary).

41. "Objectives" [outline for draft of presidential address, author unknown but likely either Harvey Bundy or Arthur Page], May 25, 1945, Harrison Bundy Files Relating to the Development of the Atomic Bomb, 1942—46, Records of the Office of the Chief of Engineers, record group 77, microfilm publication M1108, file 74, National Archives (hereafter cited as Harrison-Bundy).

42. McCloy, "Memorandum of Conversation with General Marshall."

43. On June 1, three days after this meeting with Marshall, Stimson summoned Arnold to question the general about "a bombing of Tokyo" that Stimson found objectionable insofar as it had apparently been aimed primarily at civilians and as such represented a breach "of my promise from Lovett that there would be only precision bombing in Japan." Stimson Diary, June 1, 1945.

44. McCloy, "Memorandum of Conversation with General Marshall."

45. Groves Diary, May 30, 1945, Papers of Leslie R. Groves, box 3, record group 200, National Archives II, College Park, Md. (hereafter cited as Groves Diary).

46. Groves claimed in his memoir that he had gone to see Stimson "about another matter" when the secretary suddenly turned the conversation to the subject of targeting. It is unclear from the contemporary record why Groves was summoned that morning, though it may have been related to the recent visit of five congressional representatives to the uranium extraction facilities at Oak Ridge, Tennessee. Leslie Groves, *Now It Can Be Told: The Story of the Manhattan Project* (New York, 1962), 273; Stimson Diary, May 30, 1945. Also see the account in Robert S. Norris, *Racing for the Bomb: General Leslie R. Groves, the Manhattan Project's Indispensable Man* (South Royalton, Vt., 2002), 386–87.

47. Groves quoted in Len Giovannitti and Fred Freed, *The Decision to Drop the Bomb* (New York, 1965), 40–41.

48. Stimson Diary, May 30, 1945.

49. Groves, *Now It Can Be Told*, 275.

50. Stimson Diary, June 1, 1945; Ira C. Eaker, "Memorandum for the Secretary of War," June 11, 1945, "Safe File," box 8. Also see Otis Cary, *Mr. Stimson's "Pet City": The Sparing Of Kyoto, 1945* (Kyoto, 1987).

51. Groves, "Memorandum to General Norstad," May 30, 1945 (emphasis in original), Groves "Top Secret," file 5D (emphasis added).

52. The 509th Composite Group (a unit of the Twenty-first Bomber Command, Twentieth Air Force) was a specially created B-29 unit tasked with delivering the atomic bomb. May 31, 1945, The Diary of Henry H. Arnold, Arnold Papers, Manuscripts and Records Division, Library of Congress.

53. Conant to Stimson, May 5, 1945, Harrison-Bundy, file 69.

54. Regular members of the Interim Committee included Stimson, Harrison (who chaired committee meetings in Stimson's absence), OSRD Director Vannevar Bush, NRDC Chairman James B. Conant, the president's personal representative, James F. Byrnes, Assistant Secretary of State William

L. Clayton, Undersecretary of the Navy Ralph A. Bard, and MIT President and OSRD Chief of the Office of Field Service Karl T. Compton.

55. The notes from the May 14 meeting clearly illustrated the assumption on the part of at least some of the committee members that a post-test statement should be issued:

> The inclusiveness of a public statement concerning the weapon was felt to be dependent upon the outcome of the test to be made in July. In the event that the test showed poor results, it would suffice to have only a brief notice made public by the theater commander to the effect that a dump of high explosives had blown up. If, however, the results that are now confidently expected are borne out by the field test, a more complete public statement would be necessary. Such a statement would be made by the President and should indicate the general nature of the weapon, trace the history of its development and of the controls, both national and international, that are contemplated.

In a memorandum to Conant, Bush summarized the Interim Committee's discussions and noted that among the "very frank" conversations on that day "there was a good discussion on the *timing* and nature of releases." The mention of a debate over "timing" is a key indication that there was a division among the committee members as to *when* such a release should be issued. If the presidential statement had been intended solely for use in case of an emergency (as Groves later suggested), there would have been no need to debate the timing of its release—such timing would depend entirely on the outcome of the test and/or combat use. Present on May 14 were Harrison, Bush, Conant, Groves, the president's personal representative, James F. Byrnes, Undersecretary of the Navy Ralph Bard, and Assistant Secretary of State William L. Clayton. Notes were taken (as they were at all the Interim Committee meetings) by Second Lieutenant R. Gordon Arneson. Arneson, "Notes of an Informal Meeting of the Interim Committee," May 14, 1945, Harrison-Bundy, file 100; Bush, "Memorandum for Dr. Conant," May 14, 1945, Bush-Conant File Relating to the Development of the Atomic Bomb, 1940–45, Records of the Office of Scientific Research and Development, record group 227, microfilm publication M1392, file 19, National Archives (hereafter cited as Bush-Conant). Emphasis added.

56. "Memorandum," May 14, 1945, Groves "Top Secret," file 4. It is unclear whether Groves himself wrote this memorandum or whether it was prepared by a member of his staff (perhaps William L. Laurence, a *New York Times* reporter who had been assigned to Groves to help handle matters related to publicity).

57. "Notes of an Informal Meeting of the Interim Committee," May 9, 1945, Harrison-Bundy, file 100.

58. According to the official minutes, the "consensus of the Committee relative to the proposed statement to be made by the President *after a successful test* was that the President should make only a short announcement over the radio, or possibly to Congress, concerning the general nature of the weapon and its military and international implications." The official notes are cryptic in their treatment of the latter half of the meeting, simply recording that it was eventually decided that "the nature of the statements would depend in large measure on the results of the test and of actual use, and that *changes might later be necessary in terms of the international situation existing at the time of release*." Arneson, "Notes of an Informal Meeting of the Interim Committee," May 18, 1945, Harrison-Bundy, file 100 (emphasis added); Conant, "Memorandum for Dr. Bush," May 18, 1945, Bush-Conant, file 19.

59. Stimson Diary, April 2, 1945.

60. Of the participants, who included Stettinius, Deane, Harriman, Forrestal, Truman, Stimson, and Marshall, only Marshall joined Stimson in a desire to avoid a showdown with the Soviets on the subject of Polish representation at the San Francisco Conference. Stimson Diary, April 23, 1945. See also Forrestal Diary, April 23, 1945.

61. Stimson Diary, May 14, 1945.

62. Ibid.

63. McCloy, "Memorandum of Conversation with General Marshall."

64. Stimson Diary, May 30, 1945.

65. Oswald C. Brewster to the President of the United States, May 24, 1945, Harrison-Bundy, file 77.

66. Stimson to Marshall, May 30, 1945, Harrison-Bundy, file 77.

67. Ibid.

68. Gordon Arneson, "Notes of the Interim Committee Meeting," May 31, 1945 ("this project," "must be controlled"), Harrison-Bundy, file 100; Stimson Diary, May 31, 1945 ("Frankenstein").

69. Arneson, "Notes of the Interim Committee Meeting," May 31, 1945.

70. Ibid.

71. For varying accounts of this lunch discussion see Arthur Compton, *Atomic Quest: A Personal Narrative* (New York, 1956), 238–39; Ernest O. Lawrence to Dr. Karl K. Darrow, August 17, 1945, E. O. Lawrence Papers, box 28, folder 20, Bancroft Library, University of California, Berkeley. Also see Richard G. Hewlett and Oscar E. Anderson, *A History of the United States Atomic Energy Commission: The New World 1939–1946* (University Park, Pa., 1962), 358.

72. Lawrence to Darrow, August 17, 1945.

73. Arneson, "Notes of the Interim Committee Meeting," May 31, 1945.

74. Ibid.

75. Historian Robert Newman, a strong supporter of the decision to use the atomic bombs against Japanese cities, has conceded that the outcome of the May 31 meeting might well have been different had Marshall been present that afternoon. Newman, *Truman and the Hiroshima Cult*, 85.

76. Derry, "Minutes of Third Target Committee Meeting."

77. Michael Sherry has reached a similar conclusion regarding Stimson and the bomb. Michael S. Sherry, *The Rise of American Air Power: The Creation of Armageddon* (New Haven, 1987), 295.

78. Stimson, "The Decision to Use the Atomic Bomb," 105.

79. Alperovitz, *The Decision to Use the Atomic Bomb*, 165; Michael Gordin, *Five Days in August: How World War II Became a Nuclear War* (Princeton, 2007), 39.

80. Richard Polenberg, ed., *In the Matter of J. Robert Oppenheimer* (Ithaca, 2002), 34.

81. Derry, "Summary of Target Committee Meetings."

82. Derry, "Minutes of Third Target Committee Meeting."

83. 509th Group leader Paul Tibbets later emphatically asserted that "the AIMING POINTS did not have to be cleared with anyone. Such matters were my responsibility." Paul Tibbets to Barton J. Bernstein, June 18, 1998. Personal communication, copy given to author by Dr. Bernstein. The exception to this appears to have been the city of Kokura and its massive arsenal, which was added to the target list at the behest of Marshall for reasons discussed in chapter 6.

84. Stimson, "Memorandum for Talk with the President," June 6, 1945, Stimson Papers, reel 128.

85. Stimson Diary, June 6, 1945.

86. "Transcript of Conference Held at 11 am, 9 May, 1945 with Stimson, Marshall and a Special Committee of the Senate and House of Representative Which Investigated 'ATROCITIES' in Germany," Safe File, box 2.

87. Stimson Diary, June 6, 1945.

88. For a version of this argument see Stimson, "The Decision to Use the Atomic Bomb," 107.

Chapter 6. Hiroshima and Nagasaki by Way of Potsdam

1. Scientific Advisory Panel, "Recommendations on the Immediate Use of Nuclear Weapons," June 16, 1945, Harrison-Bundy Files Relating to the Office of the Chief of Engineers, record group 77, microfilm publication M1108, file 76, National Archives (hereafter cited as Harrison-Bundy). Lawrence apparently argued for the demonstration in subsequent meetings of the Scientific Advisory Panel. Gregg Herken, *Brotherhood of the Bomb: The Tangled Lives and Loyalties of Robert Oppenheimer, Ernest Lawrence, and Edward Teller* (New York, 2002), 134; Barton J. Bernstein, "Four Physicists and the Bomb: The Early Years, 1945–1950," *Historical Studies in the Physical and Biological Sciences* 18, no. 2 (1988): 235; Kai Bird and Martin J. Sherwin, *American Prometheus: The Triumph and Tragedy of*

J. Robert Oppenheimer (New York 2005), 299. For a good summary of the early scientific dissent see Lawrence Wittner, *The Struggle against the Bomb: One World or None: A History of the World Nuclear Disarmament Movement through 1953* (Stanford, 1993), particularly 20–38.

2. Ralph Bard, "Memorandum on the use of S-1 Bomb," June 27, 1945, enclosed in George Harrison to Stimson, June 28, 1945, Harrison-Bundy, file 77.

3. Gar Alperovitz, *The Decision to Use the Atomic Bomb* (New York, 1995), 226.

4. Stimson, "Memorandum for Talk with the President," June 6, 1945, Henry Lewis Stimson Papers (microfilm ed.), reel 128, Manuscripts and Archives, Yale University Library (hereafter cited as Stimson Papers).

5. Hoover sent another memorandum urging abandonment of unconditional surrender following a meeting with Truman on May 28. This was forwarded to Stimson, who discussed it with Marshall in early June. June 11, 1945, Henry Lewis Stimson Diaries (microfilm ed.), Manuscripts and Archives, Yale University Library (hereafter cited as Stimson Diary).

6. Richard B. Frank, *Downfall: The End of the Imperial Japanese Empire* (New York, 1999), 144–45.

7. "Minutes of Meeting Held at the White House," June 18, 1945, in Dennis Merrill, ed., *Documentary History of the Truman Presidency:* vol. 1: *The Decision to Drop the Atomic Bomb on Japan* (Bethesda, 1995), 54.

8. Ibid. McCloy later recalled speaking very forcefully on the issue of modifying American surrender terms on June 18 as well as invoking the atomic bomb as an alternative to invasion. Kai Bird, *The Chairman: John J. McCloy and the Making of the American Establishment* (New York, 1992), 246; Tsuyoshi Hasegawa, *Racing the Enemy: Stalin, Truman, and the Surrender of Japan* (Cambridge, Mass., 2005), 105; Frank, *Downfall*, 143. But the minutes of the meeting do not indicate McCloy did anything more than second Stimson's suggestion of a political solution to the conflict, and his later recollections likely exaggerated the extent to which he spoke on this issue on June 18.

9. Stimson Diary, June 26–30, 1945. Stimson's message calling for Japanese surrender was heavily drawn from an earlier draft by Joseph Grew. Stimson presented his draft message to the Committee of Three on June 26, which agreed to it in principle subject to minor revisions by a subcommittee that included McCloy as well as representatives from the State Department and Navy Department. For more see Hasegawa, *Racing the Enemy*, 110–15.

10. Stimson, "Memorandum for the President: Proposed Program for Japan," July 2, 1945, Stimson Diary.

11. Stimson Diary, June 19, 1945.

12. Stimson, "Memorandum for the President: Proposed Program for Japan," July 2, 1945.

13. Stimson Diary, June 26–30, 1945.

14. Ibid., July 2, 1945.

15. Ibid.

16. Merrill, *The Decision to Drop the Atomic Bomb on Japan*, 102.

17. Stimson Diary, July 16, 1945.

18. Truman diary entry for July 18, 1945, in Merrill, *The Decision to Drop the Atomic Bomb on Japan*, 121. The content of these intercepted messages between Togo and Japan's ambassador to the Soviet Union, Naotake Sato, was in fact quite ambiguous. While they revealed that the emperor was interested in seeking Soviet mediation to end the war, they also made clear that there was no consensus within the Japanese ruling class as to what terms they would consider acceptable. For my purposes, the important point is that Stimson and McCloy believed at the time that the intervention of the emperor was highly significant. For varied (and varying) interpretations of the Togo-Sato messages see Hasegawa, *Racing the Enemy*, 120–28, 133–36; Frank, *Downfall*, 221–32; Alperovitz, *The Decision to Use the Atomic Bomb*, 233–38.

19. Henry Stimson to Mabel Stimson, July 18, 1945, Stimson Papers, reel 113. Stimson took a brief tour of the devastated German capital, confiding to Mabel afterward that "I never saw anything as sad in my life."

20. Following a meeting with Truman on July 3, the president told Stimson that "he would like to have me to be somewhere near where we could help out in the coming conference." Stimson agreed to journey to Potsdam, accompanied by McCloy, to serve as an informal adviser. Stimson Diary, July 3, 1945.

21. Stimson Diary, April 17, 1932.

22. Ibid., May 31, 1945.

23. Stimson, "Memorandum for the President: The Conduct of the War with Japan," enclosed in Stimson to James Byrnes, July 16, 1945, Stimson Papers, reel 113. Gar Alperovitz has claimed that Stimson was in fact urging a "double warning" (one warning to be delivered during the course of the conference and the other immediately prior to the use of the bomb). Alperovitz, *The Decision to Use the Atomic Bomb*, 236. The wording of Stimson's memorandum is somewhat ambiguous on this point, but my reading is that he was calling for a single warning/clarification of terms prior to the use with the bomb itself to serve as the second "warning."

24. The major difference was that Bard argued that in addition to clarification of the emperor's position and the threat of possible Soviet entry, the American warning should contain an explicit mention of the atomic bomb. Stimson was ambiguous on this point in his July 16 memorandum.

25. Stimson Diary, July 17, 1945.

26. Ibid., July 24, 1945.

27. On Stalin's eagerness to join in a joint statement to Japan at Potsdam see David Holloway, "Jockeying for Position in the Postwar World: Soviet Entry into War with Japan in August 1945," in Hasegawa, *The End of the Pacific War*, 173–75, and Hasegawa, "The Soviet Factor in Ending the Pacific War: From the Neutrality Pact to Soviet Entry into the War in August 1945," in the same volume, 215–18; Geoffrey Roberts, *Stalin's War: From World War to Cold War, 1939–1953* (New Haven, 2006), 289–291.

28. For the text of the Potsdam Declaration see *Foreign Relations of the United States: The Conference of Berlin (The Potsdam Conference), 1945*, 2: 1474–76 (hereafter cited as *FRUS*).

29. See Hasegawa, *Racing the Enemy*, 165–70, for Japanese reaction to the Potsdam Declaration.

30. Frank, *Downfall*, 343.

31. The linked questions of how close Japan was to surrender in spring 1945 and what American leaders could have reasonably concluded on this issue on the basis of the evidence they had at the time remains a matter of intense controversy among historians. The evidence on Japanese attitudes from the decrypted "Magic" and "Ultra" cables that was available to American leaders was (and still is) susceptible to multiple interpretations. Those inclined to look for signs of Japanese war weariness and a desire to seek a diplomatic end to the war could find such evidence in summer 1945. But there was also significant evidence of a determination to fight to the bitter end among both the military and many important members of the Japanese government. There is a perhaps natural tendency for historians to read these ambiguous messages in such a way as to categorically support their own position on the bomb and the necessity of its use. Thus Richard Frank, who is generally sympathetic to Truman, sees them as "authoritative, contemporaneous, and decisive evidence" that guaranteeing the emperor would not, by itself, have produced a Japanese surrender (*Downfall*, 230). Meanwhile, Gar Alperovitz, a harsh Truman critic, concludes, "*It is very clear that well before atomic weapons were used, both the Japanese and U.S. governments had arrived at the same understanding of acceptable terms of surrender*," and that all that stood in the way was a guarantee of the emperor (*Atomic Diplomacy*, 30, emphasis in original). American policymakers, however, did not generally read the messages in such a literal and absolutist fashion. Stimson, for example, was greatly encouraged by the Magic cables to believe that Japan might be close to surrender in late July. He did not leap to the conclusion that a guarantee of the emperor was the only thing standing in the way of surrender, but he was optimistic enough to push for a speedy clarification of American terms at Potsdam prior to the use of the bomb. For an overview on the English-language literature on this question see Bernstein, "Introducing the Interpretive Problem of Japan's 1945 Surrender: A Historiographic Essay on Recent Literature in the West," in *The End of the Pacific War: Reappraisals*, ed. Tsuyoshi Hasegawa (Stanford, 2007), 9–64.

32. *FRUS, Potsdam, 1:895*. Emphasis in original.

33. Stimson Diary, June 26–30, 1945.

34. Frank, *Downfall*, 216; *FRUS, Potsdam*, 2:1267–68; *FRUS, Potsdam*, 1:895–96, 900–903.

35. On the role of the JCS at Potsdam see Hasegawa, *Racing the Enemy*, 145–47, 156; Frank, *Downfall*, 219–20.

36. Barton J. Bernstein, in his commentary (p. 10) on Hasegawa's *Racing the Enemy* posted as part of the H–diplo roundtable, asserted that American leaders might have feared that "such a concession of a constitutional monarchy might embolden the Japanese to stiffen their resolve" (http://www.hnet .org/~diplo/roundtables/PDF/Bernstein-HasegawaRoundtable.pdf). Also see Wilson D. Miscamble, *From Roosevelt to Truman: Potsdam, Hiroshima, and the Cold War* (New York, 2007), 196. Both Bernstein and Miscamble also note that domestic political concerns over backing away from unconditional surrender also likely played a role in Truman's decision.

37. The strongest evidence that domestic political concerns were the determining factor in Truman and Byrnes's reluctance to make a public statement on the emperor comes from their reaction to the initial Japanese surrender offer on August 10. The only condition attached to this offer was that the United States allow the continuation of the imperial dynasty. Yet even after two atomic bombs and with the Soviet Union taking advantage of the continued fighting to advance into Manchuria, Truman and Byrnes were reluctant to agree to the Japanese terms. According to Henry Wallace's account of the August 10 cabinet meeting, Truman was concerned with a public backlash over "soft" terms for Japan. "Referring to hard and soft terms for Japan," Wallace recorded, "Truman referred to 170 telegrams precipitated by the peace rumor of August 9. 153 of the 170 were for hard terms—unconditional surrender. They were free-will telegrams—not inspired—and were mostly from parents of service men." Byrnes, meanwhile expressed concern that "we might be exposed to the criticism that we had receded from the totality and severity of the Potsdam declaration." The Diary of Henry A. Wallace, August 10, 1945 (microfilm ed.), Microfilm Corporation of America, Glen Rock, New Jersey (hereafter cited as Wallace Diary); August 10, 1945, James V. Forrestal Diary, microfilm section, NPPSO, Naval District, Washington, D.C. (hereafter cited as Forrestal Diary). For a discussion of Byrnes's domestic political motives for using the bomb and retaining the unconditional surrender formula see David Robertson, *Sly and Able: A Political Biography of James F. Byrnes* (New York, 1994), 391, 412–13, 417–19, 435–36.

38. Frank McNaughton to Eleanor Welch (notes on an off-the-record interview with Congressman Mike Mansfield), August 10, 1945, Frank McNaughton Papers, "McNaughton Reports File, August 1945," Harry S. Truman Presidential Library, Independence, Mo. Emphasis added. McNaughton was a journalist working for *Time* magazine. The same document includes McNaughton's notes from an interview with Senator Warren Magnuson, who also met with Truman on August 10. According to Magnuson's account, "Truman thought that no special concession should be made to preserve the emperor inviolate, that he was a war criminal just as much as Hitler or Mussolini, in many respects and now was trying to weasel his nation out of war, preserving meanwhile its essentially totalitarian structure." I am grateful to Barton J. Bernstein for providing me with a copy of this document.

39. Stimson Diary, June 19, 1945.

40. Hasegawa, *Racing the Enemy*, 165.

41. Stimson, "Notes for Diary," July 23, 1945, Stimson Papers, reel 128.

42. Stimson Diary, July 19, 1945.

43. Stimson, "Reflections on the Basic Problems which Confront Us," n.d. [July 19, 1945], Stimson Diary.

44. Stimson Diary, July 23, 1945.

45. It is unclear if Stimson understood the extent to which failure to add the weight of a public Soviet commitment to enter the war might prolong the war with Japan.

46. Arneson, "Notes of the Interim Committee Meeting," June 21, 1945, Harrison-Bundy, file 100.

47. Stimson Diary, July 19, 1945.

48. Stimson, "Reflections on the Basic Problems which Confront Us."

49. Joseph Davies Diary, July 21, 1945, Joseph Davies Papers, box 18, Library of Congress.

50. Colonel W. H. Kyle, "Notes of a Meeting on the Smyth Report in the Office of the Secretary of War, 11:30 A.M. to 1:15 P.M., 2 August 1945," Stimson Papers, reel 128. Gar Alperovitz has suggested that Stimson wanted to use the bomb in order to improve the American bargaining position vis à vis

Stalin and the Soviet Union. There is little evidence for this position, and it is clear that by the time of the Potsdam Conference that Stimson hoped to avoid such use altogether. Alperovitz, *Atomic Diplomacy: Hiroshima and Potsdam: The Use of the Atomic Bomb and the Confrontation with Soviet Power* (New York, 1985), 192. For another argument that Stimson was eager to use the bomb see John L. Harper, "Henry Stimson and the Origin of America's Attachment to Atomic Weapons," *SAIS Review* 5, no. 2 (Summer–Fall 1985): 21.

51. Stimson Diary, July 18 ("very greatly reinforced"), July 22 ("relying greatly"), July 23 ("evidently much fortified"), 1945.

52. Forrestal Diary, July 28, 1945.

53. Harry Truman, *Years of Decision* (New York, 1955), 416.

54. Truman's later recollections of the deliberations on the atomic bomb at Potsdam are so filled with errors as to be virtually useless. In an interview for the 1952 oral history collection *Mr. President*, Truman claimed that after receiving news of the successful test of the atomic bomb on July 16, "I went into immediate consultation with Byrnes, Stimson, Admiral Leahy, General Marshall, General Arnold, General Eisenhower, and Admiral King. I asked for their opinion whether the bomb should be used. The consensus of opinion was that the bomb should be used." Truman repeated this story in a letter to historian James L. Cate and offered a slightly different version in his 1955 memoir *Years of Decision*. In fact, this account is incorrect on two counts. First, none of the numerous contemporary records from Potsdam (including the Truman, Stimson, Leahy, and Arnold diaries) include any mention of a meeting remotely resembling that later described by Truman. Stimson's aide kept a sometimes minute-by-minute account of the secretary's meetings at Potsdam. There are references to a number of smaller meetings on the subject of the bomb, and most likely Truman created a "composite" meeting out of these scattered, informal gatherings. There is also no evidence to support Truman's contention that the subject of *whether* to use the bomb was ever discussed at Potsdam. Rather, the discussions about the bomb at Potsdam appear to have focused on the issues of timing and targets as well as the relationship between the bomb and the Soviet Union. William Hillman, *Mr. President: The First Publication from the Personal Diaries, Private Letters, Papers and Revealing Interviews of Harry S. Truman* (New York, 1953), 248; Truman to James L. Cate, n.d. [January 1953], in Merrill, ed., *The Decision to Drop the Atomic Bomb on Japan*, 1: 519–20; Truman, *Years of Decision*, 415. For more on this issue see Barton J. Bernstein, "Research Note: Writing, Righting, or Wronging the Historical Record: President Truman's Letter on his Atomic-Bomb Decision," *Diplomatic History* 16, no. 1 (Winter 1992): 163–73. One of the only historians to defend Truman's claim of a formal meeting to discuss the use of the bomb is D. M. Giangreco, "Casualty Projections for the U.S. Invasions of Japan, 1945–1946: Planning and Policy Implications," *Journal of Military History* 61, no. 3 (July 1997): 570–73.

55. After presenting a list of targets to the chief of staff on June 14, Groves recorded that "General Marshall stated he thought Kokura would be the best target primarily for reasons other than those presented in our description of the targets." The so-called Kokura arsenal was a huge military-industrial complex located east of the city of Kokura. Leslie R. Groves, "Memo to Files," June 14, 1945, and "Kokura Arsenal," [target profile], July 2, 1945, both Correspondence ("Top Secret") of the Manhattan Engineer District, 1942–46, microfilm publication M1109, file 25, National Archives (hereafter cited as Groves "Top Secret).

56. Harrison to Stimson, July 21, 1945, Harrison-Bundy, file 64.

57. July 22, 23, 1945, The Diary of Henry H. Arnold, Arnold Papers, Manuscripts and Records Division, Library of Congress (hereafter cited as Arnold Diary); Henry H. Arnold, *Global Mission* (New York, 1949), 589; Stimson Diary, July 17, 1945 ("dead city").

58. Arnold Diary, July 24, 1945.

59. Handy to Marshall, July 24, 1945; George Harrison to Stimson, July 24, 1945; both in Harrison-Bundy, file 64.

60. Truman Diary, July 25, 1945, Merrill, ed., *The Decision to Drop the Atomic Bomb on Japan*, 156.

61. Stimson Diary, July 24, 1945.

62. For claims that Truman was untroubled by the use of the bomb prior to Hiroshima see Alperovitz, *Atomic Diplomacy*, 52, 285; Alperovitz, *The Decision to Use the Atomic Bomb*, 527; Arnold A.

Offner, *Another Such Victory: President Truman and the Cold War, 1945–1953* (Stanford, 2002), 92; Ronald Takaki, *Hiroshima: Why America Dropped the Bomb* (Boston, 1995), 9–10, 99–100, 146.

63. See the July 1945 target sheets in Groves "Top Secret," file 25, and Jack Stone to Henry Arnold, "Groves Project," July 24, 1945, Groves "Top Secret," file 5.

64. Stimson Diary, May 15, 1945; Norris, *Racing for the Bomb*, 400.

65. Stimson, "Notes for Diary," July 23, 1945, Stimson Papers, reel 128.

66. From James Forrestal's account of his conversation with Byrnes, Forrestal Diary, July 28, 1945.

67. Marshall to Handy, July 25, 1945, Harrison-Bundy, file 64.

68. There has been some confusion over when and how Truman gave final approval for the use of the atomic bombs. In response to a query from historian James L. Cate, Truman claimed that "I ordered atomic bombs dropped on the two cities named [Hiroshima and Nagasaki] on the way back from Potsdam, when we were in the middle of the Atlantic Ocean." In fact, the Groves directive, issued on July 25, gave commanders at Tinian authority to use the bomb anytime after August 3 without any further instructions from Washington. Truman could, and eventually did, reassert control over the use of the bomb by countermanding the Groves directive. But absent such direct action, the 509th had full authority to use atomic bombs as they became available. Some historians have pointed to a message from Truman to Stimson on July 31 stating, "Release when ready but not sooner than 2 August" as constituting the final approval of the bomb's use. This message, however, referred to the press release drafted in Washington rather than to the use of the bomb itself. Truman to Cate, n.d. [January 1953], in Merrill, ed., *The Decision to Drop the Atomic Bomb on Japan*, 519; Truman to Stimson, July 31, 1945, Harrison-Bundy, file 64.

69. Pasco to Spaatz, 31 July 1945, Groves "Top Secret," file 5D. Hiroshima was chosen as the first target among the listed cities in large part because it was believed to be the only one that did not harbor American POWs. In fact, American POWs were killed at Hiroshima. See Gregg Herken, *The Winning Weapon: The Atomic Bomb in the Cold War, 1945–1950* (New York, 1980), 3; Robert Karl Manoff, "American Victims of Hiroshima," *New York Times Magazine*, December 2, 1984.

70. Kyle notes, July 27, 1945, Stimson Papers, reel 128. The other major topic of the luncheon was the reorganization of postwar Germany.

71. Dwight D. Eisenhower, *Crusade in Europe* (Garden City, N.Y., 1948) 483–84; Eisenhower, *Mandate for Change, 1953–1956: The White House Years* (New York, 1963), 312. Gar Alperovitz has made much of Eisenhower's criticism of the bomb in *Atomic Diplomacy*, 14, 54, and *The Decision to Use the Atomic Bomb*, 352–58. For a more critical take on Eisenhower's postwar statements see Barton J. Bernstein, "Ike and Hiroshima: Did He Oppose It?" *Journal of Strategic Studies* 10, no. 3 (September 1987): 377–89; Robert James Maddox, *Weapons for Victory: The Hiroshima Decision* (Columbia, Mo., 2004), 4; Robert James Maddox, "Gar Alperovitz: Godfather of Hiroshima Revisionism," in *Hiroshima in History: The Myths of Revisionism*, ed. Maddox (Columbia, Mo., 2007), 16–19.

72. The August 6 date reflects the time in Japan (not Washington) that the bomb was dropped. There has been much debate over the actual number of people killed at Hiroshima and Nagasaki. For a summary of this debate see Barton J. Bernstein, "Truman and the A-Bomb: Targeting Noncombatants, Using the Bomb, and His Defending the 'Decision,' " *Journal of Military History* 62, no. 3 (July 1998): 565–66, n. 43.

73. Stimson, "Memorandum of Conference with the President, August 8, 1945, at 10:45 AM," Stimson Papers, reel 128.

74. Ibid.

75. Stimson Diary, August 8, 1945 ("a complete rest"); Stimson to Felix Frankfurter ("as soon as possible"), August 11, 1945, Stimson Papers, reel 113.

76. Stimson Diary, August 10, 1945. Some historians have cited Stimson's plans to leave on vacation on August 10 as evidence that official Washington did not believe a Japanese surrender was imminent (see, for example, Barton J. Bernstein, "Understanding the Atomic Bomb and Japanese Surrender: Missed Opportunities, Little-Known Disasters, and Modern Memory," in *Hiroshima in History and Memory*, ed. Michael J. Hogan (Cambridge, UK, 1996), 73; Frank, *Downfall*, 300; Michael Gordin, *Five Days in August: How World War II Became a Nuclear War* (Princeton, 2007), 36). In fact,

the secretary's decision to leave town had little to do with his reading of the Japanese situation and was instead dictated by his failing health.

77. For a discussion of the wording of the Japanese offer of August 10 see Hasegawa, *Racing the Enemy*, 215–19.

78. Stimson Diary, August 10, 1945.

79. Stimson, "Memorandum of Conference with the President, August 8, 1945, at 10:45 AM."

80. Stimson Diary, August 10, 1945.

81. Ibid.; Forrestal Diary, August 10, 1945; Robertson, *Sly and Able*, 435–36.

82. McNaughton to Welch (notes on an off-the-record interview with Congressman Mike Mansfield), August 10, 1945; Wallace Diary, August 10, 1945.

83. Stimson Diary, August 10, 1945. Spaatz's independent decision to cease area attacks on Japanese cities forced Truman's hand. The president acquiesced in a halt to the bombing of Japanese cities on August 11, only to order that operations resume once again on August 14. Larry I. Bland, ed., *The Papers of George Catlett Marshall*, vol. 5, *The Finest Soldier, January 1, 1945–January 7, 1947* (Baltimore, 2003), 266–67, 271; *The Army Air Forces in World War II*, vol. 5, *The Pacific: Matterhorn to Nagasaki*, Wesley Frank Craven and James Lea Cate, eds. (Washington, D.C., 1983), 732; Barton J. Bernstein, "The Perils and Politics of Surrender: Ending the War with Japan and Avoiding the Third Atomic Bomb," *Pacific Historical Review* 46, no. 1 (February 1977): 8–11.

84. Wallace Diary, August 10, 1945; Groves, "Memorandum to Chief of Staff " [with handwritten notation by Marshall], Groves "Top Secret," file 25.

85. The Diary of Carl A. Spaatz, August 11, 1945, Carl A. Spaatz Papers, Library of Congress.

Chapter 7. The Last Full Measure

1. September 21, 1945, Henry Lewis Stimson Diaries (microfilm ed.), Manuscripts and Archives, Yale University Library (hereafter cited as Stimson Diary). Stimson was so exhausted as he left office that he did not compose a diary entry on this day. The entry for September 21 cited here was dictated on December 11, 1945, after he had recovered from a second, more serious heart attack.

2. Stimson's presentation on September 21 drew on his "Memorandum for the President," September 11, 1945, Stimson Diary.

3. Details of Stimson's departure are drawn from the *New York Herald Tribune*, September 21, 1945; Stimson Diary, September 21, 1945; Elting Elmore Morison, *Turmoil and Tradition: A Study of the Life and Times of Henry L. Stimson* (Boston, 1960), 643.

4. "Speech Delivered by the Chairman of the American Delegation, Henry L. Stimson at the Plenary Session of the Conference, London, February 11, 1930," Stimson Diary.

5. Vannevar Bush, "Memorandum for Dr. Conant," February 15, 1945, Bush-Conant File Relating to the Development of the Atomic Bomb, 1940–45, Records of the Office of Scientific Research and Development, record group 227, microfilm publication M1392, file 37, National Archives (hereafter cited as Bush-Conant).

6. Stimson, "Outline of Princeton lectures," n.d. [circa March or April, 1934], Henry Lewis Stimson Papers (microfilm ed.), reel 132, Manuscripts and Archives, Yale University Library (hereafter cited as Stimson Papers).

7. J. Samuel Walker, *Prompt and Utter Destruction: Truman and the Use of Atomic Bombs against Japan* (Chapel Hill, N.C., 1997), 86.

8. Robert S. Norris, *Racing for the Bomb: General Leslie R. Groves, the Manhattan Project's Indispensable Man* (South Royalton, Vt., 2002), 439–41. Army Chief of Staff George C. Marshall was also apparently troubled in the wake of Hiroshima, reportedly remarking to Manhattan Project head General Leslie Groves that "we should guard against too much gratification over our success, because it undoubtedly involved a large number of Japanese casualties." Leslie Groves, *Now It Can Be Told: The Story of the Manhattan Project* (New York 1962), 324.

9. "H.L.S. Statement at the Ausable Club, August 18, 1945," Stimson Diary.

10. On August 17, J. Robert Oppenheimer, writing for the Scientific Advisory Panel, submitted a report to Stimson on the subject of future developments in atomic energy. Oppenheimer warned Stimson that "weapons quantitatively and qualitatively far more effective than now available will result from further work" on the bomb, specifically mentioning the possibility of the "super," or hydrogen, bomb. J. R. Oppenheimer to Stimson, August 17, 1945, in *Robert Oppenheimer: Letters and Recollections*, ed. Alice K. Smith and Charles Weiner (Stanford, 1995), 293–94. Bush and Conant had warned Stimson of this possibility as early as September 1944, though it is unclear whether the secretary understood the implications of the "super" at that point. Bush and Conant to Stimson, "Salient Points Concerning Future International Handling of Subject Atomic Bombs," September 30, 1944, Harrison-Bundy Files Relating to the Development of the Atomic Bomb, 1942–46, Records of the Office of the Chief of Engineers, record group 77, microfilm publication M1108, file 69, National Archives (hereafter cited as Harrison-Bundy).

11. Stimson Diary, August 12–September 3, 1945.

12. Ibid., September 4, 1945.

13. Ibid., September 5, 1945.

14. Stimson to Truman, September 11, 1945, Stimson Diary.

15. "Memorandum for the President," September 11, 1945, Stimson Diary.

16. Stimson Diary, May 14, 15, 1945.

17. "Memorandum for the President," September 11, 1945.

18. Ibid.

19. Ibid.

20. For Stimson's doubts on the ability of the U.N. to handle the issues that would confront the world in the immediate postwar period see the Stimson Diary, October 28, 1943; July 31, August 22, 1944; January 21, January 23, May 8, 10, 1945.

21. On the difficulties of multilateral negotiations over the bomb at the U.N., see Gregg Herken, *The Winning Weapon: The Atomic Bomb in the Cold War, 1945–1959* (New York, 1980), 171–91; Barton J. Bernstein, "The Quest for Security: American Foreign Policy and International Control, 1942–1946," *Journal of American History*, 60, no. 4 (March 1974): 1023–44.

22. Henry L. Stimson and McGeorge Bundy, *On Active Service in Peace and War* (New York, 1948), 648.

23. "Speech Delivered by the Chairman of the American Delegation, Henry L. Stimson at the Plenary Session of the Conference, London, February 11, 1930," Stimson Diary.

24. William Appleman Williams, *The Tragedy of American Diplomacy* (New York, 1972), 157.

25. Stimson Diary, September 17, 1945.

26. September 21, 1945, James V. Forrestal Diary, microfilm section, Navy Publication and Printing Service Office, Naval District, Washington, D.C. (hereafter cited as Forrestal Diary); Stimson Diary, September 21, 1945; The Diary of Henry A. Wallace, September 21, 1945 (microfilm ed.), Microfilm Corporation of America, Glen Rock, N.J. (hereafter cited as Wallace Diary).

27. Stimson Diary, September 21, 1945.

28. *New York Daily News*, September 26, 1945. The *New York Times* and the *Washington Post* also featured reports attributing the Stimson proposal to Wallace (see coverage in the aforementioned papers on September 22, 24, 1945). For speculation on Forrestal and the leak to the press see Arnold J. Offner, *Another Such Victory: President Truman and the Cold War, 1945–1953* (Stanford, 2002), 108; Herken, *The Winning Weapon*, 31.

29. David Holloway, *Stalin and the Bomb* (New Haven, 1994), 131–33.

30. Lauris D. Norstad, "Memorandum for Major General Leslie Groves," September 15, 1945, Correspondence ("Top Secret") of the Manhattan Engineer District, 1942–46, microfilm publication M1109, file 3, National Archives (hereafter cited as Groves "Top Secret").

31. The memorandum called for 466 bombs to accomplish this task but suggested that a "minimum" of 123 bombs would be acceptable. Ibid. For more on the development of early American nuclear doctrine see Herken, *The Winning Weapon*; David Allen Rosenberg, "The Origins of Overkill: Nuclear Weapons and American Strategy, 1945–1960," *International Security* 7, no. 4 (Spring 1983): 3–71.

32. *New York Times*, September 22, 1945, 3. In his memoir of the Manhattan Project, Groves rather disingenuously suggested that he "wholeheartedly concurred" with Stimson's plea for international control. Groves was in fact strongly opposed to international control without first securing significant concessions from the Soviet Union. Groves, *Now It Can Be Told*, 408. For more on Groves's opposition to international control see Norris, *Racing for the Bomb*, 471–83, and *Foreign Relations of the United States, 1946* (Washington D.C.), 1:1197–1203 (hereafter cited as *FRUS*).

33. *FRUS, 1946*, 1:1198, 1203; Groves, "Memorandum for the Chief of Staff," August 30, 1945, Groves "Top Secret," file 26Q; Herken, *The Winning Weapon*, 32.

34. Evidence on Forrestal's pre-Hiroshima thinking about the bomb is scant. For a post-Hiroshima suggestion that Forrestal favored a noncombat demonstration see Gar Alperovitz, *The Decision to Use the Atomic Bomb* (New York, 1995), 333, 390–94.

35. Forrestal, "Memorandum," September 21, 1945, Forrestal Diary.

36. Stimson Diary, September 21, 1945.

37. Frank McNaughton to Eleanor Welch (notes on an off-the-record interview with Congressman Mike Mansfield), August 10, 1945, Frank McNaughton Papers, "McNaughton Reports File, August 1945," Harry S. Truman Presidential Library, Independence, Mo. I am grateful to Barton Bernstein for providing me with a copy of this document.

38. Stimson to James N. Rosenberg, October 2, 1945, Stimson Papers, reel 114.

39. Among those with whom Stimson frequently consulted were John J. McCloy, Harvey Bundy, James Conant, George C. Marshall, Dwight D. Eisenhower, Felix Frankfurter, and Henry Luce.

40. On Truman's opposition to the direct approach to the Soviets and the failure of atomic diplomacy at London see Offner, *Another Such Victory*, 108–9; Herken, *The Winning Weapon*, 36–39, 43–68.

41. Bush to Stimson, November 13, 1945, Stimson Papers, reel 114.

42. As McGeorge Bundy delicately phrased it, "Stimson had no desire to criticize the course actually followed by the United States between September and December, 1945, but he did not believe that this course represented precisely the policy and method he had in mind in presenting his September memorandum." Stimson and Bundy, *On Active Service*, 647.

43. Stimson, "The Bomb and the Opportunity," *Harper's Magazine*, March 1946, 204. The article was largely drawn from the text of Stimson's "Memorandum for the President," September 11, 1945. R. Gordon Arneson, working from this memorandum, produced the article that was published in *Harper's* under Stimson's name, perhaps with aid from George Harrison. For more see Barton J. Bernstein, "Seizing the Contested Terrain: Stimson, Conant, and Their Allies Explain the Decision to Use the Atomic Bomb," *Diplomatic History* 17, no. 1 (Winter 1993): 56 n. 78. The September 11 memorandum and the accompanying cover letter to Truman were published in their entirety in Stimson's 1948 memoir, by which point the prospects of international control had faded entirely. Stimson and Bundy, *On Active Service*, 642–46.

44. Stimson to Bernard M. Baruch, May 28, 1946, Stimson Papers, reel 115.

45. Stimson Diary, September 5, 1945.

Chapter 8. "The Full Enumeration of the Steps in the Tragedy"

1. As he prepared to depart for his new job as governor general of the Philippines in 1928, Stimson wrote to the Bureau of Insular Affairs to complain that the name of the aide assigned to him by the Bureau "suggests the slight possibility he might be a Hebrew. I should hardly care to have him in quite such personal and social relations if that were the case. . . . Sorry to trouble you about this little matter but it is a thing that one cannot do otherwise." Stimson to Frank McIntyre, January 12, 1928, Henry Lewis Stimson Papers (microfilm ed.), reel 74, Manuscripts and Archives, Yale University Library (hereafter cited as Stimson Papers).

2. Stimson to Felix Frankfurter, December 12, 1946, Stimson Papers, reel 116.

3. Frankfurter to Stimson, December 16, 1946, Stimson Papers, reel 116.

4. For more on the history of the *Harper's* article see Barton J. Bernstein, "Seizing the Contested Terrain of Early Nuclear History: Stimson, Conant, and Their Allies Explain the Decision to Use the

Atomic Bomb," *Diplomatic History* 17, no. 1 (Winter 1993): 35–72. Also see James G. Hershberg, *James B. Conant: Harvard to Hiroshima and the Making of the Nuclear Age* (Stanford, 1993), 279–304; Robert S. Norris, *Racing for the Bomb: General Leslie R. Groves, the Manhattan Project's Indispensable Man* (South Royalton, Vt., 2002), 531; Kai Bird, *The Color of Truth: McGeorge Bundy and William Bundy, Brothers in Arms* (New York, 1998), 90–100; Gar Alperovitz, *The Decision to Use the Atomic Bomb* (New York, 1995), 448–71. For a defense of the Stimson essay see Robert P. Newman, "Hiroshima and the Trashing of Henry Stimson," *New England Quarterly* 71, no. 1 (March 1998): 21–32.

5. Herbert Hoover to John C. Laughlin, August 8, 1945, Hebert Hoover Presidential Library, West Branch, Iowa, Post-Presidential Individual File, "O'Laughlin, John C." Little scholarly attention has been paid to the early conservative critics of the bomb. For more see Bernstein, "The Struggle over History: Defining the Hiroshima Narrative," in *Judgment at the Smithsonian: The Bombing of Hiroshima and Nagasaki*, ed. Philip Nobile (New York, 1995): 134–35; Robert Jay Lifton and Greg Mitchell, *Hiroshima in History: Fifty Years of Denial* (New York, 1995), 36–38; Leo Maley III and Uday Mohan, "Time to Confront the Ethics of Hiroshima," *History News Network* (August 4, 2005), http://www.hnet.org/~hns/articles/2005/080405b.html. Also see comments by Barton J. Bernstein (p. 31) in his H-diplo review of Tsuyoshi Hasegawa's *Racing The Enemy*, http://www.hnet.org/~diplo/roundtables/PDF/Bernstein-HasegawaRoundtable.pdf. For more on Conant and Niebuhr see James G. Hershberg, "A Footnote on Hiroshima and Atomic Morality: Conant, Niebuhr, and an 'Emotional' Clergyman, 1945–46," *SHAFR Newsletter* 33, no. 4 (December 2002): 1–15.

6. In a poll in *Fortune* in December 1945, only 18.3 percent of respondents expressed objections to the way in which the bomb had been used. Fifty-three and a half percent believed that two bombs had been the right number, while 22.7 percent expressed the opinion that "[w]e should have quickly used many more [atomic bombs] before Japan had a chance to surrender." For more see Sadao Asada, "The Mushroom Cloud and National Psyches: Japanese and American Perceptions of the A-Bomb Decision, 1945–1995," *Journal of American-East Asian Relations* 4, no. 2 (Summer 1995): 98–99; Paul Boyer, *By The Bomb's Early Light: American Thought and Culture at the Dawn of the Atomic Age* (New York, 1985), 3–26; Lifton and Mitchell, *Hiroshima in America.*

7. James Conant to Harvey Bundy quoted in Bernstein, "Seizing the Contested Terrain," 40.

8. Conant to Stimson, January 22, 1947, Stimson Papers, reel 116.

9. Stimson to Frankfurter, December 12, 1946, Stimson Papers, reel 116.

10. Stimson to Orlando Ward, March 21, 1947, Stimson Papers, reel 117.

11. Harry S. Truman to Stimson, November 13, 1946; Truman to Stimson, December 31, 1946, Stimson Papers, reel 116.

12. Marshall quoted in David Lilienthal, *The Journals of David Lilienthal: The Atomic Energy Years, 1945–1950* (New York, 1964), 198.

13. Bird, *The Color of Truth*, 91.

14. In addition to Stimson's memoir *On Active Service in Peace and War* (New York, 1948) and "The Decision to Use the Atomic Bomb," *Harper's* (February 1947): 97–107, Bundy helped to compose the following articles published under Stimson's name: "The Nuremberg Trial: Landmark in Law," *Foreign Affairs* 25, no. 2 (January 1947): 179–89 and "The Challenge to Americans," *Foreign Affairs* 26, no. 1 (October 1946): 5–14. Bundy also worked on Stimson's March 27, 1950, letter to the *New York Times* condemning McCarthyism. The Stimson-Bundy correspondence makes for fascinating reading and can be found scattered throughout the Stimson Papers, reels 116–21.

15. Conant to McGeorge Bundy, November 30, 1946, Stimson Papers, reel 116.

16. Stimson, "The Decision to Use the Atomic Bomb," 102.

17. Ibid., 106–7.

18. For a review of the copious recent literature on the casualty question see J. Samuel Walker, "Recent Literature on Truman's Atomic Bomb Decision: A Search for Middle Ground," *Diplomatic History* 29, no. 2 (April 2005): 315, 322–27; Michael Kort, *The Columbia Guide to Hiroshima and the Bomb* (New York, 2007), 96–104.

19. McGeorge Bundy to Stimson, February 18, 1947, Stimson Papers, reel 117.

20. On the *Enola Gay* dispute see Edward T. Linenthal and Tom Englehardt, eds., *History Wars: The Enola Gay and Other Battles for the American Past* (New York, 1996); Philip Nobile, ed., *Judgment at the Smithsonian*; Robert P. Newman, *Enola Gay and the Court of History* (New York, 2004); Michael J. Hogan, "The Enola Gay Controversy: History, Memory, and the Politics of Presentation," in *Hiroshima in History and Memory*, ed. Michael J. Hogan (Cambridge, 1996), 200–32.

21. Conant to McGeorge Bundy, November 30, 1946, Stimson Papers, reel 116.

22. Stimson, "The Decision to Use the Atomic Bomb," 104.

23. June 19, 1945, Henry Lewis Stimson Diaries (microfilm ed.), Manuscripts and Archives, Yale University Library (hereafter cited as Stimson Diary).

24. For examples of this argument from defenders of Truman's decision see Newman, *Enola Gay and the Court of History*, 136, 139; Paul Fussell, *Thank God for the Atomic Bomb and Other Essays* (New York, 1990), 5; Richard B. Frank, *Downfall: The End of the Imperial Japanese Empire* (New York, 1999), 360; Robert J. Maddox, "Gar Alperovitz: Godfather of Hiroshima Revisionism," in *Hiroshima in History: The Myths of Revisionism*, ed. Robert J. Maddox (Columbia, Mo., 2007), 12.

25. Stimson Diary, June 26–30, 1945.

26. Joseph Grew to Stimson, February 12, 1947, and Stimson to Grew, June 19, 1947, both in Eugene H. Dooman Papers, box 2, Hoover Institution Archives, Stanford, Calif.

27. Stimson and Bundy, *On Active Service*, 626 (on Grew's role), 629 (on prolonging the war).

28. Dwight D. Eisenhower, *Crusade in Europe* (Garden City, N.Y., 1948), 483–84; Eisenhower, *Mandate for Change, 1953–1956: The White House Years* (New York, 1963), 312; William D. Leahy, *I Was There: The Personal Story of the Chief of Staff to Presidents Roosevelt and Truman Based on His Notes and Diaries Made at the Time* (New York, 1950), 441–42. For more on postwar statements from military officers critical of the use of the bomb see Alperovitz, *The Decision to Use the Atomic Bomb*, 321–65. For more on the debate over nuclear targeting see Sean Malloy, " 'The Rules of Civilized Warfare': Scientists, Soldiers, Civilians, and American Nuclear Targeting, 1940–1945," *Journal of Strategic Studies* 30, no. 3 (June 2007): 475–512.

29. The Nagasaki bomb had a yield of 21 kilotons (kt), compared with a 15 kt yield for the bomb at Hiroshima. John Malik, *The Yields of the Hiroshima and Nagasaki Explosions* (Los Alamos, N.Mex., 1986), 1.

30. Diary of John J. McCloy, May 21, 1945, John J. McCloy Papers, box DY1, folder 17, Amherst College Library, Amherst, Mass.

31. Exact figures for the dead at Tokyo vary from a low number of approximately eighty-three thousand to somewhere over a hundred thousand. Frank, *Downfall*, 17–18.

32. For an argument that race played an important role in the decision see Ronald Takaki, *Hiroshima: Why America Dropped the Bomb* (Boston, 1995).

33. "Revisionist" historians of the bomb often differ dramatically on the important question of why Truman used the bomb. For example, Alperovitz has maintained (in *Atomic Diplomacy: Hiroshima and Potsdam: The Use of the Atomic Bomb and the Confrontation with Soviet Power* (New York, 1985) and his more recent work *The Decision to Use the Atomic Bomb*) that it was used primarily for anti-Soviet purposes. Bernstein, in contrast, has argued that ending the war with Japan was the primary motivation, with anti-Soviet effects constituting a "bonus." What the pioneering works of the A-bomb revisionists share is the contention—well supported by archival evidence—that whatever the motives behind its use, the bomb played a crucial role in American diplomatic calculations with respect to the Soviet Union well before Hiroshima.

34. Stimson, "The Decision to Use the Atomic Bomb," 99. The full sentence is as follows, with the part omitted from the Stimson article in my own italics: "With its aid even a very powerful unsuspecting nation might be conquered within a very few days by a very much smaller one *although probably the only nation which could enter into production within the next few years is Russia*." "Memorandum Discussed with the President," April 25, 1945, Stimson Diary.

35. Stimson Diary, May 14, 15, 1945.

36. R. D. Van Deman to Stimson, February 15, 1947, Stimson Papers, reel 117.

37. P. M. S. Blackett, *Fear, War, and the Bomb: Military and Political Consequences of Atomic Energy* (New York, 1949), 139. On Blackett, see Mary Jo Nye, *Blackett: Physics, War, and Politics in the Twentieth Century* (Cambridge, Mass., 2004).

38. Alperovitz, *Atomic Diplomacy*, 161, 289–90.

39. Barton J. Bernstein, "Understanding the Atomic Bomb and the Japanese Surrender: Missed Opportunities, Little-Known Near Disasters, and Modern Memory," *Diplomatic History* 19, no. 2 (Spring 1995): 230.

40. On the evolution of the literature on the bomb see Walker, "Recent Literature," 311–34.

41. On Groves and the Soviet Union see Norris, *Racing for the Bomb*, 387–91, 481. Also see Groves's memoir, *Now It Can Be Told: The Story of the Manhattan Project* (New York, 1962), which is unapologetically anti-Soviet.

42. Truman Diary, July 25, 1945, *Documentary History of the Truman Presidency:* vol. 1: *The Decision to Drop the Atomic Bomb on Japan*, ed. Dennis Merrill, 156.

43. Stimson, "Memorandum for the President," September 11, 1945, Stimson Diary.

44. Transcript of an interview between Stimson and McGeorge Bundy, May 30, 1946, Stimson Papers, reel 136. Stimson to Mrs. Howard G. Tracy, December 10, 1946, Stimson Papers, reel 116; Stimson to Frank R. Ober, October 4, 1949, Stimson Papers, reel 12.

45. Stimson to Bernard Baruch, June 18, 1946, Stimson Papers, reel 115.

46. Stimson to George Roberts, June 11, 1947, Stimson Papers, reel 117.

47. Responding to a concerned letter from a friend, Stimson in March 1947 confided that he, too, had "a little worry" over the implications of the 1947 Truman Doctrine, particularly insofar as it seemed to run counter to much of the work then being done by the United Nations. See James S. Rosenberg to Stimson, March 20, 1947, and Stimson to Rosenberg, March 25, 1947, Stimson Papers, reel 117.

48. Stimson to W. Kingsland Macy, October 15, 1947; Stimson to W. C. Chanler, October 15, 1947, both in Stimson Papers, reel 118.

49. Stimson to Dwight W. Morrow, April 5, 1950, Stimson Papers, reel 123.

50. Stimson's letter to the *New York Times*, March 27, 1950; Stimson to Alec P. Proctor, March 27, 1950, Stimson Papers, reel 123.

51. Stimson to Harold L. Ickes, October 15, 1947, Stimson Papers, reel 118.

52. Transcript of an interview between Stimson and McGeorge Bundy, June 14, 1946, Stimson Papers, reel 136.

53. Undated, handwritten note [circa March 1945], Harrison-Bundy Files Relating to the Development of the Atomic Bomb, 1942–46, Records of the Office of the Chief of Engineers, record group 77, microfilm publication M1108, file 7, National Archives; "H.L.S. Statement at the Ausable Club, August 18, 1945," Stimson Diary.

54. Stimson to Rev. Howard M. Lehn, April 9, 1946, Stimson Papers reel 115. Also see Stimson to James B. Conant, December 27, 1949, Stimson Papers, reel 122, for his views on the importance of religious education.

55. Stimson interview with McGeorge Bundy, June 4, 1946, Stimson Papers, reel 136.

56. Stimson interview with McGeorge Bundy, May 27, 1946, Stimson Papers, reel 115.

57. Stimson to Fredric R. Coudert, January 3, 1947, Stimson Papers, reel 116.

58. Stimson to Hamilton Fish Armstrong, October 1, 1946, Stimson Papers, reel 116.

59. Stimson to Armstrong, October 11, 1946, Stimson Papers, reel 116.

60. "Charter of the International Military Tribunal," *Trial of the Major War Criminals before the International Military Tribunal* (Nuremberg, 1947), 1:11.

61. For Stimson's linkage of Kellogg-Briand and the Nuremberg trials see Stimson, "The Nuremberg Trial," 183–84.

62. Robert Bacon and James Brown Scott, eds., *Addresses on International Subjects by Elihu Root* (London, 1916), 156–57.

63. Henry Stimson, "Bases of American Foreign Policy during the Past Four Years," *Foreign Affairs* 11, no. 3 (April 1933): 390. For more on the Nuremberg Trials and the Nuremberg Charter and their

role in the emerging multilateral institutions crafted in the wake of World War II, see Elizabeth Borg-wardt's *A New Deal for the World: America's Vision for Human Rights* (Cambridge, Mass., 2005), 196–247.

64. "A Guilty Conscience Shrieks Its Guilt," *Chicago Tribune*, January 6, 1947.

65. Stimson interview with McGeorge Bundy, June 4, 1946, Stimson Papers, reel 136.

66. Stimson to Harold Ickes, October 15, 1947, Stimson Papers, reel 118.

Conclusion

1. Ball had been employed by the War Department to work on the United States Strategic Bomb-ing Survey (USSBS), an effort to assess the effects of strategic bombing on Germany (and later Japan). On Ball see James A. Bill, *George Ball: Behind the Scenes in U.S. Foreign Policy* (New Haven, 1997). On USSBS see Gian P. Gentile, *How Effective Is Strategic Bombing? Lessons Learned from World War II to Kosovo* (New York, 2000).

2. "Address by the Honorable George W. Ball Under Secretary of State on the Occasion of the Commissioning of the Polaris Missile Submarine, *Henry L. Stimson*, Groton, Connecticut, August, 20, 1966," Papers of George W. Ball, Seeley G. Mudd Library, Princeton. The quote used by Ball came from Stimson, "The Challenge to Americans," *Foreign Affairs* 26, no. 1 (October 1946).

3. Each of the sixteen Polaris missiles aboard the *Stimson* carried an 800 kiloton (kt) warhead for a combined total of 12.8 megatons. The bomb used against Hiroshima had a 15 kt yield. Chuck Hanson, *U.S. Nuclear Weapons* (Arlington, TX, 1988), 205; John Malik, *The Yields of the Hiroshima and Na-gasaki Explosions* (Los Alamos, N. Mex., 1986), 1.

4. Jeffrey Richelson, "Population Targeting and U.S. Strategic Doctrine," in *Strategic Nuclear Targeting*, ed. Desmond Ball and Jeffrey Richelson (Ithaca, 1986), 239–40.

5. For photos of the Playboy artwork on the *Stimson*'s launch tubes see http://www.usfamily.net/web/nealandy/655pic.html.

6. Godfrey Hodgson, *The Colonel: The Life and Wars of Henry Stimson, 1867–1950* (New York, 1990), 220 ("the American Churchill"); John J. McCloy, eulogy for Stimson delivered October 31, 1950, Christ Chapel, Frankfurt, Henry Lewis Stimson Papers (microfilm ed.), reel 151, Manuscripts and Archives, Yale University Library (hereafter cited as Stimson Papers) ("the original anti-appeaser").

7. Stimson to the Committee on Public Affairs, February 21, 1936, Stimson Papers, reel 90.

8. "Memorandum for the President," September 15, 1944, Henry Lewis Stimson Diaries (micro-film ed.), Manuscripts and Archives, Yale University Library (hereafter cited as Stimson Diary) ("poverty"); Stimson Diary, June 2, 1942 ("equality and freedom").

9. Stimson to Lyman P. Hammond, June 16, 1932, Stimson Papers, reel 83.

10. Stimson, "America's Interest in the British Navy," June 18, 1940, Stimson Papers, reel 132.

11. Stimson Diary, August 18, 1945.

12. Walter Isaacson and Evan Thomas, *The Wise Men: Six Friends and the World They Made: Ache-son, Bohlen, Harriman, Kennan, Lovett, McCloy* (New York, 1988), is a journalistic treatment of the subject. On McCloy see Kai Bird, *The Chairman: John J. McCloy and the Making of the American Es-tablishment* (New York, 1992). On Bundy see Bird, *The Color of Truth: McGeorge Bundy and William Bundy, Brothers in Arms* (New York, 1998).

13. Robert A. Lovett Oral History Interview, November 19, 1964, John F. Kennedy Library, Boston, accessed via the Digital National Security Archive, http://nsarchive.chadwyck.com.

14. On American decision making during the Cuban missile crisis see Ernest R. May and Philip D. Zelikow, eds., *The Kennedy Tapes: Inside the White House during the Cuban Missile Crisis* (Cambridge, Mass., 1997). The crisis was used as a model for international decision making in Graham T. Allison and Philip Zelikow, *Essence of Decision: Explaining the Cuban Missile Crisis*, 2nd ed. (New York, 1999). For an international history of the crisis see Aleksandr Fursenko and Timothy Naftali, *"One Hell of a Gamble": The Secret History of the Cuban Missile Crisis* (New York, 1997).

15. Stimson Diary, February 18, 1916 ("ignorant as babies"); Stimson to Theodore Roosevelt, September 2, 1910, Stimson Papers, reel 19 ("the richer and more intelligent").

16. Bird, *The Color of Truth*, 351.

17. Marilyn B. Young, *The Vietnam Wars, 1945–1990* (New York, 1991), 126–29.

18. "Speech Delivered by the Chairman of the American Delegation, Henry L. Stimson at the Plenary Session of the Conference, London, February 11, 1930," Stimson Diary.

19. Stimson to Frankfurter, December 12, 1946, Stimson Papers, reel 116.

20. Lewis Mumford, *The Human Way Out* (Wallingford, Pa., 1958), 19.

21. Oppenheimer quoted in P. M. S. Blackett, *Fear, War, and the Bomb: Military and Political Consequences of Atomic Energy* (New York, 1949), 6. For more on the background of this speech see Kai Bird and Martin J. Sherwin, *American Prometheus: The Triumph and Tragedy of J. Robert Oppenheimer* (New York, 2005), 323–25.

22. "Global Nuclear Stockpiles, 1945–2006," *Bulletin of the Atomic Scientists* 62, no. 4 (July/August 2006): 66.

23. According to a 1998 report, the cold war arms race cost the United States $5.8 trillion. That figure will continue to rise given the costs associated with cleaning up cold war nuclear sites and disposing of old weapons. *Physics Today*, August 1998, 49–51. For more on the costs of the cold war arms race see Stephen I. Schwartz, *The Atomic Audit: The Costs and Consequences of U.S. Nuclear Weapons since 1940* (Washington, D.C., 1998). On the evolution of American nuclear "strategy," see David Allen Rosenberg, "The Origins of Overkill: Nuclear Weapons and American Strategy, 1945–1960," *International Security* 7, no. 4 (Spring 1983): 3–71.

24. "Global Nuclear Stockpiles," 66. The Chinese case presents an instructive comparison. The Chinese detonated their first bomb in 1964. Since that time they have consistently maintained a modest nuclear arsenal of between two hundred and four hundred warheads, a figure far below that possessed by the United States and the Soviet Union but more than sufficient for deterrent purposes.

25. On the recent debate over "usable" nuclear weapons and other threats see Sidney Drell, "The Shadow of the Bomb, 2006," *Policy Review* 136 (April–May 2006): 55–68.

26. "Memorandum discussed with the President," April 25, 1945, Stimson Diary.

27. James Sterngold, "The Next Generation of Bombmakers," *San Francisco Chronicle*, June 23, 2003, A1.

28. Blackett, *Fear, War, and the Bomb*, 140.

29. Some of the interesting new work on this question comes from scholars exploring archival sources outside the United States. See, for example, the essays in Tsuyoshi Hasegawa, ed., *The End of the Pacific War: Reappraisals* (Stanford, 2007).

Index

Page numbers in italic refer to figures